CW01430749

PEAKS

AND

VALLEYS

To Garda Ipory Buckely,
a member of the Staff of the College, and
a fine articulate humourous member and
Brilliant with the Computer.

With Sincere good wishes to you & the
family Sorry. Your support is much
Appreciated.

L Doyle

8/5/97

PEAKS
AND
VALLEYS

Tim Doyle

THE UPS AND DOWNS
OF A
YOUNG GARDA

First published 1997 by TJD Publications,
72 Park Lawn, Clontarf, Dublin 3, Ireland.

Copyright text © Tim Doyle

All rights reserved. No part of this book may be reproduced or utilised
in any or by any means, electronic or mechanical,
including photocopying, recording or by any information storage or
retrieval system without permission in writing from the publisher.
This book may not be sold as a bargain book or at any reduced price
without permission from the publisher.

British Library Cataloguing in Publication Data

0-9530126-0-3

Doyle, Tim
Peaks and Valleys - the ups and downs of a young Garda

Cover Design: Steven Hope
Printing: ColourBooks, Dublin

DEDICATION

*To my parents, Thomas and Julianne whose example was
a constant source of inspiration.*

*To my contemporaries who put the words in my mouth
and the many colleagues who implored me to write it
before it was too late.*

*To my children, Judanne, Daniel, Timothy & Thomas
who laughed and shook their heads in disbelief.*

*To my beloved Agnes, who contributed
more to my development than any human being.*

---

*Tim Doyle has just completed
30 years service in an Garda Siochana.*

. . . He is still serving in Dublin City.

AUTHORS NOTE

This book would not have been written -
not to mention published - without the financial support of
St. Raphael's Garda Credit Union Limited,
81-84 Upper Dorset Street, Dublin.

I thank them sincerely for their enthusiasm,
confidentiality, trust and sponsorship.

*The proceeds from this book
are being donated to the
Garda Benevolent Trust Fund.*

ACKNOWLEDGMENTS

I am indebted to the following:

Commissioner M.P.Byrne, for his unqualified support and contributing the introduction.

Chief Justice Hugh O'Flaherty for his kindness and providing the Foreword.

Austin Kenny, my first and greatest influence.

Anne Dempsey, for her offer to help, her editing of the book and most of all her understanding.

George Maybury, John Ferry, Chris Finnegan and Don Boyle who read the manuscript and gave me affirmation.

The Kerry Association in Dublin for providing an outlet for my work.

Margaret Galvin and the late Liam Campbell, of Ireland's Own, for advice, encouragement and publishing some of my early stories.

Cait, Denis, & Goretti for their time.

Padraig J. O'Connell, BCL. LLB for his friendship and counsel.

FOREWORD

I have known Tim Doyle for all the time that he has been a member of the *Garda Siochana*. I can vouch for his dedication, hard work - but also and very importantly - his many acts of kindness. The quality of justice, no more than that of mercy is not strained, by a well-judged charitable intervention in aid of an afflicted person from time to time.

It is a pleasant duty, therefore, to contribute this foreword to *Peaks and Valleys* the publication of which coincides with the author's thirtieth year of service as a garda.

The opening chapters are most enjoyable, providing as they do an entertaining glimpse into the world of a young boy in 1950's Kerry: from mass at Derrycunnihy to the slightly less divine raptures of Killorglin's Puck Fair . . .

With great honesty the author goes on to recount the anxiety and bewilderment that accompanied his sudden introduction to the streets of Dublin and the challenges which then faced him. Many others would have faltered where Tim Doyle persevered and eventually excelled. But life on Dublin's streets was a lot simpler then; alas, the same is true of our other cities and towns.

Perhaps the most enduring value of this book is the insight it provides into the trials and triumphs inextricable from life as a garda. To many an outsider the gardai remain somewhat of an enigma; they cannot always speak openly about their profession and the impact which it has upon them as individuals. Consequently, in the eyes of the outsider the gardai can sometimes acquire a dispassionate air which belies an infinitely more complex and emotional personality within. This book invites that outsider to step inside the uniformed world of the Garda

Siochana and realise the simple but often overlooked fact that each garda shares in the common frustration, anxiety, elation and hope that transcends whatever *uniform* one may wear.

From the foundation of the State, the gardai as a largely unarmed police force, have had a binding and benevolent effect on our society.

It is now nearly sixty four years since Maurice O'Sullivan's epochal publication: *Fiche Bliain ag Fás* (Twenty Years A-growing). I think that I am right in thinking that in the intervening time we have not had any memoirs of a general nature by a serving member of the Garda Siochana though, last year, it was my pleasure to attend the launch of John Courtney's book which, essentially, was an account of various criminal cases and written by him in retirement.

This is an engaging narrative because Tim Doyle has many interests outside his police work and the reader will learn of his love of the wild places - the mountains, valleys, rivers, lakes and sea of his - and my - native place.

I have great pleasure in commending this book to one and all.

Hugh O'Flaherty
20th January, 1997

The Supreme Court
Dublin 7.

INTRODUCTION

The click of the free-wheel of the Guard's bicycle as he entered the farmyard is recalled - Mrs. Doyle enquired - *'Any of ye see Gyp?'*, the family dog - the most likely reason for the visit! The Guard withdrew his notebook from his pocket - fright! panic! The recall of the simple things brings us back in time to a different world in the peaks and valleys of the Kerry mountains.

Tim Doyle's tale begins in the peace of rural Ireland and gives us an insight into the difficulties of making the transition from rural to urban living, while at the same time taking on the new responsibilities of police work, without adequate preparation.

Throughout the book, the struggle for the survival of the young Recruit Garda is shown. The tensions of training, the fear of supervisors, the subservience required and the emotional impact of having to cope with new duties and responsibilities are revealed.

In the midst of humourous stories, the serious message comes through. Examples of the deficit in the author's own preparedness and the lack of formal structures to anticipate problems and provide assistance are to be found throughout. The author was fortunate to meet people who helped. He grabbed at my available scrap of advice.

All recruits, and the *Garda Síochána* in general, owe a debt of gratitude to Guards like 'Little John', one valued advisor to the author. "Little John" counselled:

'Putting on a uniform does not change a person inside, only the outside. You will discover more about yourself in a split second in this job, dealing with the seven deadly sins, the ten commandments, and

many other indiscretion's than a year in many others'.
This must have been a huge task for the young Recruit to even contemplate.

A window is provided for each of us to look back - which is particularly worthwhile if it helps our steadfastness to share our knowledge in a resolve to ensure that our young students are properly prepared to cope with the heavy burden of today's workload for police.

Because of his own experience, Tim began to tutor young students - taking on the role of 'Little John'. Since then, Garda training methods have progressed to a level which few organisations have attained. A much deeper appreciation of the complimentary roles of formal and informal training has replaced the conflicts and lack of understanding, common at that time.

The good news is that Tim Doyle survived, came to love his work and was very successful. The final report on his performance from the Garda College - *'Sound man - very good at practical aspects'* was praise indeed in an era in which criticism created a hunger for recognition and for any crumb of acclaim.

Many of us will have experienced the same difficulties and the same trauma, but Tim Doyle has recorded his unique perspective on the 'peaks and valleys' of his early period in the Garda Síochána in the mid 1960's. Again, I say - *'Sound man, Tim'* - and excellent contribution to the store of knowledge on *An Garda Síochána*.

M.P. BYRNE
COMMISSIONER

Chapter 1 - INDUCTION

I was 14 the autumn the man in black came to our house.

My young brother Michael had the first sighting. He had been searching for a ball in the break of briars in our lane when the commotion on the main road distracted him. He looked through the gap where the belt of hedging had unbuckled allowing the hundred yard flap of passage thread into our yard. He heard the rhythmic click of the free wheel followed by the crunching swish of tyres as the bicycle wheels left the tar road and entered our gravelly lane.

Then he ran into the kitchen: "Moma..Moma, there's a big black man after me. I think it's one of them policemen I saw at Puck last year."

Moma was bent over the hearth poking the fire. She turned around with the tongs sprouting from her outstretched hands.
"Well, glory be to the will of God, I wonder what he wants? Fix your shirt, *a chroi*, and straighten yourselves. God give me patience. Any of ye see Gyp? The oul' peeler is probably checking dog licences."

Plainly my mother was rattled but she had one plan for all emergencies and that was to offer it up to the holy picture which hung on the kitchen wall opposite the front door. Day and night the image stared out, and she felt nothing harmful would enter while the Divine Saviour stood guard. Slowly her eyes drifted up to the face of God. Almost immediately her body loosened, and she relaxed. Turning, she hung the tongs back in its place. Next she began climbing to reach the top shelf of the dresser behind the yellow teapot. She got down the Bisto tin which contained what my father called her official documents. These included the children's allowances books, dates the cows were due to calf and the dog licence. She took this and went to the front door.

My brother and I ducked in behind her. We watched as the stranger placed his green bicycle carefully against our whitethorn hedge. Suddenly, disaster in the form of Gyp appeared from nowhere, and took up his stance between the visitor and the path to our door. We watched as man and beast faced one another.

As I waited I remembered the last time Gyp met a uniform. It was Christmas and a young relief postman had been helping out. We had been on the alert for a parcel from America. It was dusk on Christmas Eve when the postman was spotted standing on the pedals of his bike as he laboured up the road. A huge brown cardboard box sat into the front carrier.
"It's here," he bawled as he careered into the haggard. Gyp, who had been dozing, roused himself and unfolded. He took off with a flying leap and had the postman by the backside. Adroitly, Moma plucked our box from the bicycle just as it crashed into the hedge. The very one sided battle ended on the manure heap, the postman clutching a four pronged pike for protection, Gyp slobbering on the skin of his wellingtons.
"Don't show any fear."
It was my father. Typically, ladling out instructions rather than relief.
"He'll smell you. Easy now."

The big policeman could have been my father the way he faced the dog. At first the man stood perfectly still, then ever so slowly he extended one arm, palm downwards until it almost touched the animal's nose. Although I couldn't hear words, he appeared to be speaking softly.

Gyp bellied the ground, his body still balled in viciousness.

For what seemed a very long minute everyone waited.

Then I saw it. At first the merest flourish, then the long handle of Gyp's tail drooped and shook. Hostilities were over.. for the moment.

He might have a way with dogs, I conceded, but try to get by my mother. She was tiny, but now her frame seemed to fill the threshold. I knew there was no way this stranger would enter the house without Moma's permission.

The policeman walked slowly and deliberately along the path towards us, halting when his shadow lay at our feet.

"Good afternoon ma'am. Not a bad day. Can I talk to you? May I come in, please?"

For such a big man, he spoke quietly. Moma moved and beckoned him to follow, which he did, his bulk almost filling the kitchen. I dived for my favourite vantage point, an upturned butter box in the corner of the hearth which spanned the wall furthest from the door. My anxiety had been replaced with awe and interest. For me, the big man was fascinating. First, his size. Second, his black uniform and cap studded with silver emblems and buttons seemed to accentuate his majesty. There was little or no silver in our house. Now, this visitor dribbled with shiny magnificence. I sat back and studied him.

The uniform was intriguing. It encased his body snugly, was tapered, buttoned and belted perfectly. The tunic fastened over his front with four large silver buttons embossed in intricate design. There was so much to see. In all my life, I had come across only two chains. One was for tying the cows, the other for tackling the horse. Both were heavy, cumbersome and utilitarian.

Now, however, I saw a fine silver chain. It lay across the centre of his chest like a one-armed crucifix, having begun its journey by escaping from the left breast pocket of the tunic. Next, it travelled horizontally until captured and twisted into submission by the top button on the row before hanging limply, and ending its life by being hooked into the stem of the second button.

This was an enthralling piece of equipment, and when he moved, the buttons and chain rustled together, and gave forth a musical resonance. Finally, the big rectangular buckle fastening the waistband seemed like the seal of approval.

He stood fingering his cap. Moma took it from him and placed it on the clean page of The Kerryman newspaper which lined the window sill. Next, she chased the cat off the best chair under the holy picture, hit the cushion a few clatters and invited him to sit down. As he did so, I sidled over to study the cap. Its peak was ebony black and glistened just like the narrow plastic headband which was secured on either side by two small shiny buttons. Its crowning glory was the big badge. In its centre a big S snaked into a similar sized G with the words *'Garda Siochana na H-Eireann'* encircling.

He sat back, splendid and relaxed. He was spotless from head to toe and I decided he was the first really clean man I had ever seen.

I loved it when people came to our house. It created a bit of a stir, broke the monotony. This coming was special. He was a genuine celebrity. We would be the talk of the parish. And as the flames from the black turf danced in the hearth, the two adults began to talk, tentatively at first, then warming to each other until they were chatting like old friends.

My sloe-eyed sister Mary came in from school and still he sat on. Forgotten, the licence lay flattened on the table. So it wasn't the dog that brought him. So what was it? Surely he didn't cycle all the way from the village for nothing?

I knew what this powerful being stood for. He possessed enormous powers to stop people, ask questions, take names and addresses and bring them up before the court. The first policeman I had ever seen was at Puck Fair. My father pointed him out: 'That's a peeler boy. They're only spies'.

It was always prime news to fall foul of the police. To be caught without a bicycle light was the talk of the parish. Being pulled in and having one's name written in the big book in the barracks carried almost the same shame as having it read from the altar.

So what did he come for? I was about to find out. Suddenly his gaze fixed on me. The look seemed to accuse. Had he come for me?
"Tell me now?"
The face remained friendly but the eyes had narrowed and I knew I was to be questioned which increased my nervousness.
"What would your name be now?"

As I gave it, he was already firing another question:
"You have a bicycle?"
The quartet of words scorched. It was about my bicycle. My pride and joy. What about my bicycle? My mother's gaze coaxed me to her. That had always been the way, expecting me to read her mind. As usual, I

understood the signal. She had drummed it into us often enough, how to answer a question. Stand up straight and spit out the truth.

In a second I was upright.

"Yes sir, I have a bike."

He repeated my answer to himself: "You have a bike. I see now. Hmmm."

Just when I felt the topic had all dried up, he cocked one eye in my direction:

"And tell me now, is it much of a one?"

"Not bad," I said, "it has two brakes and a tail light, even though I don't be out at night much."

"Has it a bell?"

"No," I said, "I haven't one of them things, but I'll get one."

Surely he didn't cycle all the way from town to enquire about a friggin' bell?

"How long have you it?"

"Only a few weeks."

"And where did you get it?"

"A farmer I worked with during my holidays gave it to me instead of money."

I was drained from the inquisition and was convinced if he asked me had I killed Maurice Moore, (a local unsolved murder) I would have agreed.

"I see now," he said, turning for corroboration from Moma.

Then he did a terrible thing. Raising his right hand to the flap of the left breast tunic pocket, he brought out the famous notebook, leather bound with a stub of pencil stuck into the side. Slowly, almost resignedly, he turned the pages. Nearly half the book was full of writing. The whole parish must be in it. Eventually, he arrived at a clean page and wrote two sentences very slowly and deliberately, muttering particulars to himself. He asked the name of my employer and wrote that down as well.

It was the worst moment of my life. I had brought the peelers to our house. My name was in the book and the whole family was shamed.

Disconsolately, I stood with bent head and awaited my fate. The crackling fire seemed to be the only life until he moved again. Very carefully he replaced the book in the tunic pocket, fastened the small button and gently brushed down the flap with the palm of his hand.

I looked mutely to Moma. Amazingly she appeared to have abandoned me to my fate and was busy wetting the tea.

"You'll take a bite," she directed, handing him a large mug and a wedge of yellow bread plastered with freshly churned butter.

As they ate and drank, I remained in a right state. Even though it appeared Moma was taking it well, what if my father found out? He didn't often lose his temper, but when it happened, it lasted for days. The whole house was upset and in bad form. So what was my crime? I turned and stared at my tormentor who sat, talked, smiled and ate our bread, chasing the crumbs along the folds of the tunic and on to the knees of his pants.

So he ate, while I waited.

But when he stood up, he ignored me and moved with my mother towards the door. I ran ahead to remind him that he had put a blight on my life. Cornering me in the porch, he administered instant absolution. Cuffing me playfully with his cap, he gave me a gentle prod on the shoulder and a whisper of advice:

"Go easy on that oul' boneshaker, and don't forget the bell."

That eased my mind, but I still stood and watched as he talked with my mother in the yard. Then my father strode down the lane and joined them. I watched his face. I could read his moods as he had taught me to use the Maclicuddy Reeks as a weather vein. Sometimes he was sunny, sometimes cloudy. It appeared my performance was being discussed and judged. My father seemed to be nodding which was good, but I also noted the odd threatening look in my direction. Nevertheless, as they remained talking I got the impression my conduct was acceptable. Later they accompanied the policeman over the bohereen. I followed at a respectable distance and lingered until he mounted his bike and headed off towards the village.

Immediately my parent's body language said it all. Things would be all right. I was off the hook. The cause of all the trouble was in the turf shed and I needed the reassuring sight of my treasure. It was a man's bicycle, a crock in fact, but I had worked damn hard for it and it was all mine.

The cross-roads about a half mile from our house had been the place where the dream of my own bike first took shape. The ditch of Big Tom Murphy's field was a popular place for an evening. The big lads gathered there and I couldn't wait to be part of their gang. Last summer there had been great excitement when one of them arrived with a Raleigh bicycle. It was shiny black with tiny red and gold lines chasing each other along the edge of the frame. We were allowed a free examination only. The proud owner spun the back wheel, and explained the operation of the Sturmey Archer gears and the Hub Dynamo.

From that moment I had a fierce ambition to own my own bicycle. I had a mission. My mind was made up. I wouldn't be happy walking again.

Equally, I knew my parents couldn't afford to buy me a bicycle either new or second hand. So I kept my dream a secret. I had only one hope, to find a job. The farmers had loads of work, but would they hire me? Already I knew what it was to work and was considered very hardy. So all I wanted was a chance. With seven weeks of the summer holidays looming, I had that chance.

Near the end of May, a random encounter consolidated my opportunity. I was on my way home from school, rushed round a corner and straight into a pony and cart. The pony which had been contentedly grazing, changed instantly into a nervous, plunging animal. It reared and skidded, nearly overturning the cart in the process and sent me flying into a forest of nettles. As I recovered and began looking for dock leaves to soothe my simmering arms, I realised I had an audience. It was the owner of the horse and cart.
"Come on," he said, "I'll give you a lift home."

Perched up beside him, he fed me bulls eyes from a crumpled brown paper bag. I sucked them slowly, while he ground them fiercely two at a time.

On the journey, he rambled on, never giving me time to reply:
"Which book are you on? The best days of your life. Go on there, Bessie. You have my day spoilt, it's a hard life. Not enough hours in the day. Bess has a bit of a temper you, know, but seldom enough she gives out to me..."

I knew this farmer to see. He had a tidy farm but was a notorious layabout. He would milk the cows in the morning, head for the creamery and felt he had the day's work done. Normally the animal would remain tethered in the square while its master re-acquainted himself in a local pub with his best friend, Arthur Guinness.

Journey's end was his mucky yard. He slid down and looked up: "Can you untackle a horse?"
"Of course."
"There's a good lad. There's a small sup of separated milk in that tank, you might throw it to the few squealers."

Then he struck off towards the house. Later, I trailed him to his front door and looked in. He was inside, snoring loudly.

Thus our relationship began.

Each afternoon I waited and bummed a lift home from him. One evening he asked me to work for him in the summer holidays. I agreed immediately, feeling so excited I didn't ask about wages.

The lads at the cross-roads had loads of advice:
"Eat plenty for the breakfast, because most days, you'll see no dinner, not to mind supper. It depends on what time he gets tired of drinking. Ask for half a crown a day and haggle if you don't get it. Don't work too hard for the first week. Rub methylated spirits on the palms of the hands to toughen them."

The first day on the job flew. We were thinning turnips and he worked alongside me. After a few days, the weather grew hot, he grew thirsty, and I was abandoned. At the end of the first week, I asked for, and got six half crowns. In a few weeks I figured I would have the money for my bike, and then I could leave. Unfortunately, I confided my dream to my employer. And so the next Saturday he was nowhere to be found, and his wife did the dealing:
"He's gone to confession, look out for him after last Mass tomorrow."
I waited the next morning, but in vain. Of course, the lads on the ditch had a great laugh.
"Last Mass. Ha! That fella hasn't been to his first Mass yet."

Sadly, there was no mention of pay the next week either. But the following Friday, he appeared sober and in good form after a profitable day at the fair. As we headed across the haggard he pulled open the door of a disused hen house:

"This is for you," he said.

Inside lay as dilapidated a bike as I'd ever seen. It was a rusty crock, but it was a Raleigh, and when I brought it into the sunlight, it became transformed, with the tarnish evaporating before my eyes.

I promised him tireless work, and there was no more mention of money.

The bike was sacred. I cleaned and polished it until it gleamed. Then I took it up the hill for a trial run. Down Nauntinane I sped, with the tyres humming on the freshly tarred road.

The first day back at school in September, I cycled proudly into the yard. After that, travelling to and from school was the highlight of the day.

One day in October I had parked the bike in the village and returned to find an elderly stranger examining it.

"Is that your bike?" he said.

"It is," I replied, grabbing my precious possession by the handlebars and cycling home.

Now the guard had visited my house. It was later at the cross-roads that the whole chain of events was thrashed out. Apparently my employer had spirited the bike away from the fair and paid me off with his ill-gotten gains. Having left our house, the policeman had called to my employer. Words were exchanged, and money changed hands. And so, he who I thought was my tormentor was, really my saviour.

After that day, the big shadow began to darken our doorway on a regular basis. His visits shortened the winter. He became good friends with my parents. Looking back, I suppose he was lonely, and seeing that the nearest house to ours was over a quarter of a mile away my parents also appreciated the company. He would sit in front of the open fire, his hands outstretched to the blaze. An affable, friendly man with no family of his own, there was a great respect for him in our locality. He never pried, but we felt safe in his huge hands.

9

One foggy evening after Christmas he called as usual.

"I'm being transferred," he said simply.

He had the tea, but there was little enthusiasm for conversation.

Later on, my parents walked outside with him and stood talking at the gable. I loitered to listen and heard his disappointment and regret at leaving. He was being moved to a city half the length of the county away. An appeal had been lodged against the decision, but it was no use. I heard him say 'it was all due to the emergencies of the service'. I didn't know what he meant, but the phrase stuck in my mind. 'It's my job, I've got my orders, I'm bound to obey', he said. Then he gave one long look around our place, grabbed my parent's hands, gave a little wave in my direction, jumped on his bike and was gone out of our lives.

We all kept him in sight until he was swallowed up by the fog.

A terrible air of despondency almost as suffocating as the fog descended after his departure. I was heartbroken. Later that night my father spoke his mind:

"The poor man was broken-hearted. They've a tough oul' job, never knowing when they must pack up."

"Ah well, that's life. Come on, we'll offer up the rosary to the Sacred Heart for his intentions," said my mother.

The fond memory of the big policeman taking an interest in our lives persevered with us for a good while. His coming had a profound effect on my parents. Hitherto they had always referred to the police as peelers, but never again. 'I never thought I would welcome a uniform into my home, but that man was a gentleman', said my father.

My father was the best man I knew. His people came from the foothills of the MacGillicuddy Reeks, (known locally as the Maclicuddys) and it was said he hadn't been born but quarried! He was low sized and light hipped, with a strong muscular upper body and powerful arms. He was as durable as the mountains from which he came. He had had little schooling being barely able to read and write his name. But as he said himself, what use was writing when his pencil was the sixteen pound sledge? My father had other, better ways of getting his message across. He was a man of action. He didn't tell people how to do things, he showed them.

One of my earliest memories was of my father coming home from the Maclicuddys with his huge sledge on his shoulder. In one motion, he would twirl the weapon by the handle and fling it to one side, its heavy snout rupturing the grass margin. He watched as I grabbed the massive weapon, struggling to move it and finally collapsing on top of it. Reaching down, he would grab me with one arm, then with the other, he would expertly raise the sledge over his head. After this exhibition, I would help him drag the gigantic weapon to its place in the shed.

After supper each evening my father would sit by the window and my mother would hand him an old Brylcream jar which contained salve for his calloused hands. It was a local cure made from goose grease.

My mother had a richness of words whenever she wanted them. If he had the brawn, she had the brain. She was educated and read books with the light of a candle in bed at night. Another skill which attracted a lot of admiration was her ability to write a letter from start to finish without stopping to think. Her family were known as the Counsellor Sullivan's to distinguish them from other Sullivan clans in the kingdom. She came from Firies, and together my parents had put down strong roots in Dunloe. She was the boss of everything that crossed our threshold. 'I think we'll leave that to herself', was my father's verdict on anything complicated that came in the door. Whatever she said was law.

We lived at Dunloe Lodge and I was the third eldest. I was very proud of my home. I felt the address was notable. Also, our location commanded a fantastic view of the Gap of Dunloe. Directly outside our gate the roads from Killarney and Beaufort met, and a third dusty, spidery road slithered away to the Gap. Consequently, lots of traffic passed my door. As a small child I spent hours looking through the bars of the gate at the continuous trek of coaches, ponies, traps and side cars laden with foreign visitors heading towards the Gap with exclamations:
'Bravo, Belle, Magnifique'.

From the instant my eyes could form shapes I was enchanted by the Maclicuddys. They seemed to have a life all of their own, cloaked in contrasting textures as the day progressed. At morning, lazily waking as dawn pulled back her misty covers, glinting shadowy and burnished with astonishing hues at mid-day, and in the evening sultry or brooding in preparation for oncoming darkness.

Before I could walk I was a climber. Born to explore the mighty peaks, I began to practise on the double gate in front of our lodge. One day my eldest brother Danny got fed up with me, whooshed me on top of the gate and left me hanging and screeching like a stuck pig.

Sometimes the weather was frightening. The thunder lived up amid the heather and stones. It spoke, often bellowing like a thousand mad bulls. It terrified me, and I felt sure the mountains would fall on top of us. One evening when the thunder trembled, my mother pulled me to her and whispered: 'That's your Dada breaking a big rock'. God! I couldn't wait to be a sledgeman.

Just after my fifth birthday, we were banished from the Gap of Dunloe.

This change came about suddenly. My mother was expecting a fifth child. I sensed her withdrawal and grew bold for attention. The big double gate outside our door was like a magnet and anytime it opened or closed I was entwined like a spider on its ornamentation. This proved to be the catalyst that heralded our homelessness. I was then too young to realise the power the lady of The Big House had over our lives. She owned everything inside the gate, including us. Apparently, there were conditions attached to our lodge tenancy. One of the most binding was that the big gate should remain closed at all times except when she wanted to enter or leave. In that event one or other of my parents should be present to perform that task. From the cot, I can remember the hooting of the horn and my parents rushing out to minister to the Model T and its owner.

So at the age of five, whenever the gate opened or closed I clung to it, squawking my head off. Instead of receiving a sweet or lucky bag for this entertainment, the lady of the house took offence and headed for the parish priest. Her complaints encompassed not only me, but our expanding family. Apparently, she took exception to my mother's expectant state - again.
"When is it going to stop? Bringing all those children into the world. It's disgraceful. What hope is there for them? In the name of all that's holy, you should speak to her and put a stop to it."

She was not pleased with Father Sears' response:
"My dear lady, those children are the most precious creatures inside that gate," he said.

That ruffled her into action. The day that my new baby brother arrived was the day my father had a letter from The Big House. He didn't have to read too well to make out the black print on the top of the page 'Notice to Quit'. 'We have a boy, but no home for him', he was heard to mutter later.

So my brother Thomas's homecoming was more like a wake than a celebration. But within a few days, a house in the Black Valley was being mentioned. For me the name conjured images of a dark, forbidding place where the sun never shone. An image, reinforced by the litany after the rosary each night: 'Hail, holy Queen.... Mourning and weeping in this valley of tears'.

I can still remember the day in early December when we heaped our belongings into the lorry trailer and set off through the Gap of Dunloe for the valley. It was an adventure as far as Kate Kearney's Cottage. Then the hardship set in. The road petered away to a dirt track. Up close, the boulders were huge, magnificent, overwhelming. I will remember till the day I die the awesome feeling when I saw the Gap open up before me. How was it possible to gouge such a crucible out of the mountain? I looked at my father. Had he been part of it? As if to confirm he was, he pointed out the landmarks as we progressed... the Black Strame, Coosaun, Echo and Serpent Lakes, the Peep O'Day, The Gap Cottage, Madman's Seat, Gentleman's and Toas Doyle's Rock, the Colleen Bawn, the Barracks... "Four and a half miles of torture boy, but the tourists love it..."

Nature had combined with man in constructing the wonders of this rugged mountain path. On either side was a sheer drop to the lakes. Then there were sharp inclines and unbelievably acute curves in the roadway which caused us to reverse and creep forward at a snail's pace. Most forbidding of all were the towering rock faces on either side, barely necklaced together and apparently destined to fall on top of us at any second.

"Don't look up, We're at the Turnpike."

My father jumped down and ran ahead to direct us. Ahead was a huge rock, sliced in two halves to allow the minimum space to progress. The location, plus another sheer incline and a sharp right bend made negotiation very difficult. But the worst was to come in the shape of the shoulder of Corrantuathail.

Looking ahead the dusty pathway snaked upwards, disappearing and reappearing by turns. The lorry began skidding and losing ground. We ended up heaving tea chests on to the road to lighten the load. My mother got out and began to walk holding Thomas in her arms. Pushing and shouting we all helped the old truck up and over the summit until we heard my father shout we were through the gap.

Then we rested a while on a flat nothingness with the lorry snorting and stuttering behind us from her exhaustion's. The driver drew a bucketful of water from a nearby waterfall and splashed it over the foaming engine. Then we moved on again, until immediately below lay the Black Valley. All my fears gone, my first feeling was joyous wonder. The spectre of darkness vanished as the valley shimmered below. It should, I thought, be rechristened the valley of light. Specially for us, it seemed, a pale horseshoe of a rainbow hung like a bucket handle along its eastern flank, while away to the west, the watery sun splayed out shafts of golden light.

We moved down into the valley and I searched for our new home. Suddenly, we stopped outside a low slung cabin with a thatch roof badly in need of a transplant. I ran in the door - and up to my knees in water.

The first night in our two roomed home was unforgettable.

First we had the feathery drops of rain clattering into Moma's saucepans. Later we had more guests. Their arrival was heralded by a furtive scratching up in the thatch, followed by a plopping sound in the bottom of our bed.

The following day their identities were revealed when my father beat the thatch with a spade and a family of mice scattered up the mountain. I was sad that it was their turn to be evicted. The derelict house bound us together in hardship, but we were at least free and beholden to nobody. The valley people took us to their hearts and ensured that my father didn't suffer a day's idleness.

I loved our new home. I loved the ruggedness, the simplicity of life, sitting by the fire and telling stories. Even the winter was kind to us, and while the snow swirled up in the crags, it let us alone. Crossing the Upper Lake in Tangney's boat for Mass at Derrycunnihy was a highlight all its own.

However, my parents had decided that there was no future for us in the valley long-term. And within a year the county council had found us a home past Dunloe - a small cottage in the mixed farmland of mid-Kerry. Of course, the mountains were still there, demanding the continual raising of the eyelids. A vast panorama now extending along the skyline, west to the cock's comb of Glencar and east to where the gentle slopes of the Tomies dipped into Loc Leane.

Our neighbours were welcoming. Our nearest one John *Rua* Sullivan had twelve of his own to nourish but was still generous:
"There's a well behind the gate, it's yours. There's a pit of spuds above the ditch and a field of turnips yonder. Don't ever go hungry or thirsty."

In this farming country the rock-breaking sledge was put away and never used again. I grew up with other tools in my hands. Two, three and four pronged pikes, shovel, spade, slean, scythe, grubber, hay knife, hatchet and slash hook. My father was a master of all these. Patiently, or sometimes with an encouraging clip of the ear, he ingrained in me a critical respect in the care and use of all implements.

My father was always on the go. He would listen to the weather forecast on the wireless and hear that millibars were rising slowly: 'Shag the millibars', he'd say. 'Tell me, will it rain or not?'

My older brother Danny was two years older than I. Danny was tough and able to take care of himself. He was always fighting after Mass and on his way home from school. He had a deadly *ciotog*. As well as that he was a great worker and much in demand by the farmers. When he was seventeen, I noticed a change in our house. First, my mother began to write a lot of letters. It was funny to see my father watch her as the words flowed from the nib of her big, green Schaeffer pen. He was very proud of her ability: "She has a great hand. Look at them big words.

She could read the stars."

I remember one black frosty night we were all sitting around the open fire when we had an unexpected visitor. It was a cantankerous individual known locally as Ray Sunshine. He had come to ask my mother to write a letter to his brother in America.
"He lives in Boston, Mass. Now I've heard of first mass, last mass, high mass and low mass, but I've never heard of Boston Mass," he said.
"Oh, that's Boston, Massachusetts, USA," Moma said, reaching for her writing stuff. "What do you want to say?"
"Tell him.... leave me alone. I've shag all time for composing letters and I don't need any more of his effin' dollars. I've a jug full of them at home and if I brought them into town they'd only say I was living on charity. So send no more. There now. That's it."

My mother wrote the letter and at the end read it aloud: "Well, glory be," burst out Ray Sunshine, "It's above in Dublin you should be, writing books."

Another night a sad-faced widow came to see us. Again the request was for Mrs Doyle to do a letter. But this was a begging one to a distant cousin who ran a prosperous business in Chicago. The fat, vacant looking daughter who accompanied the mother was anxious to emigrate and this letter was to encourage the cousin to take her over.

Again, Moma wrote the letter and it went on its way. Three months later as we left Mass, we met the widow: "The blessings of God on you," she said. "We got an answer and they want my daughter to travel immediately. They were so taken by her letter they said she would have no problem fitting into their company."

One day a big, long envelope came to our house. It had several strange looking stamps plastered onto one corner. Its arrival changed our family forever. Danny was going to America.

And so, one morning the following November I was wakened by a fistful of hailstones bouncing on the roof. It was about five o'clock. I became aware of the soft glow of the candle as my father came into our bedroom. Quietly, he approached Danny's bed: 'Get up, boy. Get up'. My brother stood slight and pale and looked at me directly. We didn't speak. It was no time for words. Suddenly he gave a deep sigh and began to dress. Then, along with his teenage shadow, he left my room forever.

I turned to the wall, covered my head, closed my eyes and began to cry.

Later I heard the motor leaving our yard. It was the first time we had motor tyres leaving prints on our bohereeen. That evening my mother said: "I'd nearly prefer if it was the hearse that was calling."

A bit of us all sailed away in the 'Franconia' with Danny that day. I swore I would never leave home when I saw the sadness that followed Danny's departure. Soon his first letters began to arrive. Meanwhile, each night a decade of the rosary was offered for his intentions.

Danny's going changed my life in other ways. First, there was more food to go around. I grew bigger and tougher. Also, local farmers were calling me more regularly for work. It seemed I was next on the conveyor belt of labouring boys. They had their own way of trying to get the best out of you: 'Your brother was good but you'll be better. I'll train you well. You have good prospects here. We always look after the servant boy'.

Fine words, but working with the farmers was an education. Sometimes the food was plentiful. Other times I got little. Often, on a Saturday night all I got was ' the Lord spare you the health', or 'I'll be seeing your father, boy'.

I remember one farmer who was a slave driver. The first Saturday night as I washed my wellingtons under the tap in the yard, he sidled up to me:
"The wife is grousing all day about money. Wait for me at the gable of the house after tea and I'll fix up with you."

Later we met and he thrust a sugar bag into my hand. It gave a satisfactory rattle as I marched home, but on the kitchen table I counted three half-crowns, two single shillings, and about a dozen old pennies - ten shillings for 72 hours work.
"Offer it up for the Holy Souls," said Moma
"What about this poor soul?" I answered.

At this stage I had no ideas about my future, except to follow in the footsteps of the father I idolised and become a labouring man.

Chapter 2 - INCULCATION

My greatest interest outside work was football. It was through football I met the second man in black. It was the parish league final and we were up against the townies. Normally, we were the braver team, but this year Big Andy, the new guard, was in charge. He was huge. But like many big men he was a gentleman.

At half time, we got together to discuss how we could curb the big man. The trainer looked at me:
"Here's the plan. I'm putting you on him. All you have to do is soften him up. When the first high ball comes, wait until he jumps and opens up his body to catch it, then tear into him. Make sure he's off the ground when you give him the sickener."

I didn't know what he meant, but had no time to ask. The whistle went and we were away. The ball came our way, a low one. Our supporters bayed for blood. I charged in. He just grunted but kept going. I fell away, and we lost the match.

After the game, Andy sought me out:
"Shake," he said. "You played a hell of a game. You took a rasher off me though."
"That's no loss to you. I tried to knock a few sausages out of you as well."
"I felt my guts rattling right enough."

I was proud of the acknowledgement that at least I was a trier.
"You're still filling out," he said. "I wouldn't like to cross you in a year or two. You know, you'd have the makings of a guard."
"I'd make a finer blackguard," I said, and we had a good laugh.
During the next few months, I tested myself against him many times. We kicked ball a couple of evenings a week in the football field and he taught me how to use my hips to maximum effect when shouldering.

Also he remedied the timing of my tackle. We had great tussles and I began to improve with every session.

Then overnight I became head of our household. The near-fatal day my father was doing a turn for a distant farmer. Having finished work, I decided to give him a hand. A good job too, as I discovered him stretched on a desolate moor. The sight of the purple trembling lips and the agony creasing his handsome face filled me with terror. He had lain in a half-coma since morning, his ruptured heart refusing to stop.
"Thank God you came. The grey crow was about to try to pick out my eyes."

My father was 63 years old and working as hard as a man half his age. He got married at 43 and figured he had to work twice as hard to provide for us. He couldn't afford to die. What about the three others at home that needed rearing? Now he was laid up and I felt obliged to take up the slack.

Almost overnight I became a man and could go hard all day without tiring. The farmers were delighted and beat a path to my door. I had my pick of work and there wasn't enough hours in the day.

Moma, however, had other ideas.
"Do you want to be going around for the rest of your life with your backside out of your pants?" she asked rhetorically... "No son of mine is going to end up as a servant boy. The farmers will be screeching for you on a fine day, but when the weather breaks they won't look at the side of the road you walk on."

Her attitude unsettled me and I talked it over with Andy. But he took her part:
"Apart from the family there is nothing here for you," he said. "The days of the labouring man are numbered. In a few years this place will be cluttered with machinery. Soon you will have to make a decision to go. Follow your mother's advice, she won't let you go far wrong. Have you given any thoughts to joining up?"

For my part, the guards never crossed my mind. Nobody in our locality had ever joined the guards. Deep down, I felt it was a job for brainy fellows. I was only a labouring man's son. My sole interest then was to work, hand over my earnings and take care of my parents.

The letters continued to arrive from Danny stuffed with dollars. This impressed me, and secretly the notion of joining him began to take root. Moma, as usual, read my mind.
"You'll not be going to America. I reared one for the boat, and that's my quota. Something will turn up for you, my bucko."

I knew she was plotting something.

It was at that time a third and most influential guard of all entered my life. He had retired after 30 years in Dublin. He had bought a mixed farm with the wettest portion adjoining our bog. He was delighted with his purchase and would regale each passer-by with the attributes of his holding, until one day a local character delivered the perfect squelch: "Tell me now. Did you buy it by the gallon?"

This retired guard spent a lot of time hanging around the road, to the extent that people went out of their way to avoid him. He learned to counter this by perfecting the art of concealing himself in a ditch until a suitable victim appeared. I found him likeable enough except he could be very boring and repetitive. He frequently launched forth into one of several stories about life in the force in Dublin:
"Now, I remember when I was in Store Street, there was a terrible gouger living in the flats. One day the sergeant directed another big pounder of a garda and myself to go up and arrest him. When we got to the door, there was about forty locks on it. What do you think we did then?"

I soon discovered that this was purely a rhetorical question. He wanted no interruption.
One day, early in our relationship, I attempted to answer one such query and his face almost exploded in annoyance. I learned to suffer in silence and got to know his routine.

The question would hang in the air as he would chuckle a few times to himself, give a little shiver, then act out the old scenario, striding across the road, turning at the ditch and marching back again. Finally, he'd finish the story... tell how they took the door off the hinges, grabbed the prisoner, gave him a bit of a flaking, and so on.. and on.. and on...

Inexplicably my mother and himself became very great. She was spending more and more time in the dyke of the road with our new neighbour. Surely she was not carrying on with him and my father laid up?

It was the new year before I discovered what they were hatching. True to form, she caught me unawares. I had just got up from dinner one evening and was having a good stretch when she hit me low and hard. "C'mon with me. It's time you were going to be measured for the guards."

With that she turned her bicycle in the yard and I followed her. We cycled to the garda station. The door was open, and we entered a drab office. The room was empty and on a desk lay a number of hard-covered books. Suddenly the oldest looking guard I have ever seen came in a rear door. He wore a uniform trousers, collarless shirt and sleeves folded precisely above his elbows.
He addressed my mother:
"Well Missus, you're here. And I see you've brought him."
"I did," she replied. "Do you think he'll be of any use?"
"Strip lad," he commanded.
I couldn't believe my ears and looked to my mother for guidance. He spoke again.
"Only the shirt lad. Come on, now, I'm sure we've seen it all before."

Soon I felt the sharp tingle of the tape measure on my chest.
"Now back to the wall."
I did as I was told and my height was noted. "Same height as Jesus Christ. What was good enough for the Son of Man should do the *Garda Siochana*"

Lingering before our departure I overheard my mother's thanks and a promise that there would be something special for him in Larkin's Bar after last mass the next Sunday.

We heard no more for a while, until one morning I got further directives from the woman in my life.
"The garda examination is on in the Ashe Hall, Tralee, next Wednesday. Meet James Murphy's lorry at Woods's Corner at eight o'clock."

The exam hall was nearly empty. The test consisted of a paper in Irish,

English, History, Geography and Maths. I thought it was so easy, it would be impossible to fail.

A few months later came news of my success. Within weeks Her Master's Voice had more instructions:
"Next Monday at 10am, you have an interview with the Superintendent in Tralee."

The transport was provided again by James Murphy. The lorry driver was all guff.
"The gards have a great life. Not much to do, considerin'.. Most of the country people are harmless. An odd stroll through the village or a knock on a pub door now and again is all that's needed to keep them in tow. It's an up-and-coming job with a free uniform and a good pension at the end of your days."

Like all the policemen I'd known, my interviewer was big, more stocky than tall, middle-aged, heavy-lidded, his eyes showing only the merest flicker of interest in my arrival.
The interview consisted of his firing volleys of questions and nodding encouragingly at my replies:
"What span are you? What's the colour of your eyes? Why do you want to become a member of the Garda Siochana?"

I told him I spanned my height and said my eyes were brown.
"Now why do you want to join the Gardai?" He repeated the question.
I was stuck. I hadn't thought about this. It was on the tip of my tongue to reply that it was my mother's idea, not my own, but instead I smiled, stole the the last bit of James Murphy's line and laid it on him.

He acknowledged the reply and changed course again. Did I like Gaelic football? When he heard I did a bit on the field, he took a new lease of life, clapping his hands and embarking on a fierce solo run:
"Roscommon were the team of the forties. We won two All-Irelands those times and had great tussles with your county. They're a bit down this year. But they'll appear overnight like the mushrooms."
Next he cupped his hands in front of him and jigged around the floor.
"Show me how you catch a high ball?"
We ended up waltzing round the room, playing the game of our lives.
As I left, he shook my hand and said:

"Tell your father you met a footballer of the forties."

The next summons was for a medical. When the word filtered out, one local wit was heard to remark: 'It's not a medical that fella wants but a miracle. Sure, he's stone mad!'

This examination was to be held at the Garda Depot in Dublin. My sister Mary who was now teaching there met the train. I slept badly in the large, unfriendly city, got up late, gashed myself shaving and went for my interview with half a toilet roll plugging my cuts.

The surgeon was a perfect gentleman until the moment he grabbed my testicles and said 'cough'. Instead I closed my fist. He saw this, smiled, and let go. I walked up and down, called out A, B, C, and other letters on the wall. He seemed satisfied.

Later, I sat on the small wall at the entrance to the Phoenix Park and watched city life at first hand. Incessant noise. A perpetual thudding heart that never drew breath. Traffic. People. Rush. Noisy lorries, hissing buses, traffic bumper to bumper. And all of it controlled by a bunch of green, red and yellow coloured lights. And very little chat. The dearth of conversation amazed me. At home, we'd say someone had gone mad if they didn't say something in passing, or at least greet you.

That evening as I journeyed home I swore I would never live in a city.

A few weeks later a letter arrived from the Garda Depot. It referred to my medical and the fact that I had two curious teeth. This caused consternation with the mirror being plucked from the wall and shoved in front of my face. I had almost begun to suffer from lockjaw when my mother showed the letter to the ex-policeman who solved the problem. That word 'curious' should read 'carious', he said.
My carious teeth were fixed and a letter duly sent confirming this.

Three months later I was working in the bog when a second letter came. My father, who was now convalescing, ambushed the postman and held on to it until supper time. 'If you are still desirous of becoming a member of the *Garda Siochana*, please report to the Garda Training Centre, Templemore, Co Tipperary on December 29th'.

Attached to this communication was a long list of necessities to be brought with me.

My father had a great time poring, over this list and every night thereafter he would address Moma:

"Where's that letter Mam?"

"Which one?" She pretended innocence.

"Aw. The one about the guards."

Then she would reach up behind the yellow teapot and read out all the items, stopping when he grunted to allow time for him to comment.

The inventory included the following:

A strong suitcase.

A suit of plain clothes.

Two complete changes of underwear.

Two shirts.

Three towels, one of which must be a bath towel.

Two pairs of pyjamas. (Another first for the Doyle males who always slept in our pelt.)

A shaving kit.

A comb, hairbrush, nail brush, clothes and boot brush.

(What did anyone do with both a comb and hairbrush?)

A toothbrush and toothpaste.

Three pairs of black or navy blue socks.

Two pairs of black boots or shoes, new or in good repair, plain Derby pattern, round toe with toe caps.

(This silenced him totally, He never knew shoes could be described in such detail. After that on his return from Mass, he'd say 'I saw so-and-so with a pair of gards shoes on him'.)

A pen, ball-point or fountain.

(This was the one piece of equipment he approved of. He always said the guards needed a good pen for taking names and addresses.)

A list of relatives living in the Republic of Ireland giving names, addresses, degrees of relationships and occupation.

Relatives within but not including the degree of second cousin or its equivalent need only be considered. Where a number of relatives reside in the one household, the name of the head of the household will suffice. (This demand caused much soul searching and was finally 'left to herself' to sort out.)

Finally on the next to last line, an entry phrased as follows: 'if you have in your possession an outfit for participating in athletics or games, (including white canvas gym shoes and/or swimming trunks), bring it with you'.

Lastly, a directive:

'Please reply without delay stating if you will attend'.

My mother replied stating I would be honoured to enlist in the *Garda Siochana*. Having licked the flap of the envelope she placed it on the table and slapped her palm three or four times on it. Then ceremoniously, she addressed me. 'Now Tim, my strong boyo, you're signed, sealed and ready for delivery'.

A new chapter had begun.

Later, I took the garda letter and list and walked to my own spot at the butt of Nauntinane. There I read and re-read it. I was excited but perturbed. I knew nothing about the outside world and here I was with my destiny in my hands. I had been content in my secluded home and used to the simple life. I could cut turf, save hay and milk cows. I knew the call of the woodcock and the eerie, frantic twitter of the snipe as it whirred across the moor at evening time. I could track the rabbit and fox. I knew where the brown trout lay in the dark shady pools of Laune River. Now, I wondered would this knowledge be of any benefit to me in the outside world.

Memories of my earlier associations with the gardai were the only inklings of what lay ahead. I thought particularly of my first bicycle and the huge uniformed figure. Where was he now? Was he happy? I thought too of Big Andy. He had been replaced by the older garda who had measured me. Then there was the retired man who roamed the roads with his memories and had finally snared me through my mother.

There were other frightening concerns. Would I be tough or intelligent enough? Would I like training? What if I were found wanting? One thing was sure - being thrown out of the guards would be considered by my family a fate worse than death.

My mother was a changed woman and began to fuss around me. Just like the Christmas goose wandering around the yard, for me, the coming holiday would end in a parting.

One day she arrived home with a large suitcase. This was placed on the floor at the foot of my bed. Next she began to wash and iron my extra clothing and pack them within. As the weeks passed and the pile of clothes grew larger, I knew that my future was irrevocably linked with the contents of the case.

The night before my departure I went off on my own.

I had said goodbye to our neighbours. Now I visited the bog, the river, the crossroads. I looked once more at the night sky, and the full moon sitting on top of Nauntinane. I talked to the farm animals. I was very lonely.

The next day Gyp cried as I left the yard. My mother threw holy water on me while my father watched silently from the house gable. I remembered Danny's departure, and felt I too was emigrating. More than anything I wanted my parents to be proud of me. They had reared me well. Now it was up to me. No words were spoken, none necessary. We just looked, remembered and loved.

Cronin's Beetle was to be my conveyance. As the car drove out the bohereen Jack the cob ran along inside the ditch whinnying her farewell. Then we were on the tar road and I was on my way. The early part of the journey was like a funeral. Complete silence as far as Limerick. It flogged rain too which didn't help. After Limerick, Donie the driver opened up a bit:
"You'll have a nice clean shoe on you in the guards," he began. I didn't reply, just stared out the window.
"That's the Golden Vale," he continued. "No more hard work for you, boy."

I looked down at the welts on my palms and clenched my fists.

At the signpost outside Moneygall, the Volkswagen began to sulk. Later the twin exhaust collapsed, causing a pit stop. We ripped a length of wire from a nearby ditch to secure the pipes. Having got over the incline, he throttled her down, muttering that the noise would probably have the law on our tail before long.

He didn't relish going through Templemore, but skated through the side streets and followed the sign post to the big double gate. Our goodbyes were brief, the snort from the belching exhaust being the most memorable. The rain still bucketed down. I hefted the suitcase in the direction of the office. I stood at the door and watched the Kerry registration trundling back home.

I heaved a sigh and walked into the office.

I was going to wear the uniform of the *Garda Siochana*.

Chapter 3 - INCARCERATION

The office immediately inside the gate was known as the Guardroom.

Later, the reason for this became clear; day and night a member of the force remained on duty there monitoring every movement to and from *Ionad Treanala an Garda Siochana*, the sign emblazoned in wrought iron over the entrance gate.

From that day onward this nerve centre controlled me. Its strident tannoy blasted me from bed each morning with the sleep-shattering Reveille, and its haunting Last Post packed me off at night.

As I lumbered my suitcase through the door I saw a uniformed garda draped across the counter. He ignored me totally and remained staring out towards the gate with a pensive expression on his face. Soon the Guardroom filled up with other new arrivals. Silently we stood around and sized each other up. Suddenly from the door at the back, the biggest guard I had ever seen strode forward confidently. Approaching the counter his feet became entangled with a set of golf clubs belonging to one of the new intake. Stumbling slightly, he reared back and lit on the unfortunate golfer in a raucous voice:
"Get rid o' them sticks. Do you think it's Butlin's yu're coming to?"

He showed such disdain, I gave him my full attention. He had a magnificently proportioned body with shoulders at least a yard wide. From there, his trunk wedged down to a slim waist. The superb torso was accentuated by the inch-wide tackle of leather strap which fitted snugly over one shoulder and travelled diagonally along his chest to his midriff. There the harness joined forces with a more substantial and impressive belt secured round his waist with a heavy two pronged buckle.

Compared to the splendid physique, the head was a let down. Angular in shape and tilted backwards and sideways, its dominant features were

29

the eyes which gazed with a haughty, pitiless stare. His expression reminded me of our gander at home, whose twisted head, rolling eyes and hiss of opposition warned me off the ash pit. At that moment I silently christened him The Gander.

A trainload of anxious impressions beat in my every pulse. I had been lonesome before, now I was becoming more apprehensive by the minute. I didn't like the cut of this officer. Before I could rationalise my muddled thoughts, he planked himself in the middle of the group.
"Be quiet. Stand still."
He spoke in orders. His voice was rasping, high pitched, provocative and unnerving. No word of welcome. Here was someone used to getting his own way. He reeked of authority and command and I prayed he wouldn't have much dealings with us. But immediately he began calling out surnames from a sheet of paper, grinning malevolently when one or two missed their first roll-call. My prayer was not to be answered.

From somewhere on his person, he unearthed a short cane, and fondled its length as he glared at each of us in turn. Suddenly he erupted.
"Get out. Out in the square... On the double."
These orders created such urgency that there was an instant stampede of bodies for the door which immediately became jammed. He was ready, using his cane to prod free the blockage. As I grabbed my case to move, it keeled over with a loud smack. Like lightening, he was on me:
"Who're yu?"
At first I thought he said 'you whore you', and stared until he repeated the question.
"Who're yu?"
"I'm Doyle," I replied.
At this he bristled and moved closer slapping the cane against his thigh. I held his gaze more from habit than daring until he spoke again:
"Yu look a bit daft...Ha."
Then before I could dredge out a word, he had swivelled away, shouting:
"All of ye, folly me."

He strode off majestically towards the arch that split the row of buildings at the far side of the square. We dawdled behind like a bunch of disorientated goslings.

To my right I admired two separate groups of about fifty trainees marching smartly on the tarmacadam square. In unison they changed direction, turned about, and stopped dead so expertly it appeared miraculous. They were precise and controlled in their movements as they reacted instantly to the crisp, barking orders of a pencil-slim Garda instructor: 'Squad.. Attention. Quick march. Halt.. About turn.. Form fours'.
The synchronised crunch of shoe leather on the hard surface really impressed.

Passing underneath the arch the area opened out into a neatly laid out section of grass, kerbed off and dotted with shrubs and rose beds. On three sides the area was surrounded by sturdy three storied terraced buildings, while ahead stood another detached trio.

One of these was the Recreation Hall. We entered and were told to stand in one corner of the room. It was then I noticed two other officers near the stage and when our leader joined them, the three riddled us with a package of baleful expressions.

This exercise in psychological warfare reminded me of the pre-Christmas ritual that takes place in our house every year and had occurred as usual a week before I left. That morning my father asked me to hold the door of the fowl shed open as, armed with a coarse bag, he entered. Inside, the half-dozen geese erupted, plunging and staggering away from the invader. Recoiling in the furthest corner, they gnashed in terror, their plumpness an enemy to their sanctuary. There was a brief respite while he made his selection, then the smothering sack descended, signalling a horrific high-pitched gurgle of despair from the trapped victim.

Finally the doomed creature was drawn forth, its muffled cry now a quiet echo of the loud and mournful lamentations of the grieving family.

Now the same feeling of impending doom gripped me as I huddled close to my comrades. Thankfully, we were told to sit down. The officers did likewise. No sack over the head. Yet.

I scoured the three for any hint of virtue. Arising from my previous altercation with The Gander, I felt he would give no quarter. Hoping for better, I moved on. My eyes drank in the middle man. Someone beside me muttered 'Chief', and I looked with awe on this high-ranking officer. The uniform certainly impressed. The glint of gold embossed on the peak of the cap. The burnished double diamonds and bar on each shoulder. His frame seemed packaged into the uniform, and if the wrapper peeled off, I felt he would disintegrate. In contrast to The Gander, his leather tackle looked drab and discoloured. He didn't have the body for the belt.

Ceremoniously he took off his hat and planted it on the table in front of him its peak pointing suggestively towards us. As if to acknowledge his omnipotence, a shaft of sunlight splayed on him from a high window behind his shoulder. The beam enveloped him and spilled onto the table where it glinted on the heavily mossed platinum of his headgear, almost blinding me in its glare.

On his right sat another officer. At first glance he seemed puny and uninteresting, an impression I was later to amend. Giving them all the once over again, I ended with The Gander, who still wore a sneer on his lopsided face.

One by one they began to speak. After our reception at the gate, I no longer expected a welcome, and I wasn't disappointed. There was no welcome. No greeting. There was instead the official commercial:
"You are very fortunate young men to be here today having been selected to train as recruit gardai. This is no holiday camp, and your conduct here will be monitored in the strictest manner. You are hoping to become part of a disciplined force and it is our function to enforce the regulations in that regard. You are here for eighteen weeks and anyone who finds it too difficult is free to leave any time they choose."

This was the nub of the opening address. Mouthfuls of words cobbled into badly structured sentences, repeated in different ways and serving only to confuse. The impersonal delivery with which these directives were pebble dashed was off-putting. Snippets came and went:
"The gate is the sole means of entry and exit from this centre. Anyone leaving or entering must sign the book in the Guardroom. Nobody is allowed out after 11pm, except on a special pass. No fraternising with the female staff in the canteen."

No this. No that. No nothing.

And they droned on with what seemed an endless list of rules about order, decorum, personal cleanliness, rooms, time to go to bed, to get up, to eat, to pray, to study, to stay alive. Another startling piece of information was that from now on a bugle would start and end our days.

Next we were handed two printed lectures with about thirty headings relating to our conduct while training. These, in turn, were subdivided into an imposing array of regulations, duties, orders and directives. Finally, all were copper-fastened under one great commandment: 'Thou shalt obey the training personnel at all times'.

My mind trailed away from this deluge and I began to consider my fate. First impressions were not encouraging. There would be no smiles here. Our instructions would be inflicted rather than imparted. I was in for a totally alien experience.

My thoughts returned to a happier state, the sanctuary of home. While I had arrived physically, spiritually I was still at home in Kerry. I realised that assimilating these slabs of commands would be difficult when my head was elsewhere, a realisation which added to my confusion. One frightening reality was present - the certainty that many of the traits and values I had learned and cherished would now be ruthlessly shoved to one side to make room for the influx of discipline.

Suddenly, my thoughts were interrupted by The Gander's harsh voice. He told us we were about to be sworn in as members of the *Garda Siochana*. One by one we were called up to the top table and required to take an oath.

As I waited my turn, more thoughts of happier times swelled my mind. Memories of my father and Gyp as we corralled the sheep in the secluded corner of the Angle and marked them. That, at least, meant I took my first solemn oath with a smile in my heart:
"I swear by Almighty God that I will without fear, favour, malice or ill will uphold the Constitution..." and so on.
In all fairness to the people of Ireland, the Constitution and the Almighty, that oath was for me at any rate, a monumental sham.

Ideally this occasion should be a highlight of a career. No way. This was because I was not mentally prepared to appreciate what was going on. Nothing was explained. The impression was that the oath was something of no great importance to be got out of the way as quickly as possible. Further, the ceremony was performed at the wrong time - at the beginning of our training rather than at the end. I believed that completion of training would be the proper forum for such a notable administration.

I was given my registration or long number. Just like the sheep at home, I had been branded. This bunch of numbers would remain with me as long as I remained a garda. Following that initiation, we were assigned our quarters. Three to a room. I had two 'John's' with me, both from the Banks of the Shannon.

Later, as I stared out the window and noted the watery sun fall away to the west, I searched the skyline for anything resembling a friendly mountain, but found none. As I had discovered on my cross-country journey the flat belly of Ireland lacked appeal and would take getting used to. All the scenery available was a dark straggle of hills struggling for survival away on the horizon at the back of the Recreation Hall. I followed their contour until the point where they bundled up and threatened to become a mountain. However the peak was unspectacular except for one characteristic. It had a gap. Nothing like Dunloe, but the cross on the adjoining mound made me recall its counterpart on Corrantuathail. Later the hill was identified as the Devil's Bit, and I wondered if that unsavoury character would influence our training.

The call to the Angelus blared from the Tannoy - but I felt it would take more than prayers to guarantee happiness in this crazy institution.

Next, the invisible voice summoned us for tea in the canteen. This was another of the detached buildings. One side was for cooking and serving food, the remainder was laid out with formica-topped tables set for four. The atmosphere was tense - you were afraid to even blink. This was due mainly to the unnerving presence of a plain clothes member who lounged near the service area staring in our direction with a sinister expression. Later, I was to compare him to the picture of God on the wall at home - no matter what position I occupied, the hypnotic stare seemed to fall on me.

The highlight of that first day was our chat with the guards who were the previous intake to ourselves. They were delighted with our arrival because it meant some attention would be diverted from them. But for me they too were lifesavers as they explained both layout and system. For openers, they said the arch was a focal point where details of all classes and other activities were displayed. It was vitally important to check and note all directives.

They further explained that the early parade held most horrors. These inspections were used to snare and cull. They urged us to be spotless in person and clothing and to call the opposition 'Sir'. They continued with a scenario of terrifying portents. During the first days, officers apparently lashed the new arrivals with a mixture of ridicule and control disguised as discipline. It seemed their motives were to break us by eroding our self-respect and rooting out any obstinacy or laziness towards the staff and training schedules. Apparently, the mission was to make smithereens of our independence, and so clear the way to implant the perfect Garda embryo.

These revelations shocked me. My feelings of dread were confirmed. Our mentors illustrated their point with an anecdote concerning a previous batch of recruits. On their first parade the inspecting officer was hounding for blood. His victim was from the country, and had obviously been earmarked as a whipping boy:
"You didn't polish your shoes this morning?"
"No," replied the trainee.
"No..what?" cut in the officer.
"No polish," said the trainee.
"No polish.. what?" stormed the fuming officer.
"No polish brush," replied the other.

No more questions, but a verbal barracking.
From then on that recruit called even his best friend 'Sir'.

They also explained that the shoes were a favourite ploy to catch a raw recruit off balance. Apparently, on parade, a bark from the inspecting officer on the state of one's footwear causes one to drop the eyes, so concentration vanishes. This then was the signal for the blitzkrieg of shouts of 'attention, eyes front' - and a massive dollop of embarrassment.

We milked the group for every dribble of information. Apparently The Gander was the prime mover in all the skulduggery.

That night I missed the family rosary, the smell of my mother's fresh bread, the relaxed atmosphere of home and the drowsy scent of candle grease which wafted me to sleep each night. Instead, I had been transported to a small town in the centre of my country, where, under the direction of a misguided, character, I was being re-programmed to serve the state without fear, favour, malice or ill-will. How would I adapt? Later, as I tussled with the bedclothes, the haunting Last Post was a fitting end to a confusing day.

The next morning I got the fright of my life. A mournful, dreadful alarm clock in the shape of the Reveille jangled my nervous system and I was still asleep as my feet hit the ground. It was 6.45am. The last time I had been up that early was going to Puck Fair with a few cattle. Our attempts to line up for our first parade reminded me of that occasion - shuffling, stamping feet, shouts and confusion. Watching the previous class march smartly on to the square showed how it should be done.

Our group did its best. We stood to attention, then at ease but we were far from relaxed. I watched the big clock over the arch for a full half hour. As we stood the Devil's Bit spat flakes of snow on top of us. The recruit beside me was shivering. I was glad of my Varsity worsted sports jacket, compliments of Crowley's, Killorglin. Still, my face was frozen lifeless. My nose ran straight for my mouth, then iced up. Trying to accommodate such discomfort was unbearable. Standing at ease required the feet a straddle of eighteen inches with the arms extended behind the back, right hand in palm of left and thumbs crossed. As a result, reaching for a handkerchief was out of the question. All I could do was use my breath to fan the frozen icicle.

The Gander suddenly appeared, massive, overbearing, aloof. He was accompanied by the officer on whom I had reserved judgement the previous evening. Today he impressed. His head seemed small, but intelligent. The cap crammed over his ears gave the impression of shyness peeping out under the peak. His eyes were his best feature, alternatively darting or peering mischievously. He was squat, with a mincing walk. He shuffled along the rows of recruits until apparently at random he would bounce to a halt and tackle his victim. Then other peculiarities became evident. He swayed on his feet when standing still and was continually balanced on his heels. He spoke as if through a mouthful of gobstoppers, but not having heard this snappy, musical accent before, I found it fascinating. Finally, he emphasised a point by balling one fist and banging it into the palm of the other hand. He seemed quaint, with a spark of decency lurking close to the surface.

After a few days we were to see less of this officer and were left mainly to the dry-gulching of The Gander. That first parade, we got a dispensation. First and last. The following morning the reign of terror began. Both officers took the field with The Gander, in particular, scalp-hunting. He gave us the full treatment. It was a black frosty morning. We were lifeless with the cold but he seemed to relish our agony. Stalking behind his colleague, he scrutinised each individual at length. I found this most disconcerting and didn't know whether to stare back or drop my eyes. In the end I settled for a bit of both. Our mentors were right. The policy was to embarrass and belittle as much as possible.

Each morning The Gander would roar his selection of victims from the rows with his coarse, piercing voice:
"Durty buttons, uniform not pressed, shoes not polished, uniform not brushed, slovenly appearance, haircut, pace forward, pace to the rear."

The result was that disciplinary proceedings were instituted without any explanation or representation. The recruit was found guilty as charged and had to sign a disciplinary form to that effect. There was an air of secrecy about these practices and nobody dared question any decrees or punishments meted out.

During that first week The Gander pulled me three times for haircuts. It began to dawn on me that he had selected me for his flock of black sheep. During our meetings he would rear back allowing his eyes to crucify me with a tantalising stare. Next his lips would slap together in a pout, finally the words would come out in a tangle of hums and haws.
"Dile. Haa. Hair cut. Hmm... Pace forward."
The third time he lit on me, I could hardly move to save my life.
"Stand up strate, Dile. Stick out your chest."
Sucking in an overfill of oxygen, I tried.
"Look at me strate in the face."
Again I obliged, but he wanted more.

"What do you see?"

For a split second, I thought of... But I funked it.

"I see you..Sir."

Now he was smiling unpleasantly as he nailed me with another outburst.

"Don't even dream of anyone else... Ha."

Another day it was my facial hair.

"Dile. Did you shave this morning?"

"Yes. Sir."

"Yu didn't stand close enough to the razor. Ha..Humm."

How I cursed my swarthiness. From shaving once a week, it was now twice a day. I began having my hair cut three times a week. After each roasting, I presented myself to the hairdresser for further scalping. In the end I was known as 'more and more', and the overworked barber joked about the possible use of caustic soda to burn a permanent job. Already, I felt I looked so bad, I was ashamed to look in the mirror. I no longer needed a comb or brush with the bit of moss left on top of my head.

Then drill came into my life. I began to look forward to the marching, although many trainees hated it. But out there in the square I experienced an element of freedom. The instructors were good-humoured and displayed a genuine interest in their work. Immediately, they set about giving us an appreciation of proper posture, carriage and deportment, coupled with a sense of pride in the correct execution of movement.

The first few days they roared at us a lot as they fought to break us in. The first command, 'Fall-in' meant that we stood shoulder to shoulder in one line. The next order was 'Dress, tallest on the right, shortest on the left'.

This required that the tallest man take up position at the head of the line up, and on his left the rest would size off and shuffle into a straight line down to the smallest member at the end. The routine involved much jostling as no one wanted to be the shortest, but after exercising the shoulder blades a few times, we all knew our own place. The order was followed by 'Number' in which each man shouted his number from the tallest end of the line down. Then came 'Attention. Stand At Ease, and Stand Easy'. Executing these movements while stationery was meticulously taught, and involved definitive arrangements and movements of the arms and legs.

For example, the attention mode was as follows. 'Knee bent to the front, the left foot is raised off the ground and brought down smartly to the right, simultaneously the arms are brought to the sides'. There was an added refinement for the positioning of the feet: 'The heels are together in line, feet turned out at an angle of 30 degrees, knees straight, weight of the body evenly balanced on both feet'. And arms? 'Hung straight and close to the sides, hands closed but not clenched, inside of fingers lightly touching the thighs, thumbs to the front close to the forefingers and in line with the seams of the trousers'. Finally, the trunk and head: 'The body must be upright, stomach in, so as to encourage chest expansion, shoulders level and square to the front, head erect with chin slightly in, eyes looking straight ahead at own level'.

Each instruction had its own peculiarity. The vital group ingredient was to be alert for the order and synchronised in carrying it out. I quickly became proficient at the static drills. Along with that there were right and left turns and forming fours. However, being taught to march garda style was like trying to learn to walk again.

When the order 'Quick March' rang out, it meant taking a pace forward and swinging the opposite arm shoulder high, followed by a pace with the opposite foot, swinging the opposite arm and so on. 'Pick up the step', this shout caused consternation to our group those first few days. Who was out of step? Was it me? Frantic glances at each other usually ended in complete dissaray.

Then our instructor would cry 'Halt' in desperation. He would give us the Bugs Bunny stare of amazement as if we were conspiring to upset him. Almost immediately, without warning, he would spring to attention standing perfectly still. Then he would demonstrate in a fantastic exposition by a masterly drill instructor. Away in a circle he would wheel, his perfectly proportioned body compact and controlled until he arrived back to the exact spot he had vacated.
Then the banter would begin. Starting low and muffled as if talking to himself, rising to a crescendo, as he hammered home his point:
"The gate, gentlemen. The gate is wide open. I've checked. Now I just wonder how some of you arrived. Did Daddy have a helicopter and drop you in this square on your bloody hands and knees? He must have,

because most of you would find it physically impossible to walk in that gate. I've seen bad classes, but you are the worst. I don't know why I bother."

Then he would cock one eye towards the officers' quarters before continuing: "Look yonder at the tabernacle of our esteemed officers. Notice that the blinds are drawn. No doubt those benign gentlemen entrusted with your welfare and training are too ashamed to look. Beside themselves with concern they are, in case you will not succeed. Now, as for me, I don't care what cave, mountain or tree you lived in before Mammy or Daddy dumped you in my lap, all I'll say is that you have been captured, and by God I'm going to learn ye to walk."

Another day the outbursts would be different. "Gentlemen, Eureka! Zoos all over the world will soon be on our doorstep. It's the discovery of the century. We have among us the first male with two left legs. A statue will be erected on the spot. He will be famous, the original of the species. Will that member step forward." Nobody moved, not even a breath. The confidence- shattering regime had stitched our lips into an almost permanent mute state. Again the quizzical expression, with major devilment lurking: "Right gentlemen, I see you are puggled. I suggest that the member concerned should obtain a special pass and pay an urgent visit to the blacksmith. In the meantime, when I say left, I mean left, and when I say right, I mean your other left. All right?.... Left.. Right.."

We loved this man. A professional at his job and a great human being. He acknowledged us for what we were, inexperienced, impressionable and developing young men. With his unique brand of humour and slagging he brought smiles to our hearts if not our faces, and we thanked him for that.

Once upon a time my legs had been for support, for kicking football, and negotiating the many boulders and lochs of water of my homeland. Perhaps for this reason I had great difficulty in adapting my step to the regulation yard. Equally, my hands which had a lifetime of mobility when working with tools and implements were now to be plaster-of-parised rigid at the elbows. However, after the first dozen drill classes, I felt my body reacting positively. The short snappy pacing ensured an improvement in posture, and the beginnings of pride in my bearing. Out there in view of the gate and freedom, I felt that sanity existed. Back inside the arch however, the terrors continued unabated.

The rest of the classes consisted of Police Duties, Physical Training, Irish and First Aid. The first significant Police Duty lecture was about powers of arrest. 'You are bound to arrest....' all sorts of people, it seemed. Back home I had never heard of a garda arresting anybody.

Each day huge tracts of each lecture were marked out to be learned by heart. Initially, as the hand-outs were concise, this wasn't too difficult, but we were promised some savage stuff later on when studying the Road Traffic Act and Liquor Licensing laws.

The bit of Irish was very *beag* indeed. An 88, page copy book only was needed. Having inherited a *gra* for our native tongue, I looked forward to acquitting myself well. This early grounding came from my bilingual mother who had imparted her knowledge effectively. Here, an illustration of the haphazard approach towards language instruction was the subdivision of the exercise book into three segments. The first few pages covered translation of notable garda words: complaint... *gearan*, murder....*duan maru*. Indeed, murder was a word that would figure prominently in my life later on.

The middle section of the copy had handfuls of words such as *fear air meisce*, (drunk man) *teac tre tine* (house on fire) and *ainmithe air seacran*, (abandoned animals). What about *daoine air seacran*, (lost souls) I wondered?

Finally the back pages consisted of the oath, *an mionn*, the caution, *an rabad*. I thought the whole excercise indifferent treatment of our language by an organisation with an enlightened and appropriate Gaelic name.

I was fascinated with the First Aid instructions, especially the diagnosis and treatment of shock. Since my arrival, I felt as if I was permanently in a state of shock and sought a speedy return to normality. The instructor smiled knowingly when I ventured a question:
"Ah yes," he replied slyly, "Shock comes before and after pain."

For me physical training was child's play. The instructor treated us as equals, there was no 'sir', we called him by his name and we were 'his men'. He even togged in the recruit's blue singlet. However, the first time in the gym was unforgettable. He paired us off, then reached for the boxing gloves. "Right, men," he commanded, "Three minutes each."

I was no coward, but I had never hit anyone with my fists before. Nevertheless, I climbed into the ring. My opponent seemed a mild enough sort of chap, so I relaxed. Soon we were circling. Then without warning, he hit me an unmerciful puck straight into the nose. I was dazed momentarily, then lost the head and charged in swinging wildly. When time was called, we were about even.

From then on I looked forward to the gym. We climbed ropes and bars, jumped the vaults and rolled on the ground. Then came arm locks and holds. Our instructor played the role of the town bully, the city gurrier and the knife-wielding attacker as he coached these disciplines. He gave us a new insight into life on the streets: "By Christ, men, it's tough out there. They'll take you on. You know. You'll have to stand up to them. You know."

Later on he took over the First Aid instructions. Like the Physical Training he made it interesting. He was both casualty and lifesaver as he demonstrated techniques, and this approach was more powerful than any lecture. "You could save a life out there, your primary duty. You know."

Halfway through the first week we were introduced to swimming lessons garda style. At the start, many were thrilled that we would be taught to swim and lifesave. But inexperienced swimmers who had drifted to the shallow end, were quickly regrouped and told in no uncertain manner that we were supposed to be men and would start by jumping in at the deep end. If reluctant, you were nudged in and when you surfaced you were prodded under water a few more times for good measure. One desperate colleague grabbed the pole and held on. The instructor was most accommodating releasing the pole to him. 'You want it, you got it', he said as my companion slid under the water. Finally we were pointed to the high diving board and ordered to walk the plank. As a swimmer I loved this, but for others their maiden flight was accompanied by death defying laments.

And more. Next day, a notice under the arch proclaimed that the pool was closed until further notice. No reason was given. But I suspected that the unsolicited offerings from some of my terrified comrades had necessitated a clean up.

My mother's first letter came at the end of the first week. Everyone sent good wishes. People met at Mass who had read of my good fortune in The Kerryman newspaper sent their regards. Local boy does well. Why couldn't they all keep out of my life? I was under enough pressure without the eyes of the Kingdom upon me. I felt trapped and wrote home immediately telling the whole truth. I hated the place and didn't think I'd be able for it. The dribble of self-pity helped.

The Gander was giving us all a hard time. He was everywhere. His early morning attacks on our bedrooms became legendary. One morning, just as the last bugle note had shattered my dreams, our door burst open. I had been caught having a lie on. He looked at me and roared:
"Dile. Look at the state of the room. Who lives here? Ha.... Where were you reared? Hmm. Ha. Get outta that bed.."

Immediately, I obeyed, forgetting that I always slept in the nude.
"Attention," he roared. Jumping to obey I winced, suspecting that my reproductive organ had been irreparably damaged. I don't know whether it was through admiration or sympathy for my endowment, but for a split second, I thought I detected a glimmer of a smile. Then:
"Hee... Aaaw... Get dressed. Hummm. Do you think it's a nudist colony we're running here? Ha...aa."

Next morning he paid a return visit. My door was ajar and I didn't see him until he spoke.
"Haaawwww, Hmmmm, Dile."
I was wrapped around the sink, naked and lathering my face.
"Dile...Answer me."
Maybe it was the shock, but my sole answer was a rasper of a fart which shook the room. The Gander stamped his feet, swished the door a few times, then turned on me:
"You're rotten, Dile. About turn. Attention." I faced him with only my soap-spattered face for protection.
"Yu're durty. Dile. Hmmm. Ha...Yu're rotten."
"I'm washing, Sir," was all I could splutter.

"Yu'd need a shovelfull of salts to clane out your belly."
"Yes sir."
He flicked his cane and for one awful moment, I thought he was going to prod me, but he ranted on:
"Yu're all hare. Yu should shave all yu're body. Why are yu so harey?"
"It's in the family, Sir"
"The naked ape. Ha..... Ha. Hmmm."
I stared at him.
"Yu're tick. It's a book. Yu never heard of it?"
"No, Sir."
"They say we're descended from apes. What do you think?"
I looked at him. Was there no limit to this eejit's carry on? Apparently not. He moved around and looked at the lower part of my body.
"Look at the calves of yure legs. There baldy. Ha. Why's that? Hmmmm."
"From wearing the wellingtons... Sir."
"Of course, Ha. Yu're from the bog. A bog man. Clane yourself, on the double."
"Yes, sir"

His obsession with furry individuals backfired on him a few days later. It was on parade, and he had latched on to someone in the front row.
"Yu're flop. There's a thread loose on the flop of your trousers. Did you lose a button?"
"No Sir, I don't know, Sir."
The Gander ungloved, grabbed and tugged the annoyance almost in one motion.
"Ouch," spluttered the recruit as one of his pubic tendrils was uprooted. The Gander flicked the trophy disdainfully off his fingers:
"Yu'd want to be packin' yure jullery better. Ha. Ha."

His favourite ambush was the arch. One morning I was cutting it a bit fine on the way to class. Passing by that entrance, he pounced.
"Caught again, Dile, Yu're lazy. Another discipline form for yure personal file. Yu'll never last."

Almost daily the tannoy reeled off a list of offenders and we streamed from our classrooms to the staff office for another ladle of embarrassment. He was our Pied Piper and we danced to his tune.

My discipline forms were mounting up, a risky omen in the fickle climate.

One night just before curfew we were in the dormitory when we heard a step on the landing. It was a senior garda on a driving course. A friendly soul, he came in for a chat and gave us an installment of his life during training. His closest pal had been Porky, a recruit from the west with a smile for everyone. Porky had a round cherubic face, with a pink, sweltering body attached. The Gander's reign of terror threw them together. Our friendly guard took up the story:
"Porky had the room next to me. One night we were talking after lights out when The Gander burst through the door. He ignored me and began a venomous attack on Porky."
"Yu're too fat. Did yure mother spile yu? Ha. Yu'le be a waster of a Garda."
During this tirade, Porky stood to attention with his habitual smile on his face.
"Whatta yu grinnin' at? Ha..a Hmmm..m Answer me?"
"I'm happy, Sir." Porky replied.
At this The Gander swivelled around the room like a skittish Clydesdale:
"Yu're happy. Yu're happy. What are yu happy about? Yu're supposed to be training here, not going around with a stupid smile on yu're face.. Ha... I'll knock that smirk off yu."

Apparently he was as good at his his word. The next day they were lined up in the square, togged out and told to run. This was Porky's punishment. He was no athlete and had to give up, his smile disappearing with the perspiration trickling like candle grease into the unyielding tarmacadam.

That night there was a film in the recreation hall. Porky sat next to our friend. "It was a war movie," he said. "Porky was exhausted and sagged in his seat. Near the end, he seemed to buck up and take an interest in the action. However, a few minutes later he nudged me and whispered 'toilet'. I stood to let him pass. I never saw him again."

The following day at roll-call there was still no Porky. At lunchtime the news filtered in from the west. He was home. Later that evening our friend told us he saw the poster for the previous night's film fluttering

on the notice board. The film was called 'The One Who Got Away'.
Our one solace was the presence of the senior classes. They had survived, and perhaps so could we. One class was finishing training and
having been assigned their station felt free of The Gander's clutches.
Some of their stories helped too. One was about a recruit in their group
who never bought what he could cadge. Daily he borrowed towels,
soap, blades... anything and everything, so that his group got fed up and
decided to teach him a lesson.

One night they bought cream buns in the canteen and made sure he
noticed. He tracked them to their rooms, and timed his entrance when
the buns were being eaten. He was offered one - but it had been specially doctored with fresh cream being replaced by shaving cream. Even
this didn't work, so they decided they would have to resort to stronger
measures. The cadger had a mop of dark, wavy hair he doted on, washing it twice a day using shampoo bottle dregs retrieved from waste bins.
The father of one of the conspirators was an aircraft mechanic. A solution for cleaning aeroplane wings was secured and the trap sprung. Not
only was it a hair remover, it was a scalp remover as well.

A lesson was painfully learnt.

Chapter 4 - INVOCATION

One day at the end of our third week The Gander stormed into our classroom.

"How to murder yure wife. Ha. Hmmm."

We looked back at him blankly. Savouring our confusion he thundered.

"It's a film, and it's on in the hall tonight; any of ye see it?"

He moved his head from side to side as if to bring us into focus. From previous experience I knew this was a prelude to one of his tantrums. I knew who I'd like to murder given the chance and one of the few smiles since my arrival welled up inside me and crept onto the corners of my lips.

Hiding my amusement I dropped me gaze. Too late. He was looking straight at me. I knew he had read my mind and I was as good as dead. He stared and stared.

Then he took off toward me, scraping his cane menacingly along desk edges as he progressed. He was going to hit me. I kept my head down and prayed. It worked, as he went past me. About turn. Bang. His right foot shattered the silence, then he was on the return journey. He was going to flail me from behind? No. He paced up to the top of the classroom, turned and zoned in on me again. Then he attacked:

"Yu're an upstart, Dile. That's what yu are. A cur. Tink yu're tuff. Think yu'll get the better of me, do yu? Well, I promise yu one thing, I was here before yu and I'll see yu out that gate as well."

I knew I had been selected as the next victim. For the rest of the day, the incident weighed heavily on me. There was a constant, heavy, dull ache in the pit of my stomach. It was as if he had a hold of me by the testicles in an ever-tightening grip that dominated my waking hours. Sleep was restless too. The next morning, I woke again to anxiety which would not leave me. I began to imagine ways of escaping from this crazy institution.

That evening I wrote home. The letter was strewn with apologies. I wanted to leave. It was no use. I wasn't suitable. I didn't know where I'd go but I wouldn't be any trouble to them at home. But as often happens in moments of crisis, aid comes from unexpected sources. My police duty instructor had witnessed the previous days tirade against me. He was a mild, gentle, caring soul. After the evening lecture he cornered me and asked how I was getting on. I spilled my guts to him... The Gander, his discipline, the atmosphere of hostility and fear he generated. The sergeant said he would see what he could do.

The next day he told me I had a visitor. It was a priest, relaxed, friendly at peace with himself. I decided I had an instant vocation:
"Take me out of here," I begged. "I will do anything, go any place, the bush, the black babies, the cannibals. In the name of all that's holy, deliver me."
"Go easy now," he tried to calm me.
"Do you go to Mass? Write home?"
"Of course, Father."
"Well now, take it easy. Reflect on your situation, and don't make any rash decisions."

That was no good at all. What I wanted was to wear a nice soft collar rather than the steel hames that would surely be my fate in this hell on earth. Also, I felt that the priesthood was the only substitute my parents would accept.

Two days later I had a letter from home. My mother's urgings cemented the priest's advice. Let things settle. Give it a fair trial. One gem hit home. After my departure, Gyp had sulked until my first letter arrived. But her second page shocked me out of my own miseries.

Danny had been injured in a serious traffic accident in New York. He needed plastic surgery to his face and it would take some weeks before we knew the outcome.

God! This was the worst of all. My world was in ruins.

I recalled the last time I'd seen him.. the morning he left home. I thought of his youth, his inexperience. Would his looks be restored or would permanent scars from his accident remain? We hadn't even said goodbye. How was he feeling now? In pain probably, and suffering alone. Sad memories clambered over my own afflictions. My mind and his body - both scarred. What was happening to us? What was I doing in this place? Learning to be a policemen? Maybe. But forgetting to be a human being? Definitely. All of a sudden I gave in.

Forget the priest and the decent instructors. God was gone from my life. I'd go to America to help my beloved brother and shag the guards.

That evening I ate a huge tea, threw a few clothes into a bag, kicked the suitcase away under the bed and fled off across the square. Reaching the gate, I signed myself out.

Outside I stood. One thought consumed me. I had been sworn in, now I was going to swear myself out. Standing straight and proud facing the gate the square and towards the arch, I shouted:

"Fuck the guards."

I repeated this twice with venomous joy.

Then I leapt from the shadow of the hated concentration camp and surveyed the terrain ahead. Four roads beckoned. One each heading right and left circled the high perimeter walls. Ahead lay two further escape routes, one more of a lane. Three recruits walked here silently, head down. I wanted to be alone so I headed straight on. Along the tree lined avenue I marched, walking away to freedom, my back to the internment camp. At the end of the avenue the Catholic Church in the grove of fir trees blocked my progress. Somehow I felt drawn towards the open gate. My feet which seemed to have a mind of their own led me straight through the door. I found a quiet corner and sat down. Out of habit my mind turned to prayer, but I silenced it.

Then I saw her. An old woman doing the stations. She turned the corner and stood at the edge of my seat. Eyes aloft and in deep contemplation, the words gushed from her lips:

"Our father who art in heaven....Thy will be done on earth..... Forgive us our trespasses as we forgive those who trespass against us.. But deliver us from evil. Hail Mary... The Lord is with thee. Holy Mary.....Pray for all sinners. Glory be to the Father.. As it was in the beginning, is now and ever shall be..."

She was tiny and as her mouth was on the same level as my left ear, it felt like she was whispering to me. Without realising I began to repeat

49

her words. I realised then that I had not prayed since I started training.

As the hunched, shawled figure moved on, I looked up to where her eyes had rested. It was the crucifixion. I stood and did the Stations. I travelled the road to Calvary. My journey through training flashed before me by way of comparison. The symbol of the cross overhead, its partner on the Devil's Bit. I was trapped between two heavens. Since my arrival, I had been swamped in hypocrisy. Now I recognised the presence of goodness and realised that suffering and perseverance were necessary before I could claim grace. Like my Saviour, I had been reviled, ridiculed and condemned. I had been stripped, laden with burdens, and my body bruised. I had stumbled a number of times but had also received assistance.

Lingering in this peaceful place, I began to find solace, security, peace. It was as if the influence of the training centre ended outside the church door. The world was full of suffering. God on the cross, Danny alone in a foreign country. Suddenly my problems seemed minor by comparison. In this brief interlude, an old woman had helped resurrect my faith in a profound and meaningful way.

Much later as I prepared to leave the church, the venerable Canon appeared.
"I see you doing your stations, garda. We're all travelling our own road to Calvary, you know."

It was the first time that anybody, apart from my Police Duty instructor had acknowledged my rank and human condition. My earlier impressions of this prelate had been unforgettable; for his Sunday sermon, he usually dragged himself wearily onto the pulpit, where he would teeter precariously as he regaled us on the importance of remaining chaste.

'You'll go to hell', he warned.

Most of us felt we were there already.

That spontaneous visit to the church saved my career and was a major turning point. By chance I had stumbled on an oasis of peace and tranquillity. I had found someone I could relate to, who offered another perspective. Even though this God was omnipotent, he didn't demand to be called Sir. He listened and did not attack.

That night I changed. I had made a Friend and even though He never spoke in words, He was far more powerful than others who ranted and raved through my life. I discovered my own voice was rusty from lack of use. Now I could talk freely to my new Friend. I learned more about life and discipline during that one silent sitting than in the preceding month of incarceration.

The road led back to the Training Centre. The following day we got our first uniforms. Another affirmation. I felt assured that if I was going to get the gate, they wouldn't have bothered to kit me out. Also I felt both disguised and protected in my new outfit.

I couldn't wait to dress up. I wished my parents could see me getting togged out for the first time. It was an exercise in patience. The long tailed shirt with the dreadful collar stud was difficult to master, but smart when fixed. The trousers had 22 inch legs, a big backside and waist up to the navel. The tunic, badged, buttoned and belted was my favourite garment. This, along with the peaked cap, really captivated. I spent ages twirling and turning in front of the mirror. Then I sat down and wrote home the most positive letter yet.

I had survived the first month. Now, hopefully, the climate would improve.

The first morning we paraded in uniform The Gander struck with a vengeance. Earlier as we marched onto the square I had felt so proud. Positioned at the back I had a perfect view. The manly swaggers, the contour of the caps, the uniformity. Individuals yesterday. Today bound together in the blue.

In contrast The Gander was in gross form, ranting and raving like a lunatic. He seemed to consider it a huge personal affront that we had escaped into uniform. At least a quarter of us were pulled. Our new-found pride went flying over the wall. Again I thought of Danny's suffering - and this maniac in full health brainwashing us into upholding his interpretation of the law of the land.
Nevertheless I was determined he wasn't going to drive me out again. I had the uniform, and, with God's help, I would hang on to it.

Now another summit loomed - at six weeks our first examination. It engendered considerable trepidation, but except for a couple we all passed. That night The Gander's reward was to herd us into the Recreation Hall to watch an outdated film 'Murder Most Foul'. Again the title coincided with my intentions toward him - given half a chance.

At this stage, a new batch of recruits had arrived and he began his reign of terror with them.

Around that time I became aware of food. Many recruits complained about the grub, but I had few complaints. First, there was plenty of it. Porridge and a fry each morning. A choice of meat, or fish, with plenty of spuds and vegetables for dinner. Usually, a salad for tea. This, along with all the milk and buns I could stow away in the canteen meant I was never hungry.

But the physical energy expended in training had increased my appetite. I decided on a plan to ease my hunger pangs. Before breakfast and tea sittings, a buttered sliced pan would be placed on each table. We would fill the tables in rotation, four to a table. My plan was to wait until everyone was seated. Then, if I was lucky I would get a table and a whole buttered slice pan to myself - and would make short work of it. So approaching the half way stage of my training, I had developed from a scrawny stripling of eleven stone into a muscular he-man of thirteen stone.

Around that time I got a call from my home football team the Laune Rangers, to line out in a final. This meant applying for a weekend pass. These were like gold-dust and required an interview with The Gander. He gave me the grilling of my life. I didn't mind. I felt I could show him that while I might not be the perfect recruit, on the football pitch I could do my stuff. Also I was determined to succeed. I had planned to bring my uniform home as proof I was going to be a garda, and to see the expressions on my parent's faces as I wore it.

Sitting behind the desk he did not intimidate, but when he rose so too did the intimidation level. Movement fuelled his tyranny.
"Football. Ha. Are yu any use? The training here is good for it, don't yu think... Ha.. Hmm."
Gritting my teeth, I had to agree.

"Will ye make the Kerry team this year?.. Ha... They need new blood."

I answered him civilly and finally got the go ahead.

The opposing team were strong and robust. Their leader was reputed to be as hard as nails and was nicknamed *Casur*, Irish for hammer. During the early exchanges in the game whenever we met, he bit the dust. Two months of pent-up aggression had nailed the hammer. So I knew I had the brawn for the guards. But what about the brain?

Tragedy struck in the second examination, when along with over half the class, I failed. The next day I was sitting morosely in the classroom when all those who failed were summoned by tannoy to the office. Like men heading for the gas chamber, we huddled in the waiting room. When my name was called I knocked and entered. Crossing the threshold I sensed the next few moments would be perilous. Bracing myself I whispered 'careful now... easy'. But I was still unprepared for what lay ahead.

The interior was dark, and at first I could see little. Then I saw my favourite officer, seated in full battle dress on a large chair like a throne wearing an overcoat buttoned to the neck with hem almost touching the floor. He looked like a member of the Gestapo. Where lurked The Gander, I wondered? At that moment, he appeared at my right shoulder, his huge bulk bent on paralysing me. Then he spoke in his loud, threatening, deliberate voice.
"This is him, Sir. This is Dile... Dile, Sir. He's the worst. I can't do anything with him."
I was stunned.
The chairman spoke:
"Is that right, sonny?"
"I do my best Sir," was all I could manage.
"He drinks Sir," that voice boomed again, " he drank Killarney dry one night and wrecked the town."
His superior officer frowned. I was frantic. I'm for it now. I flung out the truth immediately:
"That was the day I played my first senior match with mid-Kerry, Sir."
This brought a chuckle from the chair. But bully-boy was not impressed and cut in grudgingly:
"He's not bad at football, Sir. A bit rough, but a prospect I'm told."

So this was what it had come to... Here in the gloom my hopes and ambitions were ending... Desperately I gathered myself together to fight, to deal. The only sound of life was my thudding heart as if hell bent on exploding from my chest.

I was being mentally castrated. My bark of self control was being slowly peeled back. Soon I would be pliable, putty in their hands. Was this what they wanted? I felt I was expected to fall down and offer undying supplication. But I remained standing, silent, guarding my dignity.

This was another moment of truth. I knew I didn't want to be thrown out of the guards. I didn't feel I deserved to be shown the gate, I had done nothing worthy of dismissal. One thing I knew. If banished, I couldn't face home. Neither could I expect Danny to welcome me in America. I was out in the world now and on my own.

I looked at the chairman as he mentally considered my future. This was it. My career, my uniform, everything except my soul was his for the taking. This was the worst moment of my life. He bent his head in thought and from behind his shoulder I saw the Crucifix on the wall behind him. My silent Friend. I looked to him for an answer which came in acknowledgement, acceptance, encouragement. 'You are all right', he seemed to say, 'speak your mind'. Suddenly, I was at peace and spoke: "I'm sorry I failed that exam. In all honesty, I studied hard for it and expected a pass. I don't want to be thrown out of the force and I'm asking you to give me a chance at the final examination."

That was it.

I waited. Their response would determine my fate. I had bowed to them, but at what cost? Shag them if they didn't believe me. I thought of the Casur lying felled on the football field. By Christ, if I don't get fair play here there will be a few more bodies stretched. Why don't they speak?

The chairman stared ahead. Behind me I felt The Gander's hot breath on my neck. Suddenly, the atmosphere changed:
"Killarney, what happened there?" asked the chairman.
It broke the spell. I had escaped from the abyss.

Eagerly I told him about the excitement of togging out with men who were on the team when I was in short pants, the pride of wearing the mid-Kerry colours for the first time. The chair scraped back as he rose, shook himself and joined The Gander.

They purred together while I waited.

Then they were beside me and spoke together:

"The third examination.. six weeks time. Get your act together. Quick march."

It was never quicker.

The fallout from the inquisition had a profound effect on me. Later on reflection I realised I had spoken out and it made the difference. Just as I used to do at home, but had forgotten in this place. For the second time my batteries had been recharged. I was determined to hold on. Dammit, I wanted to be a garda. I had suffered enough for it. I deserved it. There and then I decided to give the final exam one hell of a go.

That night I slept with lecture notes. The following day feeling I wasn't soaking in enough, I had a brainwave. I found the most isolated location in the centre, a toilet high up on a top floor at the end of a corridor. Each evening with my books and my brains this became my study. When a friend discovered me he said I would soon be shitting law. I became so immersed in study that waking and sleeping became entangled. One night about three weeks before the exam I woke up in a sweat. Jesus. I had fallen asleep in the toilet. Unless I reached the bedroom before discovery I was destroyed. There were several problems. First, I realised I was stark naked. Second I was a fair distance from my room and had to negotiate the dreaded arch en route.

I was in a panic. Flying downstairs, I stood briefly inside the entrance door. If I ran as fast as I could to the arch, I might go undetected. How I cursed the full moon that bathed everything in unrelenting light. Putting down my head I took off like scalded cat. I arrived in the shadow of the arch, and clung to the wall waiting for the outcry. None came. Still I was in perilous danger. I felt sure this time The Gander would get me. I'd be locked up. An to think that only the previous day in Police Duty class I had reeled off verbatim Section 165 of the Mental Treatment Act. I recalled it again:

"Where a member of the Garda Siochana is of the opinion that it is necessary that a person believed to be of unsound mind should for the public safety or the safety of the person himself be placed forthwith under care and control, he may take that person into custody and remove him to a place of safety."

Was I about to become even more acquainted with that legislation? I could envisage a meeting with The Gander in my present state:
'Dile. Yu lunatic. I always knew yu were mad. Hm. I have yu now. Yure for the mental. Ha'.

Like a lizard I remained glued to the wall, then moved forward to the edge of the arch. I peeped on to the square. It was all clear. I had a chance. Mentally I measured out the distance across the opening. Four long steps to the safety of the far wall. I took off and made it in one death-defying leap. But what was happening? The arch had turned full circle and now blew a gust of cold air up between my legs. I woke with a start. I had been sleepwalking.

Next morning, one of our group told me that around midnight I had brushed past him near our room saying I had to get back to bed. I had then proceeded downstairs at a furious pace.

That was a watershed. I realised I was overstretching myself, but with so much study under my belt, I felt very confident of the exam. Sadly, the regime had left its mark as fourteen per cent of our group had been forced out the gate each with a suitcase of shattered dreams.

I felt I hadn't been broken, just tamed a little. In spite of the hardship I had retained my dignity and pride. Now, I just wanted to get out of the place.

Two weeks to go and I noticed the barest smidgen of softening in The Gander's attitude towards me. These days when I met him around the infamous arch, he would grind to a halt like a stamping dray horse:
"Any football, Dile? Yu're a bit durty I hear. I like that. Ha. The force needs tough men..Football is good for yu, and discipline. All right, on the double, off yu go."

I also learned that my football prowess was being mentioned in high places. Word was that the Gods of football in the Kingdom had their eye on me, and I would get a station near home. That was great news. Already I was picking my favourite station in Munster.

The day of the final test arrived. I flew it. Thank God. I would be heading south. But as if to read my mind The Gander gave my tail one final, savage twist.

The day we got our stations, I was dismayed by two words:
"Dile. Dublin."

The day before my last day, our paths crossed for the last time. I was tidying my room when the furtive tread from the hall alerted me. Earlier I had floored a comrade in the shower and expected him to retaliate. Hearing the step I stood behind the door. Placing my hand on the knob I followed the pressure from outside, wrenched it open, leapt forward and let out an unmerciful roar. The Gander stood there gaping. Before I had finished, he was gone.

Maybe he was sleepwalking this time? I think not. I believe it was his grudging recognition of my determination not to be bested. Later that day we had class photographs. But I couldn't smile to save my life. My face and features had hardened.

That night there was a dance in the centre. We were each expected to parade there, produce a lady, smile and be happy. I didn't go. I didn't consider myself fit company for anyone. I felt like an overdeveloped caterpillar waiting to slough off this prison skin and fly over the wall.

True to form The Gander made his final appearance at the dance decked out in full battledress. Standing at the main entrance he blazed antagonism in all directions. Should any couple try to leave the dance for a bit of diversion, he would flush them out and chastise them for contemplating any acts of indecency within the sacred walls.

The morning of our last day arrived. A drill display followed by a meal. My parents were there for my passing out. Passing out. An apt name, indeed. My father admired the stonework in the buildings and kept telling me he needed a new shovel. As he picked up his soup spoon at dinner, he began again. He had heard the Templemore shovel was very durable. I said it was the Templemichael he wanted, and anyway the Templemore blacksmith was too busy shaping and branding new gardai to fill his order.

When I was packing on the morning of my transfer I found a single page lying at the bottom of my suitcase. This leaf had obviously become detached from my first notes entitled 'Opening talk to recruits on Attestation', and so I had never seen this message of enlightenment before. I sat down to read. It contained amazing revelations, and at this stage of my training caused a hollow laugh:

"The depot authorities expect your ready obedience, willing co-operation and respect, and these you should give cheerfully. Commence your training with the appreciation that they are your guides and helpers. Never hesitate to place your problems and difficulties before them. They will give you much help and sound advice, and in personal matters can assist since they are men of wide experience in such affairs. If you have a grievance, put it before them. It will have their sympathetic consideration and they will do their best to put matters right. Never keep a grievance to yourself. Grievances that are nursed seem to worsen and may lead to unhappiness. While you are here, make the depot your home. Regard it and keep it as such, and live as one big happy family. When you come to leave it you will go out better men and well fitted to face the future with confidence in your ability to give satisfaction in the career you have chosen."

One big happy family! Try going to The Gander with a grievance I thought.

Along with lecture notes, I had been given a Code Book of instructions with the assurance it contained the answer to every conceivable query regarding my duties in the force. While this mammoth production was not exactly set in stone, it had moved only marginally from the Stone Age, its pages being bolted together. It engendered not the slightest impulse to open it. With the lectures it was dumped on the bottom of the case.

As I packed, new misgivings replaced the old. I had a headful of law and a bellyful of discipline. But I hadn't a clue what it meant to be a garda in the real world. The only practical situations I had experienced in training were how to stop a vehicle, deal with a drunken driver and give evidence in court. Nevertheless, one day in early summer, I boarded the train at Templemore bound for Dublin. Did I feel ready? No way.

As the Training Centre was laid to rest in the Bog of Allen I was chief mourner at the graveside and offered a prayer that the Devil's Bit would serve as a fitting headstone for posterity. As we trundled inexorably to Dublin, my trepidation increased. Passenger comments made it worse: "Aren't they the young guards? Very impressive."

On arrival at Kingsbridge, a plain clothes garda directed us toward a transport van. The driver, like all drivers, was a talker:
"Y'ure going to a good busy station. It'll take your mind off things. We all had to take that first step."

All of a sudden words like cushy, handy, sound, thick and windy took on a new meaning.
But his banter reassured me, particularly when he helped me with my suitcase through the door of my new station.

As I pushed open the batwings, I thought: I've been though hell. Heaven can't be far away.

Chapter 5 - DISORIENTATION

The sergeant sat as if the chair was welded on to the lower part of his body.

Crouched forward over the huge book, he resembled a great bear with one paw moving slowly across the page. The substantial nib steered along the rows of thin blue lines, spilling out its ebony blood into a procession of beautifully formed characters. A crumpled blotter trailed in the wake of the creation, until almost on impulse, it darted forward to mop the wet script into print. Now and then the pen dipped into the narrow round-necked ink bottle which sat to one side. It was then I noticed the snow-white crested emblem embossed on the forearm, and I knew.

I'd heard about him in training. The Crown or Three Castles Sergeant, also known as the Station Sergeant or S S. He was God.

Fearing to disturb I watched reverently as the letters became words, then sentences. Three lines later at the next full stop I coughed an apologetic entry into the real world of the *Garda Siochana*.
"Excuse me sergeant. I'm the new recruit."

His eyes rolled from the page to me and back again. They were dark and watery as his ink. Reverently he closed the book, allowing his fingers to fondle the green cloth cover. Next, the body unfolded. Standing he was awesome and immaculately turned out. He slid away from the desk, paced purposefully behind me, came to attention smartly and addressed me in a deep, guttural growl.
"Do you drink?"
"No sir," I replied immediately.
"Do you smoke?"
I shook my head.
"Do you play cards?"
I dropped my gaze in an embarrassed negative.

"What good are you to me so?"

I was limp, rejected, an intruder from an alien planet, unable to understand the dialect, fit only for banishing. I could do nothing except stand to attention awaiting God's next commandment.

Suddenly he laughed, a provocative chortle, before speaking in a perfectly normal tone:
"You'll be living in, I suppose?"
I nodded, relieved that in this at least agreement had been reached.

Then I noticed the eyewitness, an utter contrast to God. A weed in a uniform. This, I felt immediately was God's acolyte, the sergeant's bully. The Bully looked adoringly at God, his shifty eyes glowing with fawning supplication. His hands moved constantly, one caressing the stub of a Woodbine, the other active in his trousers pocket.

Then God uttered a divine proclamation:
"Show him the back room."
The Bully twitched nervously and beckoned with his head.

Following him upstairs, we emerged into a long corridor with a large, derelict room at the end.
"It's a bit of a kip, but you'll get used to it."
Inside there was a manky smell of human sweat. Assorted components of iron beds were heaped inside the door with a bundle of mattresses stacked carelessly against the near wall. Opposite me stood an allotment of abandoned steel lockers, their locks busted and empty bellies gaping. Somehow I got the impression that the previous occupants had left in a hurry.

The Bully hovered near the door, the fag discarded and both hands engaged in restructuring his undercarriage through his pocket lining. Suddenly, I sensed movement on the far side of the room. At first glance this area was a wilderness except for one corner which was cordoned off. Noting my interest my tour guide sidled up:
"Keep away from that side. There's a header squatting down there in a bunker."

With that he skedaddled.

I was alone. What kind of place is this, I wondered? A cantankerous sergeant, a scruffy gaoler and a header in the corner of my room. What next? I breathed in stale air as I looked out through sealed-up windows at a baleful sky beyond. I hadn't reckoned on my new station being so squalid or disorganised.

Thoughts of training compounded my confusion. Lie down with the Last Post in cotton sheets, clean and crisp as plywood. Rise with the Reveille. Discipline. Sir this and Sir that. It seemed I had been whisked from an ordered galaxy to a suffocating planet. Impulsively I grabbed a window and whipped it open. Fresh air swept in and revitalised.

Next, I began to assemble a bed, and realised that my activity had interested the life form lurking behind the ramparts. I continued to stake my claim moving an army of disused lockers round my bed. Suddenly, Eyeball broke cover from the far end of the room. At a half jog he angled towards the door. For ballast he toted a quantity of shaving gear and a long trailing towel. The apparition intrigued me particularly because he was in full uniform. The thought that this character would be unleashed on the public was unbelievable.

I decided to pursue and investigate. I observed him still fully clothed leaning over a wash basin attacking his face with a wicked looking cut-throat razor. After every scrape his hand would thresh up the water like a piranha and splash the thin foamy liquid over his face. However, rivulets of blood chased almost every scrape, but as they gathered and prepared to leap from neck to collar, the swordsman was ready. At the critical moment the blade was dumped, and a lump of toilet paper rammed inside the shirt collar.

I left him to it.

At the far end of the corridor light splayed up through the banisters from below. Down one flight the ground floor reeked of disinfectant. There were voices coming from a room marked Recreation Hall. In I went. The radio was on, and the atmosphere was friendly. They regarded me. "How's things at the Academy?"
"Tough," I replied, hoping for the sympathy vote.
"How many sacked outta your class?"
"Seven."

"You must have been very naughty boys! Are you in the back room?"
"Yes," I replied.
"Did you meet The Squirrel?"
Instantly, I recognised the description of my room mate.
"Not really."
"Where'ye camped?"
"Inside the door on the left."
"Safe enough," they laughed.

Soon they drifted away and I began to take stock. It would take time to fit in and be accepted. I was an outsider, a raw recruit standing at the foot of a long ladder which had many slippery rungs.

I remembered my misgivings during training. What would it be like to be a garda out there in the real world? Every time I donned the blue, fixed my cap, and looked in the mirror, unanswered questions stared back. The months of incarceration had straightened my back and elbows, rammed my head full of law, and disciplined me almost to physical illness. I took it all on the assumption that when I got my station things would fall into place. Now it seemed that this was not the case. I had expected that I would be taken aside, spoken to, pointed in the right direction, made a fuss of. But instead I was being ignored, left alone and disenchanted. Everyone was engrossed in their own affairs, with no time for me.

Was I expecting too much too soon? Uncertainty and confusion had been my staple diet during training. Now it appeared that similar fare was on the menu here. What about the practical side of policing? Who would teach me that? I had hoped to meet someone my own age, but everyone here appeared several years older than me. Suddenly I felt a presence beside me.
It was God. His arrival signalled a heart-stopping silence:
"Recruit. You've heard of the three relief system?"
"Yes Sir," I replied.
"Well then parade before me clean and regular on the late shift tomorrow. Get your numbers from the Staff." He left.
"You're on The Bluffer's unit." This from one of the group, "he'll look after you."
They all laughed. I didn't know whether the joke was on me or not but smiled just in case.

Somehow it didn't feel right to enquire any more about The Bluffer then. I had been accepted, allocated a unit, authorised for tags. I was on the three relief. This meant eight hour shifts, 6am-2pm, and 2pm to 10pm on alternative days for two months. Then a month of 10pm to 6am night duty. This was an exciting moment. Mentally, I began to sort out rosters - late tomorrow, early the day after and so on. If my calculations were correct, I would be on nights for the next month. That was the way the three relief system worked: three units, each performing eight hours providing round the clock service. Already the juices of expectation were beginning to flow. The fuse was lit and I couldn't wait to explode on the public. It was beginning.

Later that afternoon after a search I discovered the Staff Sergeant hidden away upstairs in a pokey little office. Once entered, achieving an about turn to depart seemed impossible because of the clutter. He was surrounded by an enormous amount of uniform apparel. Bedclothes linen and official forms were stowed away on rickety shelves and on both sides of the table where he sat. As I came in, he had his head down and was ticking off figures in a long column.

Here at last I got the welcome I had been hoping for. He rose, scattering papers; grabbed my hand and shook it for a good while. Apart from his friendliness, his most striking features were a mop of flaxen hair and twinkling eyes. Here was a man at peace with himself. He asked me all about myself and I told him a little - but with reserve. After all I'd been through I was still not sure whom I could trust.

"You'll be forty." He handed me my shoulder numbers and letters.
"How'll I fix them on?"
"A few used matchsticks."
Grabbing my tunic, he fondled it like a tailor then expertly ripped the epaulets. He produced a blade and made half a dozen nicks on each flap before pressing home the letters and numerals.
Next, he produced the match box, beheaded a dozen redheads, carefully reboxed the sulphur and spliced the dead wood into the barrelled stubs.
"Now," he smiled, handing back my tunic. "There you go. You're district numbers. Names don't mean much round here. Most of the lads are known by their numbers, or the odd nickname. That might be confusing at first, but you'll get used to it."

"At least I won't be referred to as the Recruit," I said.

"That's a cross you'll carry until your probation is up. You'll be the junior man until another recruit is allocated to this station," he said.

I considered this implication while he busied himself. I recalled the recruits on Part Two training in the centre. Those stationed in the cities, decked out in their letters and numbers had always impressed. I was content. He spoke again.

"Now. You'll be needin' to keep warm."

Bending sideways he rummaged in a corner and dragged out a bundle of sheets and pillow cases.

"How many blankets do you wear?"

"Two will be fine." I said.

As I backed out the door he ambled after me still talking. It would take time to settle in.. the importance of time for a recruit... time to get to know the station, the party, the area, its people...

"Parading for duty. Always be on time," he said.

Entering the wash room he pointed to the mirror and smiled more information on the necessity for cleanliness in appearance and dress while on duty. I thanked him and left, arriving back at the landing. From downstairs came the sound of the S S baying out an order. Jesus! I thought, this building is upside down. Up here a decent caring Staff, a Godlike creature. Down there a self-appointed Deity who was more like an ogre.

That night lying in bed I drowsily tried to reconcile my months of training with my first day on the job. Tomorrow I would embark on my career as a guardian of the peace, the protector of life and property, preserver of the security of the land with powers to arrest and prosecute my fellow man. 'The uniform will protect you'. I'd heard it in training and believed it. Now I began to doubt. Soon I would be walking the city streets in uniform for the first time. What if something serious happened? Would I be capable? If not, could I live with failure? How many gaffes would the public put up with before ringing up to tell the powers-that-be to take that idiot off the street? I'd been mad to get up and at it, but now that the time had come I wasn't so sure. It was all the fault of my training I decided. This job was too serious to be taught by trial and error. There had to be a better way.

Learn it by heart was the daily rule in training. Now, I pick-locked my brain for one of my favourites, the definition of an archaeological object and rattled it off in the darkness:

"Archaeological object.. means any chattel whether in a manufactured or partly manufactured or unmanufactured state which by reason of the archaeological interest attached thereto or its association with any Irish historical event or person has a value substantially greater than its intrinsic (including artistic) value, and the said chattel includes ancient human and animal remains and does not include treasure trove in which the rights of the state have not been waived."

Such meaningless mumbo jumbo. What did it prove? That I could learn a bunch of almost unpronounceable words verbatim. My mind was swamped with definitions, but the question remained - could I call what I needed when I needed it? Then I thought of home and my father's painstaking guidance and practical application to farmwork: 'This is how to do it. There's a right way and a wrong way to do everything. Learn the right way first and it'll stand to you'.

Memories of home were always good and helpful. I realised the longer I was away the more determined I was to persevere. A powerful incentive to succeed was the pride on my parent's faces each time they saw me in uniform.

I finally slept.

Within minutes it seemed I awoke to snarling traffic and screaming seagulls. Apprehension loomed and stayed. My first day on duty. As I donned the blue and fixed my cap I could hardly leave the mirror in my quest for perfection. God was on the throne when I paraded before him. Again I was ignored as he remained hunched over a typewriter, with the index fingers of each hand turned sideways because they were too substantial in width to otherwise fit between the keys.

Suddenly he turned and stared hard. The look rebuked. I was standing too close to heaven. At that moment The Bully appeared and ushered me into a side room. He indicated another entrance from the far side of the corridor.

"That's yu're door," he said. "Stay there until yu're told off.

"Told off," I exclaimed. Why? What did I do wrong?"

"It's a term used for parading. After you've heard his Omnipotence,

you'll know what it means."
Sloping off into the public office he closed the door of the tabernacle behind him. I looked around me. The room was narrow, and dominated by a huge desk. On one wall, a row of substantial hooks held reams of straw-coloured paper. These appeared to contain factual information on the crimes and incidents committed countrywide.

Then the side door creaked open and the real gardai began to filter in. Unimpressive, disorganised, in various stages of dress and readiness. Each looked me over and gave the impression I was standing on their spot.

I lined up with them behind the desk and watched the sealed portals to heaven. We stood reverently and in silence, all eyes glued to the threshold of the inner sanctum. Pressure seemed to seep through the half-inch aperture under the closed door.

Suddenly the celestial gates opened and God appeared. The line up stiffened.
"Attention."
We became even more rigid. He dropped an armful of books with a thud on the desk.
"At ease."
The line up slackened a smidgen, but the tension held us tight.
"This is the new recruit."
A muffled acknowledgement in my direction.
"Accoutrements."
A clatter of batons filled the table.
"Any damage?"
He picked up one or two at random and ran a calloused finger gently along the polished surfaces.
"Notebooks."
A snap request. When surrendered for examination, he seemed almost annoyed that all were in order.

Next, he read out the current list of outstanding stolen vehicles. which we entered in our notebooks. Then, the Attention and Complaint Book was introduced, and a litany of complaints against street footballers, barking dogs and pavement cyclists were related. The Vacant Houses Book was next. So and so was on holidays - have an eye to that house.

Such mundane stuff, I thought, when would he come to real crime?

As if he had heard, God pulled back his massive shoulders, crooked his thumbs behind the flaps of his breast pockets and launched into a sustained sermon on our obligations as members of the force:

"You are responsible for the peace and tranquillity of your beat. Traffic movement must be maintained and no obstructions tolerated. Footpaths should also remain clear, in particular, any shopkeepers who stack produce in front of their premises in contravention of the law should be dealt with firmly. Now recently there has been an epidemic of shopkeepers using awnings on shop fronts and some of these are a street nuisance. Particular attention must be paid to these and should any offences come to your notice, I will be expecting a report.

"Stolen cars, broken windows or any interference with lock-ups must not go unnoticed. You will ensure that doors, gratings, cellar flaps, fanlights and places though which a thief might enter are not left open. You are prohibited from loitering, lounging or gossiping during your patrol. You must move smartly, working your beat regularly and conscientiously. On no account should you absent yourself from your beat except for a good and stated reason. Deal firmly with all breaches of the law that arise."

This was fairly inspiring stuff. And there was better to come:

"Yesterday evening a burglary was committed in Beat Number One. The report is only coming through and details are scant, but the M.O. is a broken back window. Now, I'm directing each of you to spare no effort in apprehending this culprit."

With that, his eyes pinned down one of the senior members on parade whose expression became transformed into a look of intense commitment. I sensed here was a garda who wouldn't rest until that burglar was behind bars. So on allocation of beats, I was thrilled when my newfound hero was directed to show me around Beat One.

By Christ, I swore, we'll have prisoners before nightfall!

On the street our beat rose steeply like the field that ran from our haggard at home to Nauntinane. My minder stood like a dog turned out on a bad night. Immediately, the complaining began:

"This is a stick of a beat."
I kept quiet. Suddenly like a boxer coming out for round one, he stepped forward:
"Let's go for a ramble."
His step was uneven and jerky. I tried a slow march, then a brisk walk, finally a mixture of both. He couldn't cotton on at all:
"Easy, easy. We're not pulling together."

After a few hundred yards he stopped again dejectedly and looked at my feet:
"Those George Webbs are a dear commodity. How'r your crubes?"
I looked at my ebony toecaps, then across at his tired Donaghys.
"My corns are killing me," he said.

This fascinating conversation was drowned by the dull drone of an aircraft overhead. It appeared from a slit in the sky and seemed to stand still above us. Corns stared at me:
"Never seen a plane before? None in Kerry, boy?" He mimicked my accent.
"The mountains there are too high for them." I countered, recognising the trend. I was in for a bit of Slagging The Recruit. I had expected it, part of the job. Now, I just smiled and decided to try to control the conversation by keeping the questions coming.
"Who's The Bluffer?"
"Ah, don't mind them lads. Yu've a lot to learn. We're all bluffers and you'll graduate sooner than you realise?"
"What does the S S. be writing in his book?"
I figured this would be good for another few yards.
"Oh, the fairy tales of Ireland. That's a sacred book. The facts therein are infallible and will remain forever the preserve and realm of the Garda Siochana."

I was impressed with the ease and speed of his responses. Maybe he was making a fool of me? But how could I learn if I didn't ask? I tried to conjure up some more questions but couldn't think of any. We walked in silence for a while.
"That pernickity S S. Did you hear him going on about that burglar?" he said.
"Yes," I replied with excitement. "Do you think we'll catch him?"
"You'll have a far better chance of seeing an aeroplane."

This crushing retort shut me up for a while.

Soon we came to a busy traffic intersection. I was impressed as the long caterpillar of vehicles was sawn into pieces by the mechanical antics of a red light. Corns was restless.

"Wait here," he said, before disappearing.

I stood watching the traffic and pedestrians wondering if any of them were the wanted criminal. A long half hour later Corns returned. He seemed refreshed.

"Come on," he said. "I'll show you your first lie-up."

Great, I thought, this must be the place where we can lie in wait and capture that burglar.

In an instant Corns was transformed. He took off with short snappy steps, body erect, head thrown forward like a pointer dog. We're on the scent now all right, I figured. I'll be there for the kill. This was a real policeman at work.

Such was his pace I had difficulty keeping up, and felt a sense of pride as we skimmed the path, arriving at an even busier centre. Here he became watchful, and appeared to be sussing out the area. Yes, I decided, the trap is being set. The prey must be close at hand. Eventually, he backed quickly into an archway dragging me along by the arm. It was the foyer of a cinema. Before I knew what was happening, he ushered me upstairs into the darkened interior where he scuttled ahead into a corner, proceeded to unbuckle and lie back in a comfortable pullman seat.

I slid in beside him. Micky Mouse was cavorting on the screen. I was enveloped in cartoons of sweat. What was going on? Suddenly he spoke:

"The big one is great. I've seen it three times. Wait till you see the name."

I couldn't believe my ears. Here I was stuck in a seedy cinema with all those baddies out there waiting to be caught. The main feature was the final insult... 'Carry on Constable'... I nearly screamed. Silently I did scream, and cursed and prayed for deliverance. Never in my wildest dreams had I envisaged spending my first hours of duty imprisoned in a cinema watching a skit on the police force. What would people think? I

looked around furtively but the place seemed fairly deserted. Meanwhile, my companion was laughing his head off.
"Does that remind you of training?"

What could I do? I thought of the S S and his afternoon sermon.
"What about the S S?" I whispered.
"Aw, don't mind him. That oul' vampire never goes out in daylight and only at night when he's thirsty."

Finally my nightmare was over. On the way out, I had to ask:
"Are we supposed to come in here?"
His reply was immediate and devastating:
"We're supposed to come in any place we want."

My first few hours on duty. I had walked a mile with a debilitated old character and languished in a cinema for the rest.

It was bewildering.

During my break I tried to come to terms. What if the burglar struck again? What would I say if the S S asked me how I had got on? Was this some kind of crazy initiation in which the whole station conspired? I decided that I would prevail at all costs.

As I finished my tea The Bully strolled in:
"How'ye getting on with The Bluffer?"
"Fine," I said, as realisation set in.
"Good, you'll be with him for the second half as well."

Later that evening we were allocated a different beat, and I began my questions again:
"What's the secret of the job?" I asked, a question designed I thought to reveal a lot.
The answer came back like a rocket:
"Do as little as possible, but do that bit well."

I was still chewing this over when our beat led us into an elegant area with tall distinguished buildings on every side. Ahead of us I noticed a group of women lingering on the side of the path.
"Did you ever hear of a hooker?" he asked.

I was delighted. Here was something I knew at last.

"Of course, he's the fella that bends over in the centre of a scrum on a rugby team."

"Bend over. Do they now? Not far out," he responded. "No.. Something else they didn't teach you in training. The real world.. those females over there are ladies of the night.. pavement hostesses."

"What do they do?" I asked.

"They sell their bodies to men for money. They are prostitutes."

"Oh, I see," I replied, very chastened.

As we got nearer the group, a few circled out to the edge of the path and gave a little swagger in our direction. Awkward, embarrassed I wanted to keep the conversation going and blurted out:

"Do prostitutes ever have babies?"

He turned with a wicked grin:

"Of course they do. Where do you think S S's come from?"

I had walked into it again.

The women watched us as we went past, then one called out:

"Excuse me, garda. Do you have the time?"

"No," The Bluffer threw over his shoulder. "Nor the inclination."

We continued in silence as night fell.

"How's your belly?" a question out of the blue.

"Fine," I stammered. " What's that got to do with pounding the beat?"

"A lot. You don't drink I hear. How long will that last?"

"I have the pin." I answered proudly.

"Oh, I'm sure you have - and plenty lead in your pencil as well. Any trouble with the old man? Your langer. What did they tell you it was for in training? Stirring your tea?"

Not knowing how to cope with this, I faked a laugh which unfortunately seemed to encourage him.

"Do you know what one of those women said to me one night? That the guards only think of two things, their belly and what hangs out of it!"

I decided to try to change the conversation.

"Tell me about the S S?"

Again my companion had words at will:

"He will jump at you when you least expect it. If you see him looking your way, just pray to disappear. I'll give you an example. One night the card school was set up in the public office. Suddenly there was a fran-

73

tic banging on the hatch. The S S was dealing and only a trick from game. He kept shuffling as the office kept shaking. Then he said:
"Put whoever that is in the cell. They are annoying me."
"Well, the unfortunate man was locked up for the night. It transpired he only wanted to produce his driving licence and insurance."

This was unbelievable.

And so ended my first day on the job, a bizarre mix of incidents, personalities, thoughts and provocation's, almost too much to take in.

Chapter 6 - FRUSTRATION

The next morning I was on the early shift, expected on parade at a quarter to six and out on the beat at 6am. I went to bed early but couldn't sleep. I wrestled with thoughts of the S S, The Bluffer, the ladies in waiting...All that in one day, and I had thirty years to go. How would I manage?

It seemed as if I had only closed my eyes when the cold, sharp, tingle of a baton between my thighs brought me upright in the bed.
"Forty. Five and a half bells. Get the lead out."
It was the S S. Already on duty, fully tackled. Did he ever sleep?

The Bluffer was absent from parade, gone sick, a date with the chiropodist. This brought a rare burst of humour from the SS. 'That mule would need to get more than his hooves pared'. Then, we were briefed. There were bench warrants to be executed so an extra body was put in the patrol car. A few others had paper work to catch up on. All I got were orders to patrol the main thoroughfare and keep an eye on the early traffic.

As I headed for the door The Bully ushered me towards the mess hall where he rustled up two mugs of tea. This scald felt good in my stomach as I hit the cold street.

That early shift was a bitch. Nobody alive out there. My compensation was to witness the city awakening. At home dawn appeared quickly as if by magic. It was slower in the city. Here darkness evaded eviction, lingering stubbornly in alleyways and basements until sucked from its concealment by encroaching daylight. I noted the neon lights paling as daylight strengthened and realised that in the city there was no real darkness, only a twilight.

As the city faced a new day, I faced a parcel of new anxieties. Working in a city meant working with people. I would have to smile at them, greet them, talk to them and if necessary interrogate and arrest them. I felt isolated and nervous. After the first half hour a sprinkle of people began to appear. I fancied they were looking at me, weighing me up, judging me. Yesterday with The Bluffer, I didn't notice. Today I felt under scrutiny.

During breakfast I considered my options and decided for the umpteenth time to do my best. Back on patrol I realised the pace of the city had changed. At 9am when I left for breakfast, the traffic had been heavy, bumper to bumper, punctuated by ponderous squealing buses with the conductors hanging on to the back bars.

Now forty five minutes later the traffic was flowing freely but there were many more pedestrians. Shops and business doors were flung open and my patch buzzed with the throb of commerce.

For a moment it was all too much. I lowered my head and kept walking until I found a shady porch. I stopped and rested and regained my confidence. Of course I knew what I had to do. Stand up straight. Look Dublin in the eye. This little chat proved remedial and I ventured back to my beat. There I saw another cinema and look at the title of the film being shown: 'The Long Hot Summer'. I grinned. What next?

I soon knew. An agitated woman was suddenly beside me:
"Ring an ambulance, garda. There's been an accident at the bridge. I think a man's been hurt."
With that she was gone. Turning away I tried to think. Panic stations. My first emergency. I gathered myself to look for a 'phone, and found a pair of phone boxes behind me. Thank God. In I dived.

But now there was more panic. I realised I was unable to operate the gadget. I had never before needed to use a phone. I got my news on radio, from the weekly Kerryman newspaper and the postman's knock. Now my lack of modern communication skills would shame me entirely.

Training how are you? What could I do now? Frantically I searched for instructions but the vandals had been busy. The black object with a handle protruding from its side stared back. I picked up the headset and listened. I heard a dull buzzing sound.

"Hullo, hullo," I said. It was a plea for help which went unanswered.

I turned away and noticed a long-haired youth with his nose pressed against the glass. This was my chance.

"Come here."

"Yes, mistah."

"Get in there and ring and ambulance."

Soon I had him imprisoned in the kiosk. This was my first introduction to the power of the uniform. It felt good.

"Do you know how to use this phone?"

"I do," he said, obviously amazed at the question.

"Well then," I directed, "ring for an ambulance."

He put his hand on top of the receiver and turned the handle a few times.

"I'm off," I said.

"Hey, what kind of bleedin' guard are you? Did you ever hear of 999?"

"I did," I said, "and the Man from Uncle too. Now none of your guff."

Anyway the patrol car arrived and looked after the incident.

At first I felt a complete idiot, but then I assured myself that I had used my initiative, and in some manner at least had taken care of the situation. As the day wore on, I began to realise that the sight of the uniform created incidents of their own accord. I was very visible. That brought pressure and a need to respond. But hadn't I realised the job was about people? Getting to know them, dealing with them, even correcting them.

And so it was the first tour of duty on my own was discouraging. No way, I decided, was I ready to face the public alone. But again I had made up my mind, I would do my best. There was no other option. Confessing problems to the S S was never a serious contender, it was up to me. People. People. People. I would have to build a bridge between us, and this would be a difficult and slow process. First and foremost though I decided it was vital to find a way to get to know the lads in the station.

Little did I know I was in for a crash course in colleague fraternisation. Later that night my room mate came into my dreams. Actually it was close to dawn when I woke up to a pair of staring eyes:

"Would you have a spare shirt?"

It was The Squirrel. I got up and furnished the required garment. Up to that time if I had thought of The Squirrel at all, I thought him unhappy and disillusioned - my future fate, perhaps, unless I got a grip on myself.

Now he began to talk to me almost without drawing breath. In whispered, urgent tones, I got an edited version of his life story. Apparently, he had always wanted to be a priest and had entered a seminary. But the relationship between his parents was unhappy, and when he left home, it worsened so much that his father deserted the family. When this became known, The Squirrel was asked to leave the seminary. Rather than face home, he applied and was accepted for the Gardai. Now he had spent ten years in the city hating every day of it.

All this was an eye opener. Finding someone more senior than myself suffering some of my depressions was most enlightening. The Squirrel said he despised the slagging and crudeness of some of the conversation. He hated living in the barracks. He couldn't be one of the lads which left him unpopular and classed as a recluse. He had applied to live outside the station but was turned down. I was taken on a tour behind his stockade. There I found his space was spotless. His proudest possession was a huge picture of the Sacred Heart which he kept under his bed. I explained we had its twin at home, even with the same written promise 'I will bless the house where my image is'....

After I left, The Squirrel and his dilemma weighed heavily upon me. I felt I hadn't helped him. I had no words of condolence. All I could do was listen.

Things were happening thick and fast. I was learning to communicate, take the slagging and disappear when God appeared. The next morning as I waited for the late shift, I bumped into Files.

Since my arrival I had spotted this tall, spare, delicate-looking man with two staring eyes. I was impressed. I thought he was an officer investigating some fiercely convoluted cases, particularly as he hoarded an armful of important-looking paraphernalia close to the chest. Shortly after The Bluffer and I were in the mess hall when Files put his head round the door, then withdrew it just as suddenly.

"Who's that?" I asked.

"Yerra, that's poor oul Files," he shrugged.

"What does he do?"

"According to himself he's carrying the lot of us, but really he does nothing. He is an out and out dosser, and what's more, he's getting away with it."

Soon after The Bluffer left, Files arrived:

"I'm the messman," he said, "you're the recruit."

I cringed mentally. Thanks, I thought, for putting me in my place.

"You'll get your dinner between twelve and half two. Now, make sure you're here to grab it, or it'll walk, especially the bit o' mate."

"What about paying for it?" I asked.

"Oh, The Staff will deduct. You'll have a food locker as well."

Reaching into his back pocket, he drew out an impressive array of keys, and disentangling one, handed it over:

"Make sure and lock up your food as the lachicos in this platoon will have it in their bellies before the taste is on their lips."

That afternoon at dinner the lads filled me in on his background:

"He's got a handy number, a soft tour. Four hours to order the grub for dinner and the rest supposed to be spent on outdoor duty, but being a dosser and a cribber supreme, the back door is the nearest he'll go to the street. According to him, feeding us is a full-time job, and he's always crowing about the great menus he serves up, but as you'll discover it's mostly stew and more stew."

As if he heard, in bowls the man himself:

"Good, you're all here, my family. I've great news, a treat for yous tomorrow. Sirloin.. a new hawk I've been cultivatin' has come good. Only the best for ye.."

As he sloped for the exit one of the lads called after him:

"How'r the files this weather?"

"Oh, terrible. I've an awkward one this time lads. Hair a mile long, no answer to this one, heads will definitely roll."

Producing the file cover, he pretended to open it.

"Yeah, hopefully your own," the lads shot back. "You can serve it for dinner. It'd be better than the tack you expect us to exist on."

"Ah no, lads. Ye don't know how well off ye are. The best of grub served here. Look at them grand flowery spuds. It does me good to see the recruit filling up. I'm glad to see the place is being kept clane as well, must be his influence."

Turning away, he headed for the door. A clatter of thrown potatoes landed on it before he could exit. Apparently ignoring this attack, he came back to our table:
"Did ye hear about the family that visited the zoo? Well, the place was closed and the youngsters were disappointed at not seeing the big orangutangs feeding. However, the keeper told them to come down here at feeding time. Janey.. yee're the worst I ever saw. Hopefully, the new recruit will put some manners on ye."

After he left I asked about his nickname. As usual The Buffer was not found wanting.
"That file under his oxter is his trademark. He thinks he's busy, but he's fooling nobody. He is appointed messman for six months, supposed to be elected, but there's never been a vote, he just strokes it."
"But how does he get away with it?"
"Ah sure, he's well got, being looked after."
I'd heard of these innuendoes in training, but didn't really understand.
"But how does he hang on to the job of messman?" I asked again.
"Ah, that appointment comes up every six months and he fixes it with the boss. If anyone else went agin him, they'd be creasing the half sheet."
"But is he not directed to go out on duty?"
"Ah yes, but he's a serious contender for being the greatest dosser in the job. The back door is the nearest he'll go to the street, and anyway, he's housed..."
"Housed?" I exclaimed, "what does that mean?"
"Files is housed," The Bluffer repeated, "because he can't be trusted out on his own. He has a vile temper, a danger to himself and the public. He's well connected, the last time he dirtied his bib, the boss saved him from certain discipline."

Lying back, he launched into Files's latest escapade - and acting ability.
"Jaysus, I've done it this time. There's no escape. The pension, everything gone, I might as well resign."
Files went in lamenting to the Super.
"You're a decent man. You saved me before, but this time there's no hope for me. I'm finished." He went on and on.
"But how can I help? If I don't know I can't fix it up?" the Super final-

ly asked.

The officer's soft spot had been massaged until he caved in. Then Files pounced like a rat.

"There'll be a complaint of assault, but the shagger provoked me. I lost the head and gave him a few belts but he deserved it. Thanks for saving me. You're a decent man."

And Files had survived again.

Later, I attempted to digest the fall-out from the previous forty-eight hours. Only two days gone and already I had met an amazing trio of characters. My reverie was interrupted by the SS's bellow along the corridor, causing one of my colleagues to erupt into action:

"Where's the car observer? Ah, there you are. I thought I told you to crease a half sheet on that incident this morning. If you don't give it to me pronto, I'll be serving wan on you."

Creasing the half-sheet. I grinned at the memory of Lecture Twelve, in training. It ran for three and a half pages and bore the title: 'Report Writing and Correspondence'.

It had been a Police Duty class immediately after lunch and the instructor was a stand-in. Typical of the job he had a massively ironic nickname - The Smiler.

When he turned and faced us I discovered why. His expression was a silent-movie, deadpan type, alternating between sadness and resignation.

"Paper."

His first word was uttered with the frustration of one groping in a toilet to discover there was none of that commodity.

"The half-sheet, gentlemen. Ye wrote yourselves into the job, and if you survive to the pension, you'll have to write yourselves out of it as well."

Next, he held the half sheet overhead in both hands by its edges as if it were a rare manuscript, before waving it in a half-circle before us. Then, like magic he folded the top corners together, deftly pinching the centre. Without pause, he repeated the process, bringing the left corner onto the centre divide before expertly sliding his thumb and index finger along the crease from top to bottom.

"There now, gentlemen. One of the truly venerable acts in the realm of the *Garda Siochana*. Creasing the half-sheet. Many stalwarts in our force endowed with a glibness of speech above and beyond the call dry up completely when it becomes necessary to put a few words on paper.

"Going to press. I notice your hands trembling, a common ailment. Yes, there is within the job a marked reluctance to put anything on paper. Many scribes who show inclination in that regard are dubbed as windy so and so's, or as passing the buck. But you'll go nowhere in the job without paper. Indeed, if some members buttoned their lips and wrote more, the effect would be of great benefit to the overall good of the force.

"Now back to basics. The half sheet is used to make applications, report facts, inform people especially supervisors, and record discussions and decisions. Now let's see you go to press."

For the next while I manhandled several sheets into all shapes until the instructor dropped one in front of me with more instructions.
"Gentlemen. That's a two inch crease you have there. Now the first four lines on the top right will be completed as follows: division, district, class and date, or station and date, if you make it to the outside. On the next line but one and to the left, indicate to whom the narrative is addressed. Following on, on the next line but one, comes the heading.

"All paragraphs, openings, closures and signatures must be aligned to the left hand margin. A line to be skipped between paragraphs."

Maybe it was the way he looked, his deadpan delivery or his impeccable demonstration, but that class stayed with me.

That evening as I passed the public office, the door was wide open and nobody about. Inside the Occurrence Book lay invitingly open on the desk. My heart thumping, I slipped in and read the last entry:
"Outbreak of fire at Cowans lock-up premises situated at 13 Earl Street. At 4.05am on this date an outbreak of fire took place at the lock-up premises of John Scully, Earl Street. Even though the outbreak was relatively minor in nature, two sections of the Fire Brigade under District Officer Callaghan were in attendance and adequate water supplies were available locally. The hoses were connected and the valves opened. The pressure was good..."

At this point a heavy footfall in the corridor sent me scudding away. Later I reflected and was impressed with the detail.

My third day on duty turned out to be the most emotionally difficult to date. I was on the late shift, a 2-10pm tour. At parade the S S had news: "One member for the city centre at 7pm this evening. Protest march." All eyes fell on me. The new recruit was unanimously elected. 'Don't forget your timber'. The Bluffer said after the break.

Of course I'd carried my baton in the special trousers pocket but never thought about using it. Now, that possibility was imminent.

Initially elated, I became insecure as the hour of departure approached.

Later that evening travelling to the city centre, I remembered what had been said when presented with my truncheon: 'Shove that in your pocket. You might need it'.

My vivid memory then was the feeling of security and power from the lump of timber lying snug against my thigh. But another memory jolted. This was the list of over a dozen regulations governing the use of the weapon. Now one jumped out from the pack: 'Should you break or damage the weapon every effort should be made to recover the pieces and retain them and report on the circumstance surrounding the cause of such damage'.

What a morale booster to carry into the fray!

Later in town I mingled with a large group of gardai. Our briefing had not been impressive: "We don't know what to expect. Play it by ear. Anyway, if there's a heave, don't get isolated and pray for rain."

We were huddled together in the city centre opposite the statue of Daniel O'Connell, The Liberator. As well as being a fellow countyman he had been a favourite from my history book. The national hero of freedom of expression and peaceful demonstration. I thought - here I was a hundred years on, and expected to clobber a fellow Irishman with a lump of timber if necessary.

Soon the demonstration arrived. They were complaining about housing.

Again phrases from training ran through my mind. Confrontation. Control by containment. Powers of arrest. Law Enforcement. But nothing on the wiles and vagaries of human disorder.

I remembered another sentence. 'You can't legislate for emergencies. Common sense prevails'. But what is common sense? There had been no hand-out on it. Now keeping cool seemed to be the best plan.

The gathering grew noisy as protesters voiced their opinions. I found the chanting and foot stomping the most unnerving. This was it, the thin line between law and disorder. A loose word, an involuntary action, a too hasty move, I knew these could erupt into violence.

More words from training were remembered. Discipline. Attention. Stand at ease. Big powerful gardai standing firm. But would that be enough? I hoped so. Things were moving too swiftly for an inexperienced rookie to handle. My sweaty hand caressed the baton top. I ached with nervous energy. I cursed the job. It wasn't fair sending a beginner into battle a mere three days after he'd arrived. I should have got training in crowd control.

This was serious.

The crowd moved forward apace.

I looked round me. Surrounded by colleagues I had never felt more alone. Then my gaze fell on a particularly burly looking garda and I sidled over to him:
"Do you think they'll be trouble?" I asked, trying to muster some appearance of gusto for the fray.
"If they start it, we'll finish it."
Not encouraging.
"Do you think we'll have to draw batons?"
"Don't know."
This was no good, but I persevered.
"What will happen if we have to charge?"
Again, the response was unequivocal.
"We'll hit everything that moves."
Thankfully that confrontation ended in a draw. They went home quietly and so did I. I had a lot to think about.

Looking back, my first seventy two hours in the job was a continuing mosaic of people, incidents and emotions. I realised I regarded the S S as a huge controlling influence. I disliked him but was too afraid to hate him. The damned burglar was still at large and our lack of progress hung like a fog over the station.

Physically, I decided the job was easy. Mentally it was mayhem. Why didn't someone explain things to me? Was I the first rookie to feel confused, or was there some other impediment in my make-up which made me unsuitable for the gardai?

I was still totally confused when Little John came into my life. I saw him on the fourth day's morning parade. He was back from leave, a middle-aged, powerful man with a massive head and an open, honest face. I felt I was going to get on with him and I was right. He gave me one of the few smiles I'd received in the place. And the first enquiry for my welfare:

"How'r you fitting in?"

I'd been waiting to be asked and poured out my answer. John listened patiently. When I'd finished he looked at me for a while then said:

"You're looking for perfection. Something you'll never find. They teach that in training because it is in the nature of our organisation to aspire to high ideals. But the present system of training is outrageous and won't survive. My advice is to put training on the back burner and get on with your life now. This job is 99% common sense and 1% law. Not the other way round.

"You've picked a demanding career and you're desperate to make your mark. Fine. But fresh out of training, you're now in a kind of limbo. Some people regard the guards as the most demanding job in the civilised world. I'm inclined to agree, so consider carefully what I'm going to say."

He went on to give a crash course on surviving in the Garda Siochana, and not only survive but to do so with honour.

"Expect the unexpected on duty. When unsure, do nothing. In emergencies, do something. You've probably had some problems in the streets already. Learn from these experiences. This is a lifetime job. It's all about people. Living with them, working with them, working for them. The seven deadly sins, the ten commandments and many other vagaries and indiscretions, this is what we have to contend with. You'll discover more about yourself in a split second in this job than in a year in many others.

"All human life is out there and in here. The secret is to look for the good in everyone. If you meet a friendly face, stop and have a chat. Look at people, they are your bread and butter. Get to know their faces.

"Learn how to hold your own in the station. Right now all eyes are on you, and people are slagging and bluffing to get a reaction. You'll be judged on how you respond. In you some will see their own demise. In any station you'll find a mix of characters - sound, windy, thick, well-got. In the end, most of us will back you, while a few will hope you bollix things up so that they can hide behind your mistakes.

"Some policemen figure that because of their training and power they are immune from personal or family responsibility. Of course this is wrong. We have the same problems with family, children, with grievances real and imaginary.

"The S S now, he'll grow on you. He's the product of a rigid disciplined age. The public office is his kingdom and he considers it his sacred mission to knock the corners off the likes of you. Take it handy. Don't get into any hassle with him. The job is changing and his type will soon be extinct.

"You're a thoughtful chap, but you're looking inwards too much. That's fatal. Look around you here. Take it all in, but keep your mouth shut until you find your own level. Before long you'll find a few here you can trust. Treasure them.

"Be neat, tidy and on time. Keep up the football, write home often and visit home too. It will take two years to settle."

This was wonderful stuff and I drank it all in. And thought about it again and again. Look at people. Take it handy. Now where had I heard that before. Take it handy. Keep your mouth shut. Expect the unexpected. It's all about people. Ah yes.....

Like a piece of flotsam I had found a lifeline to hang on to. I hung on.

Chapter 7 - CONSTERNATION

I shrank back from my shadow.

It splayed out across the street away from where I stood on the path. I felt afraid of it, something I once heard described as baseless cowardice.

But it was the gaggle across the street who actually inspired fear. As I stood, their leader trundled nearer, her bulky frame bristling with emotion.

Tightly the crescent formed around me. My shadow could not save me now.

"Garda, garda, come quickly."

Stumbling I followed them to the row of artisan houses.

"I'm the public health nurse," she said, "it's Mrs Nolan, number three, I'm worried about. I visit every day, I even have a key but I can't get the door open."

God, not more drama!

From day one on the job I had struggled in a maelstrom of phones, prostitutes, protests and pseudo policemen. It was all very different from what I had expected. When I stepped on to the streets of Dublin for my first period of on-the-job-training, I had imagined that my career would be brimful of adventure, excitement and fulfilment.

But in three days I had met none of it.

In fact, training so far had been more of a disaster. This was day four and I had sallied forth once more to face the world. The SS's directive had been clear:

"Forty, go down to 3 Carnowen Drive. The resident there hasn't renewed her dog licence. Investigate and report back."

Do this. Do that. No explanation. No advice. No would you, or you might. The orders and the manner of their delivery made me insecure and manipulated. Now, as I stood outside the door, I realised it was the address of the errant licence holder. And confirmation came in the form of a plaintive howl of a canine within.

The matron burst forward along the path to the front door. She jammed the key in the lock and twisted with resigned petulance. "It seems to be secure from the inside," I proffered lamely.
"I know that," she snapped back, "can't you do something?"

I stood, desperately trying to think. I was in the first stages of panic, these days a familiar feeling. Recently it had become a companion, soon it would be joined by embarrassment.

I recalled the conversation I'd had with Little John the previous day. 'Look for the good in people', he had said, 'most will respond. Get into the habit of looking at them straight in the face anyway'.
Sound, practical advice - and there was more:
'Expect the unexpected'.

Last night it had seemed remote. Not any more.

As I stood, heads turned expectantly in my direction. I looked back trying to winkle out some semblance of support but they were impassive, watching, waiting - while the dog added his fearful racket.

I needed time to gather my thoughts but none was offered.
"Here, you try it," she pushed me towards the door. As I worked the latch they crushed forward in a murmuring mass:
"She's 80, you know."
"She's been feeling poorly."
"I bet she's a goner."

I willed the key to operate, but the door, brown and peeling, held firm. Looking into the letter box I saw an empty, nondescript hall and smelt clinging dampness. The dog seemed to be upstairs. That could mean trouble. Next, I inspected the front window but the sash was securely nailed inside. Grime hung on the glass in peppery grains. Framing my face, I peered in, but could see nothing.

Nurse was at it again, apparently trying to push me through the letter-box:

"She's up there, in the bedroom. She must be ill. Can't you do something?"

I knew I had to take action, but what? Think, no way. Not a hope. Turmoil had taken my reason captive. Leave? No hope either. I had been appointed leader by virtue of my uniform. I remembered Little John's advice:

"If in doubt, do nothing. In all emergencies, do something."

Such irreconcilable counsel. The dog continued barking and the matron delivered her ultimatum.

"Are you going to stand there just doing nothing? I'm beginning to think you're not a Garda at all."

The remark dissolved my cobwebs of indecision.
"Stand back, I'm going in."

I was in overdrive now. I had taken charge and already felt better. I banged for the next door neighbour, and gained entry. I grabbed a hatchet near the back door and ran out into the garden. It felt good to have a weapon in my hands. A scrawny privet hedge divided the two gardens and without losing stride I charged through it. But I was brought down by a strand of wire hidden in the viney undergrowth. I hit the ground a fair belt knocking me breathless and sat up to discover a three inch slice in the knee of my freshly pressed trousers. I cursed roundly, and looking about, discovered that my followers had abandoned me.

It felt a lot better without the gallery.

As I surveyed the back of the building, I realised my nose was bleeding and plugged it with my handkerchief. Only my fourth day out and already my blood had been spilt in the course of duty. Suddenly one of my feet gave way and I genuflected this time on a green, slimy quagmire that smeared the path into a slide outside the back door.

Now, I was really angry. Eyes narrowed, I swung the axe, and the glass on the top of the back door crystallised under the impact. Reaching in I drew the bolts. The door creaked open and I inhaled a gust of dank air. I was glad of the handkerchief over my nose and tried to breathe shallowly. I stepped inside. A locked door to the left. A gloomy hallway ahead.

Upstairs the dog was going crazy, charging up and down the landing, paws scraping and tail swishing against the baluster rails. I went slowly towards the stairs to certain confrontation.

What protection had I? The hatchet, yes, but would it be enough? With each yard my terror grew. I tried to recall everything I knew about dogs, but the only image that came to mind was the Hound of the Baskervilles. At the stair rise, I crouched and raised my eyes slowly. The animal stood in the murky darkness, legs apart, body heaving, huge tongue hanging from massive jaws.

It was a moment of truth. The animal was on guard. I too was a guardian of the peace. Which of us would persevere? During those few seconds as we looked at each other, a flurry of thoughts raced through my brain. The Dogs Act.. 'now mark that section and learn it by heart'. Sections. I thought, that's all that will be left of me if I don't think of something fast. 'Don't get isolated'. Another gem. How does one become unisolated? Turn and run. No way. The law, the law. The answer had to be there. What was the definition of a mad dog? 'It is an offence to keep a dangerous dog within fifty yards of a public road without having it muzzled, or a block of wood of sufficient weight tied to its neck to prevent it being dangerous. Application to the District Court to get an order to seize such an animal'.

Wonderful! Was I expected to run out past my fans over to the court to inform them there was a mad dog at 3 Carnowen Drive, not to mention a possible dead body, and seek permission to act? Then, I should procure a block of wood, capture the dog and put the necklace on it.

Again no way.

From somewhere a number of fonder recollections came to mind. The way in which the big policeman handled Gyp that autumn day many years earlier and my father's advice to the distressed postman.
'Don't show any fear'.
My father. One of the people I had faith in. It was time to put it to the test.

Concealing my weapon behind my back, unplugging my nose, and pulling off my cap, I extended my hand placatingly and spoke.
"Here boy, come here... Good boy..."

All was quiet. The great growl died in the gaping jaws. The animal was transformed. Whimpering, it slithered to me and began to lick my hand. The miracle had worked.

Up close he was only an overgrown mongrel.

Now I was in charge. My first dragon slain and it was a powerful feeling.

But the peace lasted only a moment before the banging on the door brought me back to reality. I'd forgotten the posse and the old woman. I flung my body upstairs.

The first door was open and I charged in. She was there all right, buried in bedclothes. On seeing me she cringed, two bony hands gripping the ends of the quilt drawn around her jawbone. She looked like an infant but there was nothing babylike about her outburst:
"You broke into my house, you big blackguard. Whattya want? You frightened the dog," then her eyes fell on the hatchet, "and I suppose you're going to murder me now, you big bully."
"I'm a garda," I stammered, " why didn't you open the door?"
"That's my business, you big brute. I was having a lovely dream and you woke me. You had no right to break in."
"I was only trying to help."

All of a sudden I was weary of the whole debacle.
"Be off with you, you oul' peeler," she dismissed me, "if I was in trouble you wouldn't be found at all."

With that she got out of bed, forcing me out before her. Down at the hall door, she drew back the bolts. The menagerie outside gaped and moved inside. I was ignored and could only slink away up the street to the station where the SS was waiting for me.
"The dog licence?"
"Oh my..." I replied, "I forgot... I'll explain."
I told my story which sounded lame. In his eyes I had failed in my duty,

however I droned on hopefully.

When I'd finished he gave a long sigh: "The fairy tales of Ireland...."
It was official. I was a failure.

Next day I was assigned duty as car observer. This was a plum job, number three on the unit, with the car driver and motor cyclist first and second respectively. My function was to respond to the car radio, and keep in parley with the driver.

My chauffeur Jack, known as The Black was a legendary character. Already his reputation had gone before him. In a world of big men, he was gargantuan. A piebald, he was a mild man off duty but a tyrant when he donned the blue. Even though well into middle-age, his movements were graceful, even cat-like. Now, I learnt at first hand he was a woeful driver. He changed gears with a thumping sound, driving the clutch through the floor then grating the gears loudly which caused the car to leap and whine.

He parked by ear.
"You'll never make it," I said.
"Aw, I'll scrape it out," he replied. And that's just what he did, chatting over his left shoulder at me. "Sure that's what bumpers are for. See now we had acres of room. So you're the recruit?"
"I am," I replied. "What do you think of recruits?"
"When you were in liquid form, I was in uniform."
A big laugh, the rookie had been caught out again.

We were patrolling a tough area. Three youths lingered on a corner and he ground the patrol car to a halt.
"Here you," he shouted, braking, switching off and climbing out. Two of the group legged it but the third was caught and held. Grabbing him by the scruff of the neck, The Black lobbed him into the back seat of the patrol car.

We drove back to the station silently. On arrival he chased his prisoner in the back door, came out and continued the patrol. For the next while, he treated me to bursts of biblical enlightenment:
"I'm the good shepherd. I know my own but some of them don't know that yet. When they discover who I am, they'll recognise me as their

saviour. Peace on my patch to all men of good will. There go I but for the bull's wool."

Coming near tea time, he stopped the car suddenly, allowing the siren to draw breath.
"Do you want chips?"
He was already out of the car beckoning me to follow. He headed for the chipper where half a dozen people queued at the counter. Ignoring the waiting line he addressed the owner:
"They're ye are, boss. Best chips in town. Are they ready yet?"
"Not quite ready," said the restaurateur, looking exasperated.
"They look right enough. Fill up two of the big bags there like a good man. We have a few calls on hands. Out all day graftin' no time to draw breath. This area is getting very rough. We have to keep them go-boys back, or they'll take over. It looks like we won't have a proper break this evening."

Laying across the counter, he grabbed the plastic sauce container and squeezed the contents to the top. Chips were now being loaded into two brown paper bags. But The Black wasn't through:
"Shure, one decent man. Throw in a half dozen of them auld sausages as well. Those lovely brown ones over there in the corner look grand."
Soon two more bags were being loaded with lots of encouragement:
"Good man yourself. G'wan. Throw another shovel in. What a day! The place has gone mad. Good man. God, aren't they lovely. They must be the best chips in the city. And them lovely sausages, throw in another one. That's grand now. Give me a hoult of them bags. Up to our eyes we are, but we never forget to throw an eye on you're place just in case of disorder."
He was backing towards the door now with me in tow cradling the bags. He glared at the queue, finally attempting some traffic control: "C'mon there, straighten up that queue. Give that man no hassle, d'you hear, or you'll have me to tangle with. You're a decent man. Regards to the missus. Good night."

We were now back on the street. He hugged the brown bags protectively.
"We did well tonight. There's your supper now. Timing is vital when you set about plucking a hawk. You hit them hard when they have a crowd in and shame them into parting."

Meanwhile, I was both amazed and ashamed. I had heard of such activities in training but understood them to be nod and wink covert operations, not the blatant plundering I had just experienced.

But The Black, skating through the side streets of Dublin, munching fistfuls of chips and grinning to himself had no such scruples.
"There's atin' and drinkin' in these. By the way I'll need you to parade in the Petty Sessions in the morning."
"Good," I answered, "it will be my first time."

It was an enlightening experience. Just as the morning sun slanted in the high windows the bagged corner boy slunk up the stairs and entered Court 4. Already The Black was sprawled in the witness box like a tarantula awaiting his prey. He took the oath at an inaudible gallop:
"I swear by Almighty God that mumble mumble shall be mumble mumble and nothing but mumble..."
The judge leaned forward ignoring the charge sheet in front of him:
"Yes guard, what's the charge?"
"Gross obstruction and breach of the peace, Justice."
"Aha, I see. Serious, ha."
The Black pursed his lips, creased his face into a forbidding expression and nodded in agreement.

His Lordship then glared over his spectacles at the unfortunate prisoner:
"Stand up. Have you no respect? Are you guilty or what?"
"I dunno. Mebbe so, Judge."
"Gimme the facts, guard."

The Black was off reading it seemed from his notebook:
"I was on patrol and he was one of a gang hanging around the street corner. We've had a stack of complaints relating to the antics of these boys, Justice, so I urged them to disperse and they did, except the defendant. When I asked him to leave he called me a bleedin' redneck, a bleedin' rozzer and a bleedin' bogman."
"And what did you say to that, guard?" asked the judge.
"Oh, my Lord I told him that if he didn't stop bleeding he'd have a haemorrhage."
Loving this, the court erupted into laughter.
"I see, guard.... Now, let me look at the charges, gross obstruction and

breach of the peace. Anything to say?"
But before the prisoner could open his mouth the judge continued:
"I'll withdraw the gross obstruction. Breach of the peace, convict and fine two pounds, fourteen days to pay, one month in default. Next case."

The charade had almost finished me off altogether. Out in the courtyard, I tackled The Black:
"That young lad never opened his mouth to you," I said.
"Ah yes, son, you have a lot to learn."
"But he never opened his mouth."
"Aw, but don't you know well he was thinking it."

This was unbelievable, but I had one final query:
"What did you need me in court for?"
"Oh, in case I'd want you to swear up as well."
Even then I vowed silently that as regards potential prisoners at least, The Black and I would use different powers of arrest. Next day I was glad to be back on foot patrol.

Over the next few weeks and months I learned that although the *Garda Siochana* harbours many unusual characters, The Black was unique in many respects. First, he had words at will. It was said that he could curse at length without using the same adjective twice. As regards his duties, his self-appointed mission seemed to be the enforcement of the Offences against the Police Act. In his book, we were always right. Thirdly, he was a mighty slagger, and was well able to laugh at himself as well.

I had begun to realise also that the crack and the jokes were vital to survival in the force, particularly to relieve the tension in our station with an overbearing S S. Laughter was almost as important as oxygen to maintain life and morale. I saw too that slagging and humour was another vital ingredient in character building. Taking a joke against yourself as a rookie was necessary if you were to be accepted into the community of rank and file.

I heard many stories of The Black over the next while. He was a charismatic figure and attracted a following. People sat with him to hear his stories, many of them centring around altercations with the public and senior ranks, as well as tales of skulking drink and sex. He was never short of an answer. One day he came from a demonstration with a cut on the side of his head.

"Did you get the fella that hit you?" he was asked.

"No, he got away. But I skulled the chappie beside him instead."

Another night the group were discussing an officer who had recently died and The Black bowled in, in rare form after a few drinks. The adage not to speak ill of the dead eluded him completely:

"I'll tell you about that miserable baldy coot. He was always complaining that he wasn't well, and half the station would be praying that it was nothing trivial, but he invariably turned up again so he was christened Lazarus.

"Years ago he arrived on promotion at my station. The first day on parade he pulled me for a haircut. Later on during my patrol, I slipped in for a short back and sides, and on my way out who should I run into only Lazarus! He savaged me for leaving my beat and reported me for discipline.

"The day of the hearing he was all anxious to do me. 'The member left the beat without authority. It's inexcusable', he charged.

"Now, I had done my homework on the disciplinary board and heard a whisper that two of the three wouldn't mind seeing Lazarus taken down a peg. So when it was my turn to speak, I said it was like this, the Inspector directed me to have my hair cut, and while on patrol it was very quiet so I went and did as instructed.

"You were in breach of discipline," burst out Lazarus.

"I'll argue the point with you." I said.

"Continue," said the chairman.

"I felt I was entitled to get my hair cut as it grew while I was on duty," I said.

At this, Lazarus began to cough and splutter:

"Yes, but it didn't all grow when you were on duty," he finally got out.

"No," I answered, "but I didn't get it all cut either."

It was a sickener for the old baldy coot, but I won the day.

"However, he had it in for me from then on and eventually had me blocked and transferred."

"Did you go to his funeral?" I asked, not wanting this fascinating conversation to end.

"I did not then," he said. "But I visited his grave to make sure he was well buried, and do you know what I did? I went on the batter and held my water until I was nearly bursting. Then I pissed it all down on top of his grave. Showers, ha, I gave him his own back in honour of the time he blocked me."

"Tell us about how he blocked you?" one of the lads asked.

"I'm comin' to that," The Black cut in. "That was a few years ago. We were in a very dilapidated station with poor washing facilities and we began a dirty protest."

'Showers!' said Lazarus when we approached him, 'the only showers ye'll get is what the Almighty sends down from the sky'.

"That evening I was upstairs and spotted him underneath. The temptation was too much so I pissed down on top of him. Of course he decked me, and I couldn't winkle out of it."

At this stage the crack was mighty with the stories flying all over the place. The Black was in his element:

"Listen and I'll tell you a good one. A few years ago there was a brawl outside a pub and I hauled in two prisoners carrying war wounds. Next morning they appeared at the early sitting of the court charged with assault and breach of the peace. Their solicitor jumped up to cross-examine me:

'Garda, I'd like to draw your attention to my clients' physical condition. One has a severe contusion on his right eye, the other a two inch laceration on his jaw. Can you explain these injuries, particularly as there isn't a mark on you?'

"I can, judge," I replied, "It's very simple. They took me on, but they weren't able for me."

The lads loved this and called for more. The Black was only too ready to oblige:

"Once many years ago I was stationed on the other side of the city. I got to know a woman who worked as a hotel cleaner. She started at about six in the morning and I used meet her on the early tour and she told me her troubles. She was married to a toe-rag who loved the gargle and spent all her money on it."

'Will you pass the flat one morning and have a few words with him?' she asked. 'For me, it's like walking on eggs. One wrong word and I'm smashed'.

97

"I did pay the man a visit and talked to him about peace and tranquillity. But the following week I ran into her again, and this time she was sporting a huge black eye."

"You made him worse," she complained.

"This got me mad and I paid a return visit. This time there was no softly softly. I banged on the table a few times to knock some sense into him. He went for me, but I squeezed him a bit until he lay down.

"A few months later I met his wife on the street. I hardly recognised her, she was all done up like a young wan.

"How're things?" I asked.

"Couldn't be better," she said.

"And himself?"

With that she gave a big smile:

"Ah sure, I want to thank you for the great job you did. After the few clouts you gave him he was never the same. He went to hospital and died a few days later. The doctor said he must have fallen. I'm only thankful my troubles are over. God bless you in your work."

The Black was flying now and carried on: "One morning we heard that a sailor had drowned at sea and I was dispatched to give his wife the sad news. The door was opened by a large female:

"Whadya bleedin' want?"

"Are you the wid..? Sorry, I mean...."

"If it's any of your business you oul' rozzer, I'm a happily married woman."

"I see, and would you know where your husband is now, this precise minute?"

"I would. For your information he's at sea. You coppers are all questions, awful nosey aren't you? You never have answers, though."

"Yeah, well, now I've answers as well," I butted in. "Your husband isn't sailing any more. He's floating somewhere at the bottom of the sea. And having seen and listened to you, the sea monsters will be pleasant company compared to what he's had till now. So to conclude, I have answers, and can tell you that you are now officially... a widda."

A lot of the chat when gardai got together was about disciplinary matters. During my training I had fallen foul of them often, and discovered their implementation was shrouded in mystery. Now I realised I was not alone. Every member of my rank thought the regulations unfair. Our main bones of contention were that we aggravated the charges if we pleaded not guilty and were subsequently convicted. Also we had no warning before summoned to answer an allegation and on occasion statements of complaint could be withheld from us. The only positive effect of this was that if you were under investigation, you got a lot of sympathy. Indeed, some members were looked on as heroes for standing up for themselves.

This was The Black's original claim to fame. He was a legendary survivor having coped with as many enquiries as his summers in the job. Most of his convictions arose from confrontations with either the public or his superiors.

All regulation breaches were investigated by an officer in the same manner as a crime. While trivial cases were dealt with by a ticking off, The Black's dispensations had long dried up. In his case all enquiries resulted in the drafting of disciplinary charges on a misconduct form. Known as Form D1, this was the most dreaded piece of paper in the force.

The punishment meted out depended on the severity of the charges and previous conduct. An enquiry resulting in a conviction was known as being blocked. The penalties arising from this ranged from reprimand, caution, fine, transfer, reduction in rank to dismissal. A combination of penalties could be a terrifying cocktail. For example, being blocked and transferred was considered too close for comfort to being asked to hand in your uniform.

And so the more I saw the more enthralled I became with the lore of The Black. His number one follower, The Bluffer, fed my need for more stories. One concerned an inspector who took a dislike to The Black. This officer was always spotless. One day he spotted The Black on the beat with his tunic pockets unbuttoned.
"You are improperly dressed, garda."
"And so are you," was the answer back in a flash.
"Why, what's wrong with my dress?"
"See that belt," The Black pointed to the Sam Browne around his superior's waist. "It should be around your head as a halter, you auld jinnet."

Not surprisingly this was a blockable offence and The Black was transferred to south west Ireland where the shady peaks and the lapping waters might restore him to a state of grace. In this they signally failed.

One day he was walking down the only street in the village when a car drew up beside him. Inside were a couple of Americans:
"Tell me, officer. Are we on the right highway for the Magg Gill i Coddy reek? We've just flown into Shannon on a 'D.10' and I'm on my way to renew acquaintance with my forefathers."
"Well, now," The Black replied, mimicking their transatlantic drawl. "I just arrived here meself compliments of a 'D.I' but I'm not interested in visiting the remnants of any mountainy tribes who might claim my relationship. I suggest that you have some of that savvy and shag off back to where you came from."

The most illuminating conversations in the barracks centred on sex. The lack of it, its abuse and other typical talk. Here too The Black had it all figured out. He was a genuine barrack rat, jealously guarding his batchelorhood and only once came within an ace of being captured. A few days before the wedding, the woman concerned decided that he should go to confession. He made it to the door of the confessional before turning back, but a few of the lads had arrived and eventually he was horseboxed inside.
"Now, my good man tell me your sins," said the priest.
"Well, father to put it in a nutshell, I've done it all."
"I see, but you'll have to be more specific."
"I can't father."
"I've heard it all before, my son. I'll give you absolution. You'll feel better."
"It's not you I'm worried about father, it's them shaggers listening at the door."
With that he burst out, his contrition and his marriage plans in equal tatters.

The priest looked after him: "The worst ever.. his soul must be as black." And so the nickname came and stayed.

On and off duty, I listened and took in all the yarns. Soon it was easy to smile and laugh in all the right places. The Bluffer himself was the subject of many tales. A constant whinger he rarely worked a full shift without going sick. Once, a Superintended cornered him.

"Tell me," he asked, "how many teeth in the human mouth?"
The Bluffer gazed at him, mouth open displaying a fine set of molars.
"I haven't a clue, sir."
"That's very strange," said his boss, "because according to my information the human mouth contains approximately 32 teeth. And according to your sick record, you've had 76 extraction's in the last five years."

On another occasion when The Bluffer was a recruit a visiting entertainment came to his district. It consisted of some magnificently proportioned young ladies who removed virtually all of their clothing during their act. There was a public outcry and the gardai were requested to investigate.

The Superintendent sent an officer and the recruit in civvies. They filed their report and the authorities directed that charges of indecency be laid.

This was red hot news in holy Ireland and the court was packed. At his summing up the judge informed the court that he had been impressed at the sincerity and innocence of the recruit garda and would be guided in his final decision by the recruit's opinion. The Bluffer was summoned back to the witness box.
"Now tell me Garda, were you upset and disturbed while witnessing the act."
"Yerra, no Justice," The Bluffer replied immediately.
"And why not garda?"
"How could I Justice? Wasn't I on duty!"

On another occasion The Bluffer was reprimanded for repeatedly walking around with his hands in the pockets and finally summoned to his superior's office. Enter The Bluffer and slams to attention.
"Why do you slouch around with your hands in your pockets? It gives a bad impression, why do you do it?"
"It helps me think Sir," said The Bluffer.
The officer was a bit of a character and began to draw him out.
"What do you be thinking about?"
"Oh.. Sir.. Plotting my next move," replied The Bluffer.
Just then the phone rang in the office. Now, everyone knew The Bluffer considered all incoming calls as unecessary servile work. On the rare occasion he was forced to answer the phone he kept up a continuous,

'Hullo.. Whose there? Hullo... It's a faulty line'... Then he would sum-
mon another member, hand him the phone with instructions, 'can you
hear what that person is saying?'

Well on this occasion the officer directed The Bluffer out of his pose.
"You might move in the direction of that phone, exercise one of your
hands and listen to what that caller has in mind?" he said.
To make matters worse it was the Chief and his first query was what the
said Bluffer was doing in the Superintendent's office. Of course The
Bluffer got a red ear from the Chief and was directed to perform point
duty at the busiest intersection in his patch until the end of the month.

All these stories proved to me what it took to gain respect from colleagues. I needed something similar to prove myself. A minor run in
with authority in which I would come out on top - or a good case.
Something special was definitely needed before I would be accepted
into the inner circle. And I knew I wanted to belong.

So how to do it? Often as I lay in bed at night I mulled over my days. I
felt tantalisingly close to a secret that everyone but myself was privy to.
I was in a desert, fasting, beside me a large tightly covered pot of precious lifesaving liquid. Occasionally the pot cover would lift for a few
seconds then close just as quickly. If I was to prise open the secret, I
would have to time my move with perfection. Timing was the key.

As I lay, I looked at the lectures in the suitcase on the top of my locker.
They were undisturbed since my arrival, becoming more and more irrel-
evant. What a sham! The job was nowhere near the words contained in
them. I had been slagged in the mess about my incident with the dog in
the woman's house. It was their way of telling me I was a bit of a pup
myself. The word was I hadn't done well, still only a mongrel pup.

I had to act fast if I was to recover ground. Get to know the lads. Learn
to live with them. But how? What I needed was something to put my
name in lights. As it happened, it was the S S who decided my fate.

102

Chapter 8 - TRIBULATION

"Do you know your Sub/District yet, Forty?"
"All except No 5 beat, Sir," I replied.
"Well then your month of nights is starting on Monday and you can do a foot patrol in that area for the month. Did you have ere a prisoner yet?"

That was a barb. I replied in the negative as he knew I would. But he had given me an answer to my dilemma. The month of nights would be a godsend. I'd cut loose and fill the place with prisoners.

On the first day of the month we had to cover the early tour as well as the night one. As a concession this curtain-raiser was split, with half the unit doing four hours each. You can imagine who got the lie on that morning - not the recruit. The night tour was a 10pm-6am shift with parading time at 9.45pm. The first night I burst from the station and headed off with deadly intent. I was, in fact, delighted to be working in darkness for a change. I didn't have to face the public, only the baddies who, I felt, would introduce themselves before long.

Four miles of a circuit and three hours later I was tired, hungry and fed up. I had seen nothing remotely like a potential prisoner. The beat was a hard slog. The first mile was a tree-lined avenue, with houses set well back from the road. It was uphill then for the next while, then a wheel left to some shops and a few public houses. It continued into a group of factories and building sites, then new houses, left again and I was back to the start. I began to notice the shape and perspective of the shops in the dark where their roof outlines were starkly outlined.

After my break, I toured my beat again this time with more care. I checked all lock ups, turned door handles in shop doors, examined gratings and checked out alleyways. I inspected parked and unattended cars and lorries. Already The Bluffer had warned me to double-check my beat before I reported off. This was vital as if anything out of place was discovered by the oncoming patrols the SS would crease the half-sheet. But there was nothing.

After the first week I was a jaded, dejected and constipated young garda. It was almost impossible to stay awake for eight hours of darkness - two hours to kill before midnight, six hours after. A month in the twilight zone. And at the same time, a new affliction befell me. I couldn't sleep during the day. All I managed was a half stupor, dozing intermittently, waking with a screeching headache. After the first week I was in a permanent daze. The 4-6am part of the shift was the worst. My feet were sore and stiff and my body was screaming for relief.

Like many facets of the job I began to realise that applying for leave was a law unto itself. To obtain annual leave, each member had to indicate at the beginning of the year when they wanted a summer and a winter break.

The second type of leave consisted of a monthly allowance of two days and four nights off during day and night duty respectively. I discussed the possibility of a night's leave with The Bluffer but he was not encouraging. 'Being the recruit you have two chances,' he said 'none and fuck all'.

The first night on parade I noticed The Bully canvassing the unit and filling in their selections on the monthly calendar known as the altar list. All weekends were booked up immediately and when I asked if I would qualify for a night off, all I got was the ash from The Bully's Woodbine.

The list was pinned up in the glass cabinet in the parade room, but I still didn't feel competent to put my own number down. Nights off were solely at the whim of the SS. At the end of the first week I asked The Bully again if an approach to the SS would yield anything. 'He'll ate you', was the unhelpful response.

The granting of leave was conditional on the SS's moods. He seemed to take little leave himself. 'The exigencies of the service' was one of the main reasons leave was refused. Typically the SS made his own rules. Once I saw him making a fist of a leave form and flying it towards the fire in outrage: 'Can't be spared. Refused'.

There was only one other possibility. The chance of a morning off. This perk was granted to a night duty member who had to attend court the following morning. In my state of grace, this did not apply.

The first hours after a meal break were a killer. During the rest period my joints stiffened up. But no one cared. I was pitchforked out again and expected to do a complete re-check of the beat. The month of nights was becoming extremely difficult.

Another problem was I began to feel sick and unwell. Up to then I could eat thorny wire without any ill effects. Now the three relief system had thrown my eating and sleeping habits out of kilter and I was suffering. I had lost my hearty appetite. At nine o'clock each night the nervous energy began to work up. Then, in anticipation of four hours without food, I lashed into the grub. But there was no relish, I was eating for the sake of eating. And I was getting very constipated. Sitting on the throne was often more promising than productive.

I'd been warned of all this by The Bluffer:
"Go easy on the breadbasket on nights. You need time to adjust."

Most of the older members had cast iron stomachs. At break time the frying pan was king of the kitchen. Everything was fried and most offerings ended black because the pan was rarely cleaned. Onions were a favourite dish, fried bread and beans a delicacy. To see the gooey beans being ladled on to the greasy bread nearly made me throw up.
"Rump steak. It will keep you going on the beat for hours."
This was The Black as he chomped a lump of meat that looked like the sole of a shoe.
"Watch his jaws," The Bluffer nudged me. "That head should be preserved in the Wax Museum to frighten bold children."

One night after the parade halfway through the month the SS joined me in the corridor and said he was coming with me. I was delighted at the prospect of such exalted company on my patrol. The first thing that struck me was that outside his office the SS was a different man entirely. He seemed enthusiastic, approachable, and I thought I might be able to ask him some questions. But it was he who began the interrogation.

"Do you know the regulation beat?" I answered in the negative. "Two and a half miles to the hour," he announced. "On nights, patrol next to the buildings, day time nearest the kerbstone. All accessible places should be visited in rotation during your tour of duty."

This exchange seemed to put him in good humour and he began to talk about everyone that passed.
"That young buck. I put manners on him one time. See the respect he has for the law now. You must teach them to respect you. If you don't you're lost."

Later: "Did you see that pair getting out of that car? They're not husband and wife at all you know. I should come out more often."

Later still the revelry from a public house on the corner drew him like a magnet. "Now, now what have we here? Time, give it to me - summer opening hours?"
I rattled it off, but if expecting marks out of ten, I was disappointed.
"Drinking. The ruination of many's the good man's health and family. The abuse of the liquor licensing laws is rampant in this city. Aye! it's well after closing hours. It is our duty to stamp it out."
"Yes sir," I replied excitedly. "Will I go to the back door?"
"What? Yes, do that. Off you go."

I scooted round the corner and took up position. I was perspiring with excitement as I listened for the evidence to support a prosecution. My first big case... and the SS. I would be in his good books. Feverishly, I listened... Yes.... sounds of glasses clinking. Money changing hands, voices raised in merriment. At last.. the lectures were coming good, and I would be in at the kill.

From the front I heard the SS roar into action. A loud batter at the door followed by a bellow.
"Guards on public house duty. Open in the name of the law. The premises is surrounded."

Immediately the place became a graveyard. The lights were doused and a furtive tramp of feet grew in my direction. I stood aside just in time as the back door was flung open. A stampede erupted from within. With coats over their heads they flew by me along the alleyway.
"Come back, Gardai on public house duty," I shouted imitating my SS

as the blob of drunken humanity continued to spill onto the street.

I was reaching to capture a straggler when the bulky uniform appeared from the corner.
"Let him go. The one I want is still inside, he won't escape."

We were met at the front door by the cringing publican.
"Oh it's yourself Sergeant. I thought it was someone playing a joke."
"Well, you let some jokers out the back all right, but I know every mother's son of them."
"Oh! I had an awful awkward crowd in tonight. Couldn't clear the place at all. You came just in time, I was just going to ring up. Take the weight off your feet, Sergeant."
"No, I'll stand here out of your way beside all these half-filled pints. You work away. I need to make a few notes."
"Now Sergeant, never mind the notes. Would you like something? A nice corned beef sandwich and...."
"Not hungry," the SS snapped, taking out his big Parker pen and laboriously unscrewing the cap.

His quarry licked his lips anxiously as he wiped down the counter beside us. I might as well have been invisible for all the notice anyone took of me.
"Not hungry. Well, will you have a sup?"
He reached behind him on the shelf, hefted up a bottle of Old Irish, swept a tumbler from under the counter and placed it within a few inches of his tormentor's nose.
"Well, now the recruit has almost been trampled to death by the hordes you let loose on the back lane. Give him a mineral there to soothe his nerves," said the SS.
The mineral was poured in record time and placed before me.

The publican eyed the Old Irish hopefully. It could be his lifesaver if the sergeant was thirsty enough.
"I have lovely fresh rashers in the fridge Sergeant. Would you like a nice toasted sandwich? It must be nearly your break time. C'mon now, drink up.."
But the SS had apparently been transformed by the big bottle whose swirling smoky contents was wafting away all antagonism.
"Ah Paddy, old friend," he crooned, fondling the label as some rare and

most beautiful object. Then, suddenly, he erupted.

"Swill and ullage."

"What?"

"Swill and ullage. Your customers were swilling pints and were so anxious to get out they knocked over the table full of drink there by the back door. And this bottle is not full. The technical name for the quantity of which a bottle of alcoholic beverage falls short of being full is ullage."

"Well now, you have a great head, hasn't he, guard? Here's a full bottle," said his supplier, fetching up another.

The SS cradled the replacement bottle, silent for a while, then he spoke. "Give the recruit another orange. I'll just have a quick one while I'm waiting for him."

He uncorked and filled the tumbler, drank so quickly and repeatedly that soon the liquid had dipped half way down the label.

Then he turned toward me:

"Are you all right? You look a bit pale. Barman, give that young lad another orange and while you're at it, I could murder a pint. And what happened to those sandwiches you were crowing about?"

Food and drink were supplied immediately and just as quickly dispatched. Before leaving he turned at the door, his face once more a mask of officiousness:

"That was a serious breach tonight. Nevertheless, seeing as you expressed genuine regret, I will reserve judgement for now and will get back to you when I've made my decision."

We stood outside:

"Respect, that's vital. There has to be fear before respect is forthcoming," he said.

As we walked he seemed content with life. I desperately wanted to talk to him, to try to get to know him, but I didn't know where to begin. And so we walked in silence until he turned to me:

"You did well back there. You kept your mouth shut, that's vital in the early days."

This was great. I jumped at the opportunity to keep the conversation going:

"What about prisoners? How do I catch them?"

"There's plenty of them around. Your first arrest will be a milestone. The sooner you get one the better. Remember if you think he's up to something bring him in and we'll find something for him. If you see a fella hanging round late at night, you can be sure he's got nothing good on his mind. You'll have to look for them though, they'll not give themselves up. But there's enough to go round and you'll get your quota if you're good enough."

The last four words said it all. If I was good enough. It was up to me to prove my worth to my superiors.

I felt I had achieved some kind of understanding with the SS but I was wrong because two nights later on parade he tore strips off me:
"Forty.... Where's that prisoner? What have you been doing for the past fortnight - counting stars? You're the greatest waster of oxygen I've come across in ages. Not a screed of an arrest. This won't do. The Superintendent will be asking about your progress. Now, I'm directing you to get out there and do the job you're paid to do. I'm demanding a prisoner by the end of the month."

I was stunned by this attack and the burden it placed on me. What could I do? There was no magic formula for an arrest. It was a spontaneous reactionary act and I had to go by the book.
What to do? If in doubt ask a man of experience. I decided to get advice from one of the senior members. The first one I met was The Black whom I ambushed the next night in the back yard:
"Where in the name of all that's holy am I going to get a prisoner?" I asked, "it's so quiet out there. Nothing happens."
His reply was swift:
"Son. If there's nothing happening you'll have to make things happen, won't you?"
I remembered his dealings with the corner boys. Is that what he meant? Surely that wasn't the correct way to arrest people?

Later, walking my beat I thought of the gardai I had known at home. I had wanted to be like them, easygoing, relaxed, keepers of the peace. Here I was just a few weeks on the job being pushed out in the dead of night to bring back a live prisoner and only seven days to do it in. For five nights I went forth. Five mornings I came home with nothing except an ever-increasing ball and chain of worry.

To actually physically deprive a human being of their liberty, bring them to the station, then to court, take the sacred oath and give truthful evidence against them. That was my quandary, and a massive stumbling block to my progress as a garda.

The second last night I saw a prisoner - but I hadn't caught him. The patrol car spun to a halt in the yard and the four doors opened in unison. The Black was first out and I saw a shape being hurled along the corridor. At the far end of the hall was the SS. spraddled, blocking the prisoner's way:
"Aha, caught you again, you hoor. Didn't learn your lesson last time. I knew you'd be back." He grabbed a hold of the prisoner and gave him a bit of a throttling.

"Aw, Jaysus Sarge, I know I'm ordered out of the gaff, but you know yourself I had to get a cut out of the missus. You're a man of the world, you understand."
"I don't understand. I haven't any of your tom cat habits, so leave me out of it."

Later as I was leaving The Black whispered in my ear. "Wait outside the front gate. I'll have a present for you later on."

Just after midnight the patrol car pulled up. A rear door opened, a woman jumped out and ran towards the station door. I stood looking at her when The Black roared at me:
"Catch her quick before she gets to the station. That's Woodbine Annie. She's your prisoner."

I took off after her but could only get as close as the smell of drink as she led me into the public office. The SS jumped up when he saw her:
"Annie, what are you doing here?"
She uttered a shriek and the two seemed to converse through eye contact till the SS looked at me and grunted:
"Prisoner?"
I could only nod.
"Drunk, I suppose?"
Again, I nodded, feeling better by the minute.
"Place of arrest?" the SS asked, uncorking his pen.
"The station," I muttered.
"Manner of arrest... Quickly now."

"Well, she appeared outside the station with drink on her and ran in here before I could get at her."

"You didn't formally arrest her then. Put a hand on her? You have to put your hand on her to arrest her, restrain her liberty. Your arrest was illegal. This prisoner is in unlawful custody. Go on home now, Annie, there's a good girl. As for you Forty, give her a shilling for her trouble. Now back on your beat and bring in something worth catching."

Finally, I was out on the street on my last night of night duty. I was patrolling my beat morosely and arrived at a junction where sewerage pipes were being laid during daylight hours. Arising from this there was a huge hole in the road and general traffic disruption at all times. Suddenly at a distance I made out a shape approaching fast. It was a cyclist with no front light.

At last. My prisoner.

Confidently I stepped out onto the road, raised my right arm and waved my torch as I'd learned in training. The cyclist slowed, but when he was about ten yards from me he dropped his head and drove the pedals like a demon straight at me.

I stood my ground, and as he drew abreast I launched myself at him. The timing was perfect. But unfortunately, the impact sent him sprawling bike and all into the hole.

Instantly my ecstasy became agony. What had I done? I listened but there was no sound from the black depths. Far away a bell tolled mournfully. It was midnight. I blessed myself. God forgive me, I thought, what have I done?

The cyclist had to be seriously injured or dead. This was the worst yet. In my desperation for a prisoner, I'd killed one.

There was no escape. Or was there? A furtive glance around. The place was deserted. Nobody had seen me. I fled from my nightmare to the sanctuary of the station and up the back stairs to my bedroom. What was I to do? I wasn't cut out to be a policeman. Quickly I ripped off the now-hateful uniform and began to pack my bags. Next I sat on my bed. I would wait until the morning when I would be off duty and could escape unnoticed.

But as I sat and waited and dawn crept over the city, a new thought came and would not go away. I had to go back. I had to know how the man was. If I didn't I knew I wouldn't get another moment's peace. Shortly after nine o'clock I crept out the back door of the station and retraced my steps to the intersection. Approaching the road-works I nearly died. The hole had been filled in.

I reeled across the road and stood grappling with this new development. Suddenly a voice intruded:
"Are you looking for a start?"
"No, no, actually, well, the fact is I'm a garda at the local station and we had a report that some fella fell into a hole here last night."
"That's right," said the foreman amicably. "This morning when we arrived for work there was a fella stranded in the hole with his bicycle roaring to be dragged out."

A wave of indescribable happiness swept over me. But the story wasn't over yet:
"The funny thing was he kept repeating a crazy story that he'd been attacked by a black Panther. Would you believe it? In Dublin!"

So I had been reprieved. But I was still in limbo, cast somewhere between past training and present reality. Again, that perennial question, how to reconcile the two? I decided to seek out Little John again. The day he was back from temporary transfer I was waiting for him. I spilled it all out, going over every minute since we last met. He let me talk, nodding encouragement until I was spent.

Then he began:

"Teething problems, we all had them. Take your time, don't rush things. The ABC is be on time for duty, be clean and tidy and always be ready to help people. The latter is the cardinal rule.

"Let me tell you about my days as a recruit. I was a Taca Siochana. I joined in 1939, the start of the Emergency and the Second World War. We were only temporary gardai and could be let go at fourteen days notice. We had less pay than the regulars and no pensions. We were known as the cut-price guards, a fierce derogatory term. In those days guards had to be in barracks before midnight; known as the Cinderella's we were. It was regimentary stuff; a throwback from the military era

112

because no one knew any better. By their nature disciplined forces are slow to change. But barriers are being broken down, and if it is to flourish, the force has to move with the times and adapt. So you've come in at a time of change, and you will be involved in that change.

"I've said it to you before and I'll say it again. Putting on a uniform doesn't change a person inside. Only the outside. In your case you are what you were, a country lad trying to come to terms with law and discipline as you wander around the streets of a strange city, and so much has happened to you in the last six months that you haven't had time to separate the good from the bad.

"You're in a different world. You're expected to observe, decide, intervene, manhandle people if necessary and then justify what you've done. But what about feelings? They don't go away, and it'll take you time to assimilate everything.

"Watch people as you pass by. They'll stare at you. It's a natural reaction to the sight of the uniform. Some members don't notice. They've their heads in the clouds spotting for Aer Lingus. Then again your appearance will affect people in different ways, to some you're a comfort, to others you're a symbol of oppression. It's all to do with your powers and how you apply them. You mustn't go out of your way to "do" people. You must give the impression you have no option and are doing no more than your duty. Mostly everyone has an experience with a member of the force at some stage, it can be good or bad. If someone has had a bad experience with a garda, and you are their next experience, and it's good, then you can turn the negative into positive. A smile, a kind word is invaluable. Remember, that person you hassle today may have a whisper on a serious crime tomorrow. They need you and you need them.

"Another aspect of the job is its unpredictability. It's like a load of buckshot, no pattern. No matter how much you plan, some happenings are outside your control. You'll walk into them accidentally; you decide on a whim to patrol a quiet cul-de-sac; all of a sudden, there it is. A crime. An incident. At times you must be strong and able to use your baton instantly. At other times you must put on another skin, smile, give directions, offer assistance. This ability to adapt is difficult, but necessary, if you are to persevere."

113

He left me with a lot to think about. Teething problems, live through it, take your time.

What toll would it take on me? The Bluffer, The Black, The Squirrel - would I end up like one of them? Who knows? No time for whinging, just get on with it.

I had survived the first eight weeks - just.

As weeks grew into months I continued to be moulded and developed by my new life. I took part in a crazy football match, visited the Garda doctor, had my first Chief's inspection. And for my first Christmas away from home, I got a most unwelcome gift - a transfer to the Border.

Chapter 9 - CONSOLIDATION

"You saw it, guard. Number eight. He assaulted me. Do your duty. Arrest him."

If ever a young man had dreamed dreams and woke to an unfulfilled reality, or set out on a mission boldly, or wished a single wish, that was me.
Now my dreams had come to life, tightening my chest with excitement.

"Did you have ere a prisoner yet?"
The question from my S S, the occasion and tone of delivery had burnt into my soul and become a personal crusade. During the intervening three months I had been involved in arrests, but usually the scent was picked up by others and I was employed solely as back-up, therefore enjoying little triumphalism at the kill. More than anything, I wanted to track down and arrest unaided my very own prisoner. Till then I would regard myself as a mere half-garda.

In the meantime, my existence revolved around this quest. Conveyor-belts of prisoners paraded before me. Ghostly figures humanised on every encounter with the public. Expectation. Disillusionment. I'd lived with both.

As time passed I began to attach conditions to my quarry. To pursue, snare and take a scalp single-handed would serve as my initiation. But I now wanted a prisoner of substance with a bit of action attached. So I decided to preserve myself until I met some gruesome behaviour at which time I would leap into action - to the terror of the evildoer.

Since the unforgettable set-to with the cyclist, the S S's rhetorical question had been confined in my treasure chest and padlocked by the morale-boosting counsel of Little John.
"Take it handy. Don't rush things."

But now, here he was, a prisoner, gift-wrapped, on a plate. Was my deliverance at hand?

I was on duty at a soccer match. There was something exciting about fellas in togs chasing a ball of wind and I had been enjoying the match, despite the fact that the players consistently refrained from handling the ball which was for me an alien bashfulness.

There was a big crowd in a lean-to shed behind me and when the players appeared, their supporters rose the roof, welcoming with wild abandon the most notable team members: Mugser, Barrel-arse, Heron-head and their particular favourite, the Swan. He was the goalie bolstered by his fans with shouts of encouragement:
"C'mon the Swan."

As he took up position his first action was to pace out the distance between the posts and to decide they were too wide apart. Next he grasped one of the uprights and tried to uproot it. Failing this, he measured out to the square, marking a few divots here and there with his heel, as if warming up for the hop-step and jump.

From the start of the game the ball remained in the opposite half of the field with virtually all players engaged in a frenzy of short, tapping kicks, darting runs, sideline throws, name calling and handwaving.

Only once during the first quarter did the ball stray in the direction of the Swan. He fondled it, his fingers wafting over its contours, until almost on a whim, he held it at arm's length before pirouetting and flinging it overarm to a team-mate. The latter tapped it a few times then prodded it back again towards the Swan who seemed to let it roll towards the unguarded net, before diving expansively and laying on it like a playful tom-cat.
The crowd roared its appreciation:
"Me oul' flower. Swan Lake. Give us another."
For an encore he gave a few paddles before rolling sideways on to his feet and cupping the ball in his arms. Next, he placed it gingerly on the ground, tapped it gently forward and high stepped after it to the edge of the square. Just as an opponent encroached, he gobbled it up, shaded his forehead with an outstretched palm and fixed his gaze on the far reaches of the field.

"Give it air, Swan."

The crowd were revving him up and in obedience he swung his right foot in a wide arc, coughed up the ball and let fly. Disaster. The ball skewed off his foot and trickled a mere half-dozen yards to one side.

I knew countymen of my own who could lob the half-hundred weight a similar distance without taking off their coat.

There followed a tremendous schmozzle, with the previously defending team attacking like demons and the unfortunate referee scurrying among them.
All of a sudden like a spoilt child, the referee grabbed the ball, ran from the pack, for the sideline - and me.
"You saw it guard. Number Eight. He assaulted me. Do your duty. Arrest him."

The referee wore a whistle draped round his neck, and not one but two watches on a spindly wrist. He dropped the ball between his feet, flapped an arm in the direction of the pitch and grappled with his note-book.
"Assault. He meant it. We're all the wan, you and me. Trying to keep order."

Behind me the crowd booed.
"Bleedin' get on wit it, ref, ya auld Mollie."
"Yeah, gard, book him. The oul' gobdaw. Or them other shower, go on, run them in for false pretences, paying good money, I ask you."

The referee smelt of perspiration and after shave.
"I'm doing my best. Keeping the peace out there. That hooligan you saw it, didn't you?"

When in doubt do nothing. I thought of Big Andy. His big laugh had been the only censure. I'd witnessed plenty of rows on the football field but never a hint of anyone being arrested. I thought of my S S and his reaction should I appear before him having arrested a member of his favourite team. I know who'd be put in the cell.
From then on I'd be known as 'After Eight'.

It was time to act or to speak. I spoke:
"I don't think much of the altercation. I would consider it kinda accidental."

I surprised myself with the outburst. And as the referee stared back, I was way ahead doing something I was becoming mighty proficient at: double-checking my decision. Gut feeling, was promising, but better dredge out the legislation just in case. Powers of arrest for assault...... but there were so many different types of assault. Occasioning actual bodily harm, grievous, wounding and common assault. That was it... common assault. Yes. Common law powers of arrest. 'A garda is bound to arrest any person who commits a breach of the peace within his view if he cannot otherwise prevent it'. Ah, now I have it, a breach of the peace: 'An attempt or offer with force or violence moved against the person of another'. Aw, forget it. Common sense. The gospel according to Little John.....
'In all emergencies, do something. If you're not sure, do nothing.'

"No," I said, " there'll be no arrest. I'll report the matter but I'm taking no action now. I think the match should continue, but that's up to you."

My first public statement and I hoped I wouldn't live to regret it. At least the crowd near me agreed and harangued the referee into restarting the game. A few toots on his whistle seemed to revive him.
"All right, I'll continue, but if there's any more trouble, it's the Black Maria you'll be calling."

As usual it was all the fault of my S S. If he had been on my side, I wouldn't be within an ass's roar of any soccer match.

But it had been a bad weekend all round.

And it started as if it was going to make me famous.

The previous Friday, a letter had roused me to fever pitch:
"The Kerry County Board request that Garda T Doyle be granted leave to play for Kerry on Sunday next."
The S S stripped his teeth.
"Rovers are playing in the park next Sunday," he said.
"Yes, but I've been chosen for my native county."

"The exigencies of the service. Leave refused."
I was obviously fuming, and noting my lack of subservience he put the boot on my neck with his next remark:
"You'll have to decide which is more important, Gaelic football or the *Garda Siochana*."

That was the end of it. I was confined to barracks and destined to watch my first soccer match. Later when I compared it with Gaelic, it appeared tame with neither team capable of scoring even a good wide. But at least peace was the winner.

The following day, anxious to work off my anger, I grabbed my sports kit and headed off for the football park with The Bluffer and The Black as sparring partners. As soon as I warmed up, we had a bit of a kick around, but after a few minutes they were in a state of collapse.
"Give us a breather," croaked The Bluffer.

They repaired to the sideline maybe to make daisy chains while I began to practise on my own. But as I launched myself off the ground to grab the ball from orbit, I lost my balance, and returned to mother earth with a crunch landing on my left elbow.

I was gripped immediately by a spasm of pain. Later back in the station, I met the S S on the corridor and told him of my injury. Impatiently he grabbed my sore arm at the wrist and swung it like the handle of the pump in our haggard. Knots of pain shot through my elbow. First aid, how are you? But he had made his diagnosis.
"You're for the garda doctor tomorrow."

Next morning the Garda Medical officer had a clinic in a nearby station. By the time I arrived the long, shallow waiting room was half full of members swarming round the door, clumped together as if they, or I, suffered from an incurable disease. As I listened and heard their ailments, I learnt that a 'flu bug' had apparently felled the lot of them.
They had all the symptoms - from wheezing, spluttering coughs to king-sized nasal discharges into crumpled handkerchiefs. The symptoms grew in volume whenever the doctor's door was open.

As I sat I monitored the transformation as each patient left the surgery. In contrast to their previous demeanour, the rate of recovery appeared miraculous. Having crawled in, they fluttered out, beaming and waving a piece of paper as if they had been granted an executioner's reprieve. Finally it was my turn. The doctor ignored me as he bent over his desk and called out:

"Name and station?"

I furnished these details.

"Lie."

At first I thought he was accusing me of an untruth, but then he limped towards me and motioned me towards a settee:

"Com'on now. Hurry up. On your back. There."

Before I realised it, I was horizontal with him leaning on my sore elbow. I opened my mouth to tell him of my trouble but before it was fully ajar, he filled it with two pudgy fingers and more orders:

"Open wide. Come on, now. Wider."

I obeyed and within minutes he had left me and was over at his desk and scribbling in his prescription pad.

"Yes! another case of laryngitis."

I was thunderstruck. He rammed the note into my hand with further instructions:

"There now, a week off.. isn't that what you want?.. Get that bottle from Hamil..."

"But doctor," I interrupted, " it's my elbow."

"You're... What?? Why didn't you tell me in the first place? Wasting my time. What happened it anyway?"

I told him. He grabbed my arm, examined it superficially and began scribbling another scrawl on fresh notepaper. "You're for Jervis Street."

The hospital casualty department was bulging. Eventually a nurse took my particulars and pointed me towards a corridor with instructions to wait until my name was called. I was soon whisked in behind a curtain and my upper garments peeled off.

The doctor was young but knew his job. He felt my elbow with soothing, manicured hands:

"So you're an athlete. I'm into rugby myself."

As he tended to me I told him my rugby story. One year during a triple crown decider we had been busy roofing a turf shed with a bit of extra help. Soon rain drove us indoors and we sat round the radio listening to the game. One of the helpers seemed to be in direct communication with the field of play with an intimate knowledge of all the Irish side. Soon however, we realised he didn't know an oval ball from a hard boiled egg. The commentator was giving great coverage to one player continually grabbing the ball on the blind side. Then our resident expert blew his cover: 'Isn't yure man a great player for a fella with only wan eye', he said.

The casualty officer enjoyed that as he plaited a sling for my arm and having fixed it in place told me to rest it up. Finally he gave me a sick note and said I was to abstain from work for a week before returning to the Outpatients.

I was in no hurry back to the station. I wondered how I would be received. Here I was, hardly a wet day out of training and getting myself injured needlessly. Different if I had gone down in the line of fire, but chasing a ball? Would I be considered too soft, or worse still, a faker?

With these dismal thoughts I slid in the back door of the station and skimmed up to my room. The familiar surroundings soothed my anxiety but it soared again when I realised that elementary maintenance such as washing and dressing would be difficult. I was slumped on the bed when The Bluffer approached.
"You got a bad fall. Is there bone damage? We thought we heard a crack."

This vote of confidence, courtesy of an eyewitness was just the painkiller I needed, so after a while I drifted down to the mess hall. My good spirits evaporated when The Black strolled in:
"It's a great job. Ha. Paid while yu're on the sick. Keep waving the white flag there, boy. It's good for a month at least. You should shag off home for yourself. See The Staff, he'll organise it."

Later that afternoon I delivered my sick note to The Staff.
"Hmmm, elbow bruised, much pain?"
"Not as bad as yesterday."
"Yes," he continued, "any slagging from the mess?"
"A bit.. Advice, more than anything."
"Yeah. I can imagine. You'll be all right in four or five days. Meanwhile

rest the limb, hang around and show the face."

I took his advice and planned to remain in the station when my relief was working in case they would think I was dossing. The scheme worked well as that evening when I bowled into the mess hall I met The Owl for the second time.

The Owl was semi-retired. He dressed in uniform pants, shirt and collar stud. The only time he donned the blue was at election time and for inspections.
I had first spotted him three days after my arrival at the new station. A big, heavy, elderly man, Old Pat, alias The Owl, earned the title because of his tendency to slumber quietly in any corner he found himself, but taking all in as well.
He was one of the few God addressed in a civil manner.

Now, I had a Squirrel and an Owl to keep me company. My menagerie was increasing.

My injury brought myself and The Owl together the day after my sick report. I had been in the mess hall for a while when I noticed two soft chairs facing each other at the far corner and a body planked across them. When the Angelus rang at noon, he stood up and prayed, his eyes flickering across me, but far away.

After his 'amen' he pulled the chairs apart, turned one around, slumped down and looked across at my injured limb:
"So you're the young fella?"
I nodded.
Like his counterpart in the feathered fraternity, he had a wise face. I desperately wanted to talk to him as he was meant to have influence with the S S but in deference to his seniority, I felt I should wait for him to speak first. However, all that was on offer were contented little yawns, and afraid that he would drift from me I opened the proceedings:
"What part are you from?"
"West of the Shannon, boy."
He spoke in a haunting monotone that seemed to trail away back to his homeland.
"How are you getting on with himself?" he asked.
This was an awkward one, seeing as they were buddies, but I decided to

be straight:

"Hard to know. I'm doing my best, but he's hard to please, isn't he?"

"You're not fit to judge him yet."

I accepted this, nodding in agreement - anxious for him to continue, which he did.

"We grew up in the era of a civil war, a lawless country developing into a free state but the sight of a uniform was still guaranteed to turn many a stomach. Memories of tough times linger and are hard to dislodge. Some will go to the grave with us."

He continued talking as much to himself as to me:

"We were the prehistoric guards, symbolic of an era when all the job needed were big, tough, uneducated bogmen who did what they were told without answering back. That's the way it was, and it was bred into us from day one.

"The first thing I'll say to you is this: the S S is carrying this job. He's the most powerful man in the station, and he'll guard his reputation and domain until he walks out the door for the last time.

"The man is indestructible. He has his own way of doing things. He's been compared to a snail with horns, prodding and intimidating all before him, but that's his nature and he knows no other way.

"You mightn't understand this now, but carrying a rank within the force is not easy. You have to stand back from situations and look at the over-all picture before you act. He has a lot on his plate and to my way of thinking, he is doing the job to perfection. When things are handy it's easy to take charge of men, but when the pressure is on, that's when the real skippers stand up and are counted.

"You'll have to accept his ways if you want to survive. He gives the impression of being tough and hardhearted but underneath he is hon-ourable and will not wrong you. Indeed, you'll find no better man to keep you on the straight and narrow if you respect him and don't act the blackguard.

"Do your bit of work and don't be afraid of mistakes. We all made them. If you make a hames of something, own up to it immediately. Don't put it on the long finger hoping it will go away. It won't. Most come back and become a file. Some grow hair and develop a life all of their own. If he doesn't know in advance that something is wrong, you're up shit creek as he will go through you for a shortcut then wash his hands of you without blinking an eye. Remember, a policeman who was never in trouble never did anything, so if you're out there, you'll definitely run into some awkward cases. That's when the S S will be on your side and will even bend over backwards to give you a dig out. We all joined up to do our bit the best we could. Along the way some got side-tracked, others prospered. Influences and choices, that's the key. You'll have to choose carefully whose jotter you're going to copy."

He stopped talking at last, but I wanted more.
"How do I satisfy him?"
"I'll answer that by asking this. What does he see when he looks at you?"
"Inexperience, green, I dunno..." but he cut across me:
"You're a rough, uncut diamond badly in need of shaping. You're full of enthusiasm but that can be a hindrance in the beginning. You'll have to get the corners knocked off before you fit in."
"How can I fit in?" I asked.
"Time and experience," he said. "At the moment you're full of regulations and laws; but it's out there in the street that the real learning starts. You need to be pared down a bit, learn to get on with the lads, suffer a bit of hardship. An auld fella told me when I started out, good judgement comes from bad experiences.
"The S S may roar at you but he'll teach you as well. Don't stray far from his headlines. He'll give you your head, he has to, as he can't afford to baby-sit anyone with some of the hard chaws he has to deal with. Now and then he'll let off a bit of steam, sometimes leave you to stew, but in the turn of a hand, he'll lay off. You're a fast learner, I think, and anyway this oul' job has a way of gettin' in on you. Can you make sense of all that?"

I nodded.
"Good," he said " because it's time for my snooze." Then he stretched out luxuriously, threw his head on his shoulder and drifted to sleep.

As I sat I thought about what I had heard. So the S S had been testing me, hounding me for a prisoner, raiding the pub. The Owl had embossed it again. The pride, the bond, the job. Being part of something enduring. It seemed to prove once again that no matter how lackadaisical some members appeared, each cared about the job. As The Owl said: 'it has a way of getting in on you'.

Next morning a group of us, including The Owl were chatting in the mess hall. Suddenly I heard a ferocious bang outside the station. Before I could blink there was a dash for the door, The Owl bringing up the rear but moving with a speed I would not have thought possible. I remained stuck to my seat until God's arrival uprooted me:
"Where's the rest of them hiding?"
"They went.. They ran..." But he stopped me.
"They did, some sight. Well, you're fit enough. Throw off that sling, stick on the tunic and button up. There's a bit of a tip outside the station."

I learnt a lesson from that incident. The live-in brigade were ripe for all emergencies. When God roared it didn't matter whether you were on or off duty, you responded. And he wasn't going to allow a minor impairment of one of my wings to stop me from doing my duty either.

Over the next few months I heard more of The Owl's wisdom. One day I came in on a heated discussion about promotion. Suddenly The Owl piped up:
"If they repealed the Old Pals Act, it'd be a great job."

Another time we were discussing the lack of opportunity for further education. And again the Owl splintered the chat:
"The polis is only a job for academic failures."

Just like The Black, stories of The Owl's past exploits were numerous.

Once, many years before, he'd been stationed at the edge of a city and dealt in a corner grocery shop. The shop changed hands and the new owner proved to be a bit of a schemer.
The Owl's first purchase was a bottle of milk, for which he passed six old pence over the counter as payment.
"One pint of milk guard, yes, price five pence halfpenny. I've no change, so I'll give you three of these six-a-penny suckers instead," said the owner.

The Owl found himself on the street with his pint and three sweets. His first impulse was to throw the aptly named confectionery away but on reflection he pocketed them. He decided that the shopkeeper was not going to sweet-talk him into any future submission.

Later on that day The Owl donned the blue crossed the street from the station and took up duty beside the shop. He waited until a few customers were inside, then went in himself, took another bottle of milk and marched with it to the top of the queue.

"Aw it's yourself garda, another bottle of milk, that'll be.."

"Yes," The Owl cut across him, " I know the price, five pence halfpenny. Here it is, five pence and I'm returning your three suckers in lieu of the balance."

On the fourth day of my enforced idleness, God rose up before me in the mess:

"Yu're better. Parade before me tomorrow. Late tour."

That was all. The cure. A miracle or a divine decree. Even though I still had a few days of my sick leave to go, it was time to throw off the bandages, take up my bed and walk.

Some days later I met my Superintendent for the first time. I was about two hours into an early patrol when a mist chased me back to the station for my waterproof. I was leaving by the back door again when a furtive scratching sound in the corridor alerted me. Looking round I saw someone fiddling at one of the doors. I went up to him:

"Are you all right there?"

"Whoa.. Who're you?"

All of a sudden it hit me. This was the District office and the tall, gaunt individual in front of me fitted the description of the officer in charge of my district. He seemed disorientated as he searched for the latch on the wrong side of the door. Trying to be helpful I banged on the light only for him to cringe away Dracula-like from the illumination.

"Jaysus! turn it off. Who're you anyway?"

"I'm the recruit," I was getting used to admitting it at this stage.

"The recruit. I see. Hmm. Did you see the Detective Sergeant on your travels?"

"No, Sir. Do you want me to get him for you?"

"What? Yes, do that. Tell him there's a burglary at Murphy's licensed premises and to meet me there as soon as possible."

I was delighted at being the bearer of important news and made for the public office. God was there writing in the Occurrence book but before I could speak, The Bully appeared and the look on his face bulldozed me back into the corridor:

"I've fierce important news for..." I burst out, nodding towards the Almighty's back. But The Bully shushed me and beckoned me away.

"Hould your whist. C'mere till I tell you. Himself took one of his turns this morning. He wouldn't even open the post. Ran me back out with directions to dump it back in the letter box." 'Let some other shagging skipper open it', he says. " I think it's all to do with the chief's inspection in a few weeks time. What ails you, anyway?"

All of a sudden my news palled.

"It's the Superintendent," I replied. "I met him going into his office. He told me to inform the Detective Sergeant that there was a burglary in Murphy's pub and to meet him there. It must be serious."

At this The Bully cocked his nose and sniffed the air.

"Funny now, I've been in the station all morning and that's the first I heard of the incident. How's the boss looking?"

"A bit under the weather, I thought."

"Ah, that's it. He's in the horrors and after a cure. Say, did you put ere a few summonses in yet?"

"A bicycle light. It's coming up in a month's time. I suppose it's time I was getting a few more."

"It is," said The Bully, "especially with the Chief on his way. He's due in a month's time. He's not the worst though he sometimes loses the run of himself and doesn't know his own mind. When the whim hits him, he gets his back up over nothing and tears strips off everyone, but then he can be as nice as pie. Loves to hear himself talk. We let him spout away. Now I'll get The Black to give you a hand filling in a page or two of your notebook."

The following afternoon The Black and myself lined out together.

"I know a great spot," he said. "The new white line on the sharp corner of South Terrace. It's a cert. You'll be the Chief's pet. The last time he was here, he lit on us all for not enforcing the Road Traffic Acts."

Before long our traps were laid. But everyone appeared super law-abiding that particular evening. Then, The Black twigged the problem:

"It's the traffic passing on the far side that's doing the damage, tipping off the approaching drivers. I'll soon put a halt to their gallop. You stay here, it'll be easy pickings from now on."

He crossed the road, sauntered up a bit and flagged down the oncoming traffic on his side. This gave me all the nearside to plunder and I pulled in the first few that sailed over the continuous line. Knowing I was being monitored by the arch predator, I laid down the law sternly, pointing out the relevant breach of the Road Traffic Act and demanding identities. But once I produced my notebook and started writing, the excuses flowed like gravy. Some almost cried, others swore allegiance to the forces of law and order, promising it would never happen again, and begging me to 'please, please give them one chance'.

As my pen wavered, they hit me again:
"Never been in trouble in me life, Gard. You're new, aren't you? From the country. Kerry, isn't it? Recognise your accent. I was there on my holidays, lovely place, grand people. You seem like a decent chap. Ah g'wan, give us a chance, just one, it'll never happen again."

These heartrending pleas dried up my pen. I felt it would be victimisation to book someone for slipping over a four inch white line. Different if the car was a banger with a feast of summonses flourishing on it.

Eventually, I succumbed to my better instincts, sealed up my notebook and issued cautions to all concerned. Suddenly The Black was beside me.
"Whattya at?"
I told him the truth. I hadn't the heart to book decent people for such a minor indiscretion.
"Right," he said. "There's only one thing for it so."
Looking at his watch, he ordered:
"Start writin. Time... Date.... Place. At 4pm on this date... at South Terrace stopped motor Vehicle number...."
I looked up at him in amazement but he continued urgently, "C'mon, write.... stopped James Murphy, address.. put in Main Street. Pick out any town you like. Driving.. make of car, registered number,. something current... Offence. Breaking a continuous white line. Excuse..... Sorry, I was going too fast. Okay, here's another. C'mon.. Keep writing."

And he recited off two more. All I could do was follow instructions to the letter until several pages of my notebook looked very presentable. "That'll keep you going. There only bogies. It's a bluff for the Chief....Once I heard of a desperate member scabbing a few names off the obituary column. Dead safe they were. Ha...."

The Black still spouted out before turning away leaving my mind in flitters and my official notebook desecrated with fictitious names and addresses.

Within a few days, however, I was able to complete a genuine half-dozen pages of my notebook. It was my first serious accident. A boy cycling home from school had come a cropper against a JCB. His leg was splintered, I was left with his screams ringing in my ears and no sign of an ambulance.

Images from training came when I needed them. I remembered my first-aid instructor demonstrating how to secure a suspected fracture on one of our group he put lying on the gym floor. Armed with this, I tied the belt of my trousers round the youth's shin bone, stopped a passing car and had the casualty in hospital in a jiffy. Lingering, I saw how the staff set about reducing his pain, and I experienced a sense of satisfaction about my part in the accident.

That night I had a wonderful experience as his parents sought me out and thanked me profusely for saving their only son. The accident report filled a few pages in my notebook, including a double-page spread for a rough sketch. It instilled in me a resolution to act in all emergencies and made me realise that I would prefer to be guilty of a sin of commission rather than omission.

So, in preparation for the arrival of the Chief and the expectation that he would interrogate me about the investigation, I pored over the details. For the first time, measurements, point of impact, debris, admissions of driving, production of documents and oral warnings became not theory but practice. I even revisited the scene when off-duty to ensure I had all the facts.

Filling out the report in the accident book seemed like a daunting task, but when I copied the headings from previous entries and added my own details, the finished product looked acceptable. The S S complimented me on my handwriting, but as usual added a rider:

"You haven't investigated an accident until you've done a fataller."

The nights were closing in. Summer was giving way to autumn and I was into my fourth month on the job.

My beat was there to be prowled. The main street was a frenzied glut of movement. The rest was a labyrinth of streets dotted with factories, offices, shops and houses, busy or quiet depending on the time of day, but all expecting the garda to ensure that peace and tranquillity reigned.

I peered and pondered as I bowled along on my patrols. Most of my thoughts had been distilled from the preaching of Little John, The Owl and even the S S. These had put the bit between my teeth on many issues, but the most daunting task still remained - facing the public.

Nevertheless I was learning all the time. Every time I donned the blue was different. Each day was a new challenge. When things were quiet, I felt at ease. But when called into action, my uniform often felt a ton weight. Invariably I set out intending to give all comers the benefit of a friendly face, but often the sheer volume of people made this impossible. My plan worked best when I stood at an intersection where I was visible and could monitor every type of individual. Attitudes varied from the 'howye', to the nod of recognition, to the sullen 'I don't like you', or 'what are you looking at me for?'

So I walked and looked. I began to realise that observing people - compulsory for the job, was also becoming personally irresistible. As my mileage mounted, so my ideas changed. People were often not what they seemed. I had been well aware of the adage not to judge people by appearances. Now I realised how true it was. For instance, an unkempt longhaired youth often turned out to be educated and respectable. Others with an aura of breeding were regularly revealed as spiteful, narrow-minded bigots.

Similarly I was surprised at the different reactions of people who sought my help. Some, to whom I donated only a minute of time were generous in their thanks or even wrote letters to my superiors. Others whom I went out of my way to help, often left with a mere grunt of acknowledgement.

Then there were the parents who used me as a bogeyman. Usually women, they approached me clutching children at arm's length.

"You're bold. Will you stop it once and for all? Look, there's a guard. He'll take you away and lock you up. Won't you guard? That's it. Look, he says he will, and throw away the key. Here, take him guard."

Outwardly I had to smile and be pleasant. Inwardly I thought it's you, the parent who should be locked up.

Other pests who wanted to be seen talking to the garda, haunted my beat armed with the news of the day. But their talk usually consisted of rehashing the headlines - with predictable comment.

"That's a terrible case. I don't know what the world is coming to. Why isn't there a law against it? What are you guards doing about it?"

Finally, there was the vehicular traffic or mechanically propelled vehicles, a long-winded title for a car or lorry. I was becoming adept at judging speed and distance, as well as the different shapes and makes of vehicles. Slowly I began to get the hang of dressing down each approaching vehicle. First, I focused on its condition. If it was a banger, my eyes went to the driver, the road tax and number plates. Gradually, my eyes became accustomed to flicking off the bonnets and labelling each vehicle in my mind with split-second timing, until I became almost expert at targeting those suspected of contravening the Road Traffic Acts.

Understandably it was impossible to pin-point all traffic, but while patrolling I did my best, facing the oncoming traffic as Little John had explained: 'Keep your beam so that you can be seen. It's not your seeing them that is as important as their perception that you can see them'.

The driving public were wonderfully diverse. I thought the coolest were the bus drivers who expertly manoeuvred their double deckers at peak traffic. The lone car drivers displayed the most mannerisms, the most disgusting when they excavated, inspected then sometimes digested the contents of the portholes of their nose.

I came to the distinct impression that most people's personalities changed for the worst when they were behind the wheel of their private jam jars.

The prospect of discovering a stolen car always made the pulse quicken. Once or twice I thought I spied one in the distance but invariably it sped away into a side street before I could check the list in the back of my notebook. I was still learning how to deal with the motoring public, in particular, in confrontation situations such as check points. Often I heeded Little John's advice: 'Prosecute but never persecute'.

I usually began with a smile to which most people responded. If the vehicle yielded offences, then normally a bit of severity was introduced into the proceedings. Things cooled down even more if I considered the breach of the Road Traffic Acts serious enough to warrant further action. The demand for identification often transformed a smiling citizen into an angry, wheedling or abusive one. My own smile soon faded on those occasions also.

While most people were easy to get on with, some had endless complaints about life: noisy traffic, badly parked vehicles, loud barking dogs or dangerous shop awnings. I finally discovered a foolproof way of dealing with these. First, I allowed them let off steam until they began repeating themselves. That was the signal to whip out my notebook and began to record every word. At this point some were transformed, warming to my attentiveness and polishing up their complaint. Others recoiled, and faded from the scene when asked to identify themselves.

Throughout my life humour had been a constant companion. (He deserted me during my training and first few weeks on the job, but finally returned). It was always said that a streak of devilment ran deep in our family, and I could usually see the funny side of most things. Further, since coming to Dublin, the station live-in atmosphere had spawned a continuous stream of incidents with a capacity for comedy. But I soon learned there was a time and place to laugh and if something comical happened on the beat, any appearance of mirth was usually out of order. The station mess was the altar where such offerings were placed for the enjoyment and benediction of all.

One day I brought home my own story to the gratification of the mess. I had been walking along a tree-lined avenue when I was called urgently:
"Garda, garda, come quickly, it's little Mickey, he's in the toilet."
The woman's child had locked himself in. Since the case of the old

woman and her dog, locked doors had become Public Enemy Number One, and I decided this time I was going straight in.

"Mickey, come here," I called to him through the keyhole. He came.

"Now," I said, "stand well back from the door."

He backed away obediently, and I took a run at the door. Bang! It wasn't much of a door but there was enough spring in it to send Mickey flying head first into the toilet bowl.

I thought of a new entry for the garda Manual.

If forced entry to an occupied bathroom is contemplated, please ensure the toilet seat is down.

As the days rolled by and the Chief's inspection drew nearer, the station became a hive of activity. Washing. Cleaning. Dusting down and checking of records. All rooms given the once and sometimes twice over. Yard brushed. Approaches tidied.

The day before the visit, God read the Commandments at parade time.

"Haircuts for all. Best uniform, spotless. Gloves. Regulation shoes, and, of course, all accoutrements. Notebooks. Gimme them now."

He scrawled a mark on each before continuing.

"There'll be a drill display in the yard in honour of the occasion. I'm sure you'll all be looking forward to a good leg stiffener."

The Squirrel seemed very nervous of the approaching inspection. So much so I suggested we should get together before it, and give each other a tidy up. He agreed, but I got the impression he would give anything to escape the ordeal.

Soon, too soon, the day of inspection dawned.

Chapter 10 - INSPECTION

On the dreaded day of inspection I woke in a cold sweat of anticipation and noticed The Squirrel's bed had not been slept in. I tidied round my billet while throughout the station fellows ran hither and thither and jammed in front of every mirror checking their appearance. Outside, beneath a dark, menacing sky, the S S never looked better as he prowled the four corners of the yard, his eyes constantly on The Bully who was parked just inside the entrance gate.

"Right," he roared at the newly promoted sergeant who had arrived on transfer: "Line them up and give them a run at the drill."

My thoughts went back to training as we drew together in two rows. Little John and I led off. Approaching the perimeter wall, I dragged my feet in expectation of the 'about turn'. It came all right but in two halves:
"About," I lifted my leg and swivelled in anticipation of the second half of the order, only to breast up The Owl who was still ploughing forward behind me. Further back the regiment had backed up so tightly you would need a grappling hook to prise us apart. But somehow we negotiated the half circle, straightened up the traces, and took off from the other end - though The Black's ponderous stride and The Bluffer's mincing gait made it impossible to keep the step.

Suddenly, the S S gave a shout that shook the place:
"C'mon outta there."
All eyes turned to The Squirrel slinking out the back door and scampering to the tail end of our group, his crimson socks flashing into a sea of black.
"Oh Janey," whispered Little John, "colour blind."

The splash of colour was like a red rag to the S S as he gored The Squirrel:

"Take that person without regulation socks out of my sight. Immediately."

The Squirrel had shimmied in beside me but at the last command he took off again in a beeline for the entrance. The S S motioned me silently to follow him.

"Your colour blind," I said to him in the bedroom as we emptied his plastic bag containing socks of all colours of the rainbow.

"I am, but don't tell," he implored.

Back in the yard we were under starter's orders to have another go.

"The recruit will be the leader," the S S proclaimed. "Ye all watch him and for all our sakes make an effort. Right. We'll do an about turn."

To my way of thinking sloppiness was no substitute for effort, but the S S seemed happy enough. Anyway a signal from the gate put an end to the rehearsal. Now for the real thing.

We all lined up again facing the entrance just in time to see the sleek black motor slither into the yard. It's appearance and solemn progress reminded me of a funeral procession but the body that alighted was very much alive.

On either side of me The Squirrel and Little John almost swelled me out of the line-up but I countered with my expertise in the drill square as I soldered them back. Earlier I hadn't been apprehensive about facing the inspecting officer, figuring I'd gone through the mill in training to become immune to such protocol. But suddenly the pressure mounted when I realised the Chief had glided away from his welcoming party and was folding his eyes over each of us in turn. As with all senior officers, his movement style and his uniform ensured that he smouldered with the prestige associated with his rank.

The Superintendent and the S S still clung to him as they manoeuvred him in a walkabout. As they neared me, I had an opportunity to inspect the Chief.

I have always felt our storyline is not in our palms but in our faces. The Chief had worn the years well. His face was broad, unlined and good-natured, supported by a thick chunk of neck and well-nourished jowls.

The hat was on sideways, almost jauntily. The width of his shoulders was accentuated by the row of emblems, double diamonds and bar. In common with most officers I had met, his shoulders were sufficiently broad to accommodate the array. From there down, he was in decline, the most pronounced detraction being a sprouting belly viciously constricted by the twin-pronged buckle of Sam Browne.

Next he moved toward us. This was what was most dreaded: the inspection routine. The young sergeant called us to attention. I froze my body, something that had been pounded into me in training. My thoughts, however, were a different matter, they continued to move and swirl. I was the recruit, the lowest of the low, not even a rank to call my own. Also I was the latest model and would be expected to be perfect. I closed my mouth tightly and fixed my face with a look of intense concentration - unnecessary as it happened as the chief strode by with downcast eyes as if it were a boot inspection.

Our next serving was drill, and true to form we made a hash of it. The rookie sergeant called out the commands but his quavering voice did not instil confidence.
"Squad attention. Ah.. Right turn. By the right. Or left... Ah... Quick march."

I was off like a greyhound with Little John holding form at my side, but we had only crossed our feet a few times when the Chief erupted.
"Squad. Halt. The worst I've ever seen. Like drunken sailors. Right turn. Sergeant. I'm taking over."

Now my drill movements were light years ahead of the rest and when I made the turn I had a perfect view of the routine. It was pitiful to observe. Fellas swinging arms and legs all over the place, bouncing off one another, milling together as they sought mutual security. At the far end, The Black and The Bluffer were almost waltzing in the turning circle.

The Chief hauled back and told us what he thought of us. He commented unfavourably on our carriage and bearing, the fact that most of us had forgotten we had shoulders and how we had allowed our chests to become part of our bellies. Next, he lined us up facing him and gave a few warm-up orders:

137

"Squad attention. Stand at ease. Stand easy. Stand at ease. Attention."

Amazingly his directives seemed to straighten all backs and sharpen all reactions.
"That's better. Now sergeant. Take over."

This time The Black and The Bluffer led off as if in a fettered three-legged race. As leaders they dictated the pace and picked up the speed. The next couple of rows, referred to as 'packing' by the S S contained some extremely large individuals who were caught for speed, resulting in a continuous back up of bodies. The remedy was a hasty about turn but the young sergeant seemed to have been struck dumb. Ahead I could see the two leaders scurrying onwards, and closing in on the laurel hedge which encroached round the back of the station directly on to their path. Squinting sideways, I noted the drill sergeant was about to issue the appropriate order. I stiffened my body in readiness but no words came. A quick glance confirmed my fears. His lips quavered but he couldn't get the words out. At that moment the two leaders reached the hedge, glanced at one another and in unison plunged into the thicket. Beside me the sergeant found his voice and shouted:
"Squad, turn."
Then under his breath he gasped: " For Christ's sake, turn around."

Luckily by this stage the Chief had lost interest in our safari and was in deep conversation with the S S and the Superintendent at the far corner of the yard. But the omniscient God had eyes in the back of his head as he turned and glared. He was about to let rip when the heavens opened and brought us indoors.

Inside the parade continued. The S S commandeered our notebooks and passed them to the Chief who flicked through the written pages until he reached a fresh one. He scrawled his name and dated the page before stacking the notebooks carefully on top of each other.

Next he sat back and launched into a lecture on deportment and dress. He exhorted us to carry ourselves smartly while on duty and especially to look after our health.
He then moved to the maintenance of peace and tranquillity allied to the prevention of crime. He included in his sermon such clauses as the necessity for visibility while on duty, cultivating local knowledge and

getting to know ones patch and its inhabitants. I was impressed by his torrent of words which flowed seamlessly, pausing only for the merest flick of a prompt from the crumpled half sheet in his hand. Next, he marked our cards on the need for courtesy and civility toward the public, reminding us we were public servants paid from the public purse. Finally he preached on our return of work and stretching back, began to really lay it on the line:

"Yesterday your detective branch had a significant capture. A noted burglar was arrested following painstaking detective work culminating in a dawn swoop. Once captured, such was the weight of evidence that he confessed. Now, what I want to know is - what were the rest of ye doing while this villain was plundering the District?"

I looked over at The Bluffer and thought of our afternoon at the cinema while robbers roamed free.

It was lunchtime. Before dismissing us the Chief turned to the S S and the Super, then back to us:

"Gentlemen, you are fortunate to have as supervisors men of the calibre of your Superintendent and Station Sergeant. They demand exemplary standards and it is obvious that you are responding to their importuning. Thank you for the excellent turnout and good day."

We adjourned to the mess hall where uniforms were loosened and tea made. The Bully continued to give us a running commentary as the inspection progressed:

"Good news, lads. He's in a hurry. Finished the books now. Just the premises left. He'll be gone in half an hour."

We stayed in the mess hall until he tore in with another bulletin:

"Jaysus lads.. any fags?"

Everyone knew this was the prelude to a juicy bit of gossip and half a dozen cartons were pushed under his nose.

He lit, took a long pull and exhaled in a cloud of smoke and words:

"D'you know what? You couldn't be up to them detectives. D'ye remember that spiel this morning about the great capture?"

"Yeah," cut in The Black. "They had nothin' all year and yesterday morning they made a burst, whipped in a soft thing and he calved after dinner."

This brought a laugh, but The Bully was smacking out more smoke signals with huge pulls of the weed:

"Well, listen, you'll never believe this. We all know that the little canary sang goodo yesterday afternoon, but early on his tongue was in a knot and it took a bit of physical persuasion from the Detective Sergeant to unsettle him. Unfortunately during the course of its travels his swipe hit the partition, rupturing it severely. This morning the S S spotted the damage and compared it to the Titanic:

"We're all sunk," he growled.

"Leave it to me," said the Detective Sergeant, "we'll cover it up."

"Yu're noted for that," said the S S.

"Well, when the Chief inspected the detective office what did he find on the wall but a holy picture? He was very impressed and said he will be recommending that all stations in the division display similar religious images. Them plain clothes fellas. I wonder where they got that picture?"

I could have told them. Under The Squirrel's bed.

The Bluffer reappeared later with the best news of all.

"He's pulling out."

Someone gave a little cheer, but The Bully shushed us all as the sound of the steel tips sent shivers along the corridor.

"It's the boss."

Instantly the S S was balanced on the saddleboard:

"Ye did all right."

That was it. He turned and pulled the door behind him as if serving notice that the conclave could continue undisturbed.

Immediately in the release of tension the banter began:

"Hey, Black. You surely have some old story about a Chief you came across, just to honour the occasion, like."

"Yes, Chiefs. Aye. Someone once said the last good one was an Indian."

The Black's response drew a few laughs, and he was away:

"For instance, himself this morning, not the worst by any means. Didn't get the back teeth up yet. I'll tell you about a real Chief though. Did you ever hear of Polish? He was a different deck of cards entirely. An original of the species. He was legendary. Always immaculately turned out, you could shave yourself on the top of his shoes. It was rumoured that he plastered a bit of the black stuff above the hairline as well which is how he got his nickname. Everything to do with the job was his hobby horse. It was said he could rattle off the disciplinary regulations verbatim. His favourite breaches were; drinking, the slightest departure from strict sobriety, marrying without leave and conniving at or knowingly being an accessory to any breach of discipline.

"But more than, anything he specialised in haymakers of questions from the Manuals of Law and Police Orders.

"Now, Polish was married and on one occasion his unfortunate wife was involved in a minor scrape when driving the family car. Well, Polish held a court at home and acted as prosecutor, judge and jury leaving the unfortunate woman to defend herself. Of course, she hadn't a hope and was convicted and disqualified for life. Legend has it that the code of silence prevailed thereafter, with him addressing her only via the family dog."

The Black was now in his stride and the yarns came thick and fast:
"I first met Polish many years ago when I was doing the stations of the cross in the wild west. It was during a general election and I was on duty in an old schoolhouse. I'd heard he was pernickety so I decided to make a good impression. As he got out of his car, I was there:
"Good morning, Sir," I said.
"T'is not, what's good about it?"
I was flummoxed.
"Well," I said, " things are all right here anyway."
"They're not then," he said, cocking his head and starting on me.
"The Noxious Weeds Act."
He spat out the words at me, then swivelled away at a half trot for the five-bar gate on the far side of the road. I was glad of the few minutes respite because I wouldn't recognise a noxious weed if it was served up to me at dinnertime. I followed him.

Arriving at the fence he turned on me again:
"Look at that field. The noxious weeds are rampant. It's your duty to stamp out this outrage."

Suddenly he took his hands from the gate and began fiddling around his midriff, undid the flap of his pants and without taking his eyes off the yellow carpeted field proceeded to urinate on it thoroughly, talking as he performed.

"The propagation of noxious weeds is widespread in this area. In fact the manners of some people hereabouts are atrocious, no respect for the organs of the state."

His own organ was in grave danger as a pot-bellied wasp appeared and began buzzing around it before he finally stowed it away.

The Chief's reputation increased with his mileage as he continued to make smithereens of every station in his jurisdiction. His pet questions were on obscure pieces of legislation which he asked in his peculiarly whinging voice, and no matter how you answered, he followed with an amendment or caustic comment. His knowledge was impressive. Once he was queried on a point of law.

"If you went to the trouble of looking up the relevant section on page so and so in the Manual of Laws and Police Duties, third line from the bottom you would discover the answer," was his answer.

Rumours of his arrival spread wholesale terror. Once he met a wily sergeant who had the reputation of being a bit of a hob lawyer. However, he too came to grief when Polish came calling:

"Tell me now. Seizures under the Illicit Distillation Act. Could you brush up on the various items encountered when dealing with this?"

The skipper fielded with confidence, rattling off the details. Wash. Potale. Singlings. Grains and Coolers. But he cooled down to such a degree that he ran out of steam before the end. Polish raised his temperature to boiling point before leaving him floundering:

"Aha, you forgot one. The Worm, the spiral tube through which the distillate passes from the still to the receptacle."

The result was that sergeant bore that insidious nickname forever after.

And so the Chief's reign of terror continued and all sergeants had been humbled - except one.

We'll call him Sergeant Pat. He served in a one man station on the verge of the Atlantic. He was reckoned to have never been beaten on paper, never caught out in law, and above personal reproach. So much so that everyone held their breath in anticipation of the Polish visit. People prayed that - like his namesake our patron saint - Pat would prevail.

Finally the great day dawned when Polish drove into Pat's patch. It wasn't long before battle commenced:

"Tell me, sergeant. What should you ensure if a travelling cinema set up in your village?"

"Oh then," replied Pat. "Two days notice would have to be given to your good self. The Cinematography Act regulations would have to be complied with and also the structure involved must conform with the plan attached to the licence which should be produced for inspection by the licensee."

"All right. And tell me now, if you saw an aircraft flying low over the town, what offences, if any, could the pilot commit?"

"He must fly at such a height to ensure it will land outside the town should its engines fail. Also, it is forbidden to carry out any trick or exhibition while flying over any populated area or any meeting for games or sports, except as arranged in writing by the promoters. And lastly, it would be unlawful to fly low and, thereby, cause unnecessary damage to any person or property or drop any article except ballast (fine sand or water) or other articles by direction of the Minister."

This was ballast on Polish's head all right. But he merely grunted acknowledgement and jammed the trottle in search of more air pockets:

"What identification mark must be carried on the aircraft?"

Again Pat had his landing gear in fine fettle.

"The nationality E.I. in the case of *Eire*. Marks must be clearly displayed on the underneath, sides and top of the aircraft. Also, there must be a metal plate affixed to the body showing the owner's name and address, nationality and registration marks."

This was the first of a steady convoy as Polish sniped out questions with relentless regularity and Pat just as monotonously fired back perfect answers.

Then Polish moved into top gear and to his favourite piece of legislation.. The Fishery Act.

"Tell me sergeant: close season for eels?"

"Oh now, usually from the tenth of January to the first of July during which time the use of any instrument other than a single rod and line for the capture of eels is prohibited."

"And in the case of net fishing for salmon and trout?"

"The annual of not less than 168 successive days. Now, it varies in different localities but generally occurs between the first of August and the first of April the following year. The weekly between the hours of 6am on Saturday and the same time the following Monday. The daily between 8pm and 6am the following morning during open season, and only in fresh water within particular rivers with certain exceptions."

"The governing of bulls. I suppose you know that as well?"
"Yes Sir," Pat replied amiably. "Bulls calved between January and June inclusive on the 31st March in year following: bulls calved between July and December on 30th September in the year following."
"All right, all right." Polish pulled in his horns momentarily, then attacked again.
"The Oil in Navigable Water Act. Now as you have jurisdiction over a maritime station, can you tell me the exceptions to the escape of oil into a harbour or territorial waters?"
Again, Pat wiped out that slick:
"Accidentally, if all reasonable efforts were made to prevent same, under the direction and with the authority of the local harbour authorities and for safety on the occasion of a fire on board."

Polish was throwing all caution to the wind and now took to the high seas:
"Smuggling.. Now sergeant. Suppose you had to carry out a search for such goods, what are your powers?"
 Pat scuttled this one as well.
"I can stop any vehicle or conveyance to ascertain whether any smuggled goods are being transported therein. Persons driving or in charge who refuse to co-operate are guilty of an offence. Fine £100. Section 203 Customs Consolidation Act 1876 refers."

In desperation, Polish headed for the hills:
"On my way here I noticed fields full of sheep. Now sergeant. Section 4 of the Clean Wool Act has particular relevance to their control. What is that?"
Pat had his shears ready and set about fleecing all before him.
"A person who shears sheep shall before or during that act separate from the fleece all wool in which a prohibited substance is present."

Polish, realising he was being skinned alive tried again:

144

"Yes sergeant. I see. And tell me now the Forestry Act 1946. Could you give me the felling regulations?"

Again, Pat's axe was well sharpened:

"It shall be unlawful for any person to cut down or uproot any tree over ten years old unless not less than 21 days and not more than two years before the commencement of cutting or uprooting, the owner or his predecessor in title or some other person on his behalf shall give to the Sergeant in charge of the station located nearest the tree a notice in writing in the prescribed form of his intent to cut or uproot such tree. Section 37 of the Forestry Act 1946 refers, penalty £5 in respect of each tree cut down in contravention thereof."

Begrudgingly Polish acknowledged defeat and asked for the station records.

For a solid hour he canvassed these, word for word, entry by entry, but all he got was perfection. Finally, only one segment remained - the inspection of the station premises. But here again Polish was put to the pin of his collar to find a speck of dust or anything else out of place.

Finally he entered a disused room, the last to be inspected. His sole welcome was the slanting sun spiking in the window and filling the place with the auburn glow of early evening. Again the place was spotless - and he was about to turn away when he saw it.

"Aha," he almost shrieked, pointing to the spider's web hanging like a suspension bridge from two corner walls.

"Any explanation sergeant?" Pat was flummoxed, and Polish gleeful:

"You know your law and your records are spot on; but now we'll see how good you are on paper."

And so a week later the 'Please Explain' arrived.

"An explanation is required for the presence of a spider's web in the upstairs accommodation. In particular, I am desirous to ascertain:

(1) When the room was least cleaned?

(2) Was the particular area in question dusted and if so, how did the web remain intact?

(3) What efforts are being made to ensure there is no re-occurrence?"

Pat spent the morning racking his brains for a solution. After all the years - caught in a web.

Meanwhile the grapevine had been working overtime as colleagues prayed for Pat's vindication. With a heavy heart, he went over the encyclical again and again. He climbed the stairs slowly to the offending room. Over in the corner the frail tapestry gloated - an enduring talisman to his misfortune. Pat whipped out his baton and scattered the membranes to eternity. He stood, walked, looked and thought. Finally, he sat, dozed, dreamt and slept.

Sometime later he woke with a start. He had been asleep for several hours. Turning he looked at the area of torment and then for the first time that week he smiled.

Jumping up he rushed downstairs and began to write:

" Re Divisional Officer's Inspection on the....
" Referring to the above, I reply as follows:
"The upstairs room in this station was cleaned as usual at 9am on the date of your inspection. Immediately thereafter I checked the room and all was correct insofar as there was no spider's web visible within. At 4pm when we entered, you noticed the web and correctly brought it to my attention. Now, since your departure I have monitored the habits of the spider fraternity within this premises, in particular, the family who seems to have squatters' rights in the corner of the upstairs room.

"In addition since your communiqué, each morning at 9am I have inspected the habitat of the spider clan. My exhaustive observations have led me to discover that the spider family do not appear to take rest. Each morning I remove their web and withdraw, but each afternoon on my return, I discover their network reformed in the same location. Therefore, it is an undisputed fact that the aforesaid web is being constructed twice on a daily basis. Now, if you wish I can further monitor the movements and lifestyle of these amazing creatures, but as you will appreciate, doing so would mean the neglect of other duties. More permanently the spider clan could be destroyed. But this might be contrary to the most auspicious precept in the realms of the *Garda Siochana* - the protection of life.

"Finally, you will no doubt be aware that the control of spiders is not at present covered by any sanctions. Perhaps a man of your outstanding intellect should raise the matter with the relevant authorities and ensure suitable legislation is enacted forthwith."

The Chief knew the cocoon being spun for him and admitted defeat. He scrawled a dozen works on the file and fired it back to Pat:
"Spin a web..Spin a yarn. You can certainly do both. Explanation accepted."

As usual the tale was greeted with great acclaim.

Back in the job, for me things remained uneasy until football came to my rescue. Here at least I was confident of an inspection I could pass.

Chapter 11 - PERSPIRATION

A highlight of that autumn was my selection on the Mid-Kerry team in the Kerry Senior Championship football final. My call up was unexpected. Having made my debut the previous summer I had lost out since due to my unavailability.

My selection gave me a great lift especially when word spread throughout the station. For the first time there was the acknowledgement that I was something other than 'the recruit'. Also I had learned from my previous mistakes. There was a big difference between demanding and applying for leave. This time I sussed out The Bully and The Staff and both put in a good word for me. I think The Staff put in two as he was a native of West Kerry, our opposition. At first he threatened to take me into protective custody for the duration but then went out of his way to get me off - with his blessing.

The day of the match was showery. There was an unforgettable moment before the start when high above the cheering came Big Tom Murphy's unmistakable bellow:
"That's young Dile there. He's a gard in Dublin. T'will take a lot to bate the trained man."

Big Tom was a great benefactor to all the lads who grew up around my place. He gave us the field besides the cross-roads where many of us chased a ball for the first time. His accolade lifted me. A trained man? The assumption that it would be a factor had not entered my head. Also the timing of the revelation was crucial, giving me confidence at the start, and an edge during play.

The game itself was a blur. The ball came my way frequently during a torrid first half and without fondling it too much, I lashed it as hard and as far as I could in the opposite direction. At the final whistle, the cup crossed Sliabh Mish into Mid-Kerry for the first time in almost sixty years.

Back in the station I got an unexpected welcome. Someone had rung and told them I'd done my stuff and should be rewarded with a pat on the back or a day off. There was no smell of a day off, but my little bit of fame didn't go unnoticed, and the following week The Kerryman also paid tribute by giving me a paragraph all to myself.

Arising from this publicity, I discovered I was getting a bit of a reputation which helped raise me from my doldrums.

One day I had a caller at the station. Would I play a game of football? Would a cat drink milk? Our team was only a scrap one while the opposition was strong. We had it hot and heavy and after the game I heard two fans discussing our performance:
"That was a tough old game," said one.
"Well, it's not called the Kickham Cup for nothing," replied the other.

Within a week my athletic expertise was tested to the ultimate. It was an Inter-District match in the Garda Grounds, Phoenix Park. This was the premier Gaelic competition within the Dublin Metropolitan Area and never were games contested with such vigour. Sergeant Mick ran our team and togged out himself in case we were stuck. He was a mother hen and took a personal interest in all the players, even to the extent of sending us little notes in advance of fixtures.

My first sighting of the ground was not impressive. It was dreadfully uneven. Later I was to discover it was positively treacherous, notably around midfield and both squares. Overall it was the poorest excuse for a football pitch I'd ever seen, its deficiency all the more surprising given the vast acres of splendidly laid out football pitches lying idle around us.

In contrast to the field the dressing room looked fine. But on closer inspection it proved to be only a shell with two dilapidated rooms. Later on, we did our togging out from the boot of a car.

Even before play began it was obvious this was to be no ordinary football match. A number of ingredients served to make it unforgettable. First, the starting time came and went, a dragnet of excuses being trotted out to delay proceedings;

"We've three in court. A few on the way. A couple called out on duty at the last minute. One of our cars broke down."

This foreplay - in every sense of the word - was exhausting. Looking for gear, waylaying the referee, trying to pull a fast one, coupled with half-glances at the opposition hoping they weren't flush took its toll. In particular the appearance of a county player served to raise the hackles or bolster the aspirations as the case may be. Within seconds his pedigree was being assessed by the opposition:

"He'll be minding himself for the county. Give him wan early on. He's a bit windy. First ball let him have it."

I should have known it wasn't going to be friendly. There was no shake hands. Instead my opponent kind of scratched himself against me before trying to cripple me with a look of undiluted hostility:

"You're a recruit?"

I said I was.

"Then, for your sake I hope the academy taught you all about blood sports."

There were no pitch markings or flags whatever. This didn't matter as by the time the game began, the crowd on the near sideline had swelled and stretched to both corners. All the play seemed to concentrate on that area, with the string of supporters imitating the frantic convulsions of a conger eel as they followed the play up and down.

"The ball's out."

"No way, only the man."

"Which way is it going?"

"That way."

"No, it went out off yure man."

"Who's doing the line?"

"Him."

"No. Not me, him."

"It's a hop ball."

I've never seen so many powerfully built men in togs before. Luckily most were unfit but with enough breath to last a quarter, and in my case, for the opposition to bear down on me with deadly intent. The fact that

I had a bit of reputation gave them license to lay it on without pity, and it wasn't long until my skin rippled from a few riveting tackles. When I rearranged my gear at half time I discovered a swarm of abrasions in the most unusual body areas.

It was the era of the tough man. If you weren't able for it, you had better keep away.

Of course the opposition didn't have it all their own way either. The game was building up to a humdinger egged on by the sideline crowd who mixed encouragement and diatribe with language fit to take the leaves off the trees.

"Burst him. Break him up. Or even kill the bastard."

On the field the sorting out process continued. One particularly stylish player who had been slowed down with a bloody nose complained bitterly to the referee:

"He done me nose in, ref."

"Aw go on outta that. Pity about you. If you were able, you'd do me just as fast," retorted his opponent.

We got as far as half-time intact and Mick used the break to cool us down and soup us up.

"Say nothing to the ref. I think he's on our side. Now, if we could get their centre-back to lose the rag, we'd be away in a hack."

He also had the form book on the opposition at the ready and laid it on us.

"Their full back now, deadly under a high ball but he's on nights and up all day in court, if you graze him out the field and give him an odd run to the sideline, he'll not be able to stand."

But like all great schemes they dissolved within seconds of the start when hostilities resumed between rejuvenated teams and skirmishes broke out all over the field. That was when the referee made a fatal mistake. He began to exceed his brief.

Apparently this ref was just passing by when pressed into service. It was claimed later that he was an Englishman who had been employed to carry out a survey of the fauna and flora in the Phoenix Park. If that was the case, he learned a lot that day about the rare species known as the 'Garda Siochana at play'.

I knew that appointed referees were notorious for not turning up, so before a coin was tossed, it was necessary to procure a neutral official to fill the role. Normally there was a good scatter of spectators, and if a member of the public would do the job, he was accepted, otherwise an agreed garda candidate was appointed. On this occasion, the honorary role fell on the Englishman. Before the throw in, he confessed that he had never seen a Gaelic match before, never mind adjudicating on one. This was dismissed by the team mentors who issued guidelines for him on throwing in the ball, standing in the middle of the field, keeping the time - and letting us at it.

He kept his head till half-time. But on the restart he had one rush of blood after another, affected perhaps by the amount of actual gore being spilt. Anyway, he began interfering. His worst ability was his fleetness of foot which meant he could appear instantly at the heart of a schmozzle.

I thought of The Black's advice on dealing with disorder.
"Don't be in any rush to get there. Let them flake away for a while until they get a bit tired. Then move in smartly and mop them up."

This referee did the opposite, reefing fellows apart, exceedingly difficult as some were really dug into each other. He began to compound the annoyance with a litany of exhortations delivered in high pitched grandiose tones:
"Come. come, now constables. Cease this folly forthwith. It is most unbecoming. Tut tut, my, my, come, come, let's have some order and decorum."

All this had an unfortunate effect on the players. A section of hardchaws turned their aggression back on him:
"Aw, g'wan with you ref."
"What about that black hoor? He started it all."
"Look at my shin?"
"Let the play flow. A bit of rough and tumble won't kill us. We're not nancy boys."

I was beginning to harbour a certain sympathy for the hard pressed official, decked out in a pair of well worn wellingtons and an oversized track suit donated by the guards.

Eventually, he burst from the circle and laid an almightly spiel on us all: "You are undoubtedly the most uncivilised band of ruffians it has ever been my displeasure to encounter. Such lack of discipline and 'esprit de corps'. It's unforgivable. Considering the fact that your Depot is not too remotely distant, one would not expect this reprehensible behaviour to be perpetuated in such close environs."

The mention of our superiors and any regard they had for our behaviour exploded the possibility of a truce and inflamed some of the participants. They were exhausted anyway, and hell-bent on a row as the best way of ending the contest:
"Who are yu to tell us how to play? Who asked yu in the first place? At home with your rosary beads you should be. Go on. Shag off with you, we'll finish it by ourselves."

But the referee was made of stern stuff. He responded by demanding names. This really incurred the wrath of those giving most lip. Now, when asked for their identity they clammed up. Others began demanding his name, his father's name - and insinuating that his father was not married to his mother when the son in question was born.

The referee responded with another stinging attack. He lambasted us with a spiel of law including a treatise on the Phoenix Park Act which decreed that he had limitless powers within the environs to quell any disorders, and furthermore, all concerned were bound by law to disclose their identities to him.

This was too much. The players retorted if he had power, they had twice as much. That was it. He flung down his whistle and laid a final scathing outburst on the pedigree of all present:
"The civilities are over. I am now adjourning to your depot where I propose to seek out your Commissioner, ply him with the salient features of this debacle, and have you removed, by force if necessary, from the environs. Now, good day."

He then set off at a trot.

Now this scenario was a new one even for battle-hardened veterans who had upheld the honour of their stations through the blood and mud of many gaelic pitches. Some felt this activity had escaped the pages of the disciplinary regulations and could not be censured. Others weren't so sure. It was Mick who gave the verdict:

"Whatever comes of it, it'll not be in our favour. This calls for diversionary tactics."

All eyes fell on me. Oh no! not the recruit being sacrificed again.

"You're the fittest. Hit off across the park and head him off before he reaches the Depot gate. We'll start up the wagons and follow you round the road."

What could I do but obey?

The ref's lead was substantial but his course erratic and I caught up with him at the depot gate. Thankfully, he was out of breath and needed time to rest against the railings. Almost immediately a carload of deputies arrived and he was persuaded to go for some refreshments. Passing the Zoo he remarked that the railings around it were lower than the railings around our depot - but already relationships had improved and we laughed dutifully. We adjourned to a tavern in Parkgate Street where his recollection of events was liquidated from his memory.

In those days virtually every garda Gaelic game was strewn with controversy, be it a disputed score, a line ball or an appealed decision. The most testing time of all was when the ref's whistle called a halt, the notebook was produced and an identity demanded. Usually this meant more raised hackles among the players and a counter-question;

"What's the charge?"

Nearly ever game was punctuated with a falling out, and many a reputation was made and lost during these hot-blooded encounters. When the game started it was every man for himself and if you clattered one of the opposition you had fifteen pairs of paws waiting to plaster you. Nevertheless, no matter what happened on the field, when the game was over, everyone shook hands and that was the end of it.

Playing sport at the optimum level of expertise was impossible for a member on the regular. While most players were big, strong, and had commitment and skill, the job deprived us of the extra zip to compete consistently at the highest level. I discovered that performing on the evening of an early day was always a lottery. If you rose at 5am, tiredness enveloped in waves all day, there were headaches, a sore throat and no appetite. But we were all in the same boat.

Around this time I made my first appearance in the summons court. The entrance door was heavy and creaked loudly as I pushed it open. This brought a bellow from the bench:

"Silence in court!"

I slid into the nearest seat, then realised I had joined those waiting to be prosecuted.

Looking up I realised the owner of the deafening voice had terrifying eyes. They belonged to the garda in charge of the court who sat on the judge's left hand. Realising my mistake I crossed the aisle to join my colleagues.

Now, my only goals were to get to the box without stumbling, utter the oath without stammering, read out my prepared evidence and hope no awkward questions were asked. I felt reasonably confident, seeing as all I had up was a summons for a bicycle light. Having gathered myself together, I looked up to discover the ogre had been transformed. He was now gazing benignly in my direction, with the glare reserved solely for the opposition who sprinkled the seats opposite the aisle.

He jumped to his feet:

"Gards to be sworn."

I was abandoned as all my colleagues shouldered their way to his side. He counted them before turning towards me:

"Are you going to swear or stare?"

By now deeply embarrassed I resurrected my lone summons and surrendered myself to him. I realised that each of my colleagues clutched a bible, it reminded me of a prayer group. He thrust the Holy Book into my hand.

"Are you in the state of grace?"

"Oh yes, like yourself."

I felt I was now breaking even, but he snapped back.

"Take off your cap."

I went to comply only to discover I was already bareheaded. But he had moved on:

"All right, hold on tight. Everyone repeat after me, I swear by Almighty God that my evidence to the court in my several cases...."

Was this another nudge at my lone miserable offering?

But later when I had given my evidence I was rewarded with a single smile. I knew I had passed the test.

All these escapades put more mileage on my clock, introduced me to other colleagues and meant that ever so slowly, I was finding an identity.

The Staff whom I visited each Thursday to collect my pay always had a few words for me. One perennial question was:
"Do you write home?"
"I do."
"How many pages?"
"Several."
"Do you send money?"
"A few bob."
"Do you go to Mass and say your prayers?"
I said I did, but he had more.
"What did you have for breakfast and tea?"
"Oh the usual, a bowl of porridge and a bit of bread."
"Good man. None of them minerals or new fangled crisps. Don't forget the bit of fruit. Remember the regular can be a killer on the breadbasket."

Living in had its compensations. It was handy for work and the bit of grub. But it had its downside as well. Being the recruit I was caught for all sorts of chores. If a broken window was reported in a shop or office, I was the one sent to stay until the keyholder came in and secured his premises. Any accident within walking distance of the station, Forty was the boy.

But plenty of sticks meant plenty of experience.

Chapter 12 - INITIATION

The year skipped on and suddenly I was nine months in the force. It was my second tour on nights and having failed to raise a prisoner during the first tour, I still carried the torch in more ways than one.

Halfway through the first week I had a moment of truth. Like all such, it was totally unexpected, and grimly illustrated how a few steps in any direction could lead to a fateful encounter.

I had been on a busy street corner late at night marvelling at how hitherto indifferent drivers became instantly law-abiding when they saw my uniform at the traffic lights. Braking carefully, stopping dead on the line and canvassing me for approval.

After a while I pulled back to the shadows of a shop front. I had hardly brought my feet together when suddenly a car careered through a red light. It had to be stolen or have a drunken driver behind the wheel but was out of sight before I could note the registration. The vehicle had to be intercepted. It had already torn through another red light up ahead. I had to send out an all station message immediately and ran for the phone box beside a flat complex. This time the 999 worked perfectly, and I passed the descriptive particulars and direction of travel to the Control centre.

It was now after midnight. I looked up at the new flats and for some reason began to stroll towards them. As I came nearer, the clamour of violence gushed out of an open doorway, breaking the quiet and filling me with nervous apprehension. I knew the feeling of old - paralysis stabbing like an icicle. But the uniform drove me on.

From inside the open door, two shapes came into view, a man and a woman. His back was to me as he tossed her along the hallway, her frail body crunching against a radiator. He was bulky, with a shaven head and a mass of tattoos on both arms.

Once, years ago, I had seen a tinker woman being cuffed by a man in the corner of the fair field at Puck. She was a wild, red-haired woman and gave as good as she got. But this woman was weak, defenceless. There could be no hesitancy.

Leaping through the door I laid hands on him before he could turn. He was hard at the edges, but when my grip tightened, his skin stretched and softened till he submitted.
"Go aisy, man," I cautioned, loosening my hold, only to grab again as his bulging eyes betrayed malicious intent. Watchfulness had been drilled into me by Little John:
"Your eyes are your greatest weapon. Other people's eyes tell a story as well. Watch them all the time, especially in conflict situations. A drooping eyelid or a blink can be the clue that he's going to go for you."

Now I read his inclination just in time as he dived toward me. Good job I had a firm grip of his upper arms as I swung him off target and he bounced his head against the wall. Turning he moved forward threateningly. I stared back, watching his eyes, and mouth:
"Get outta me gaff, pigface."

I stood my ground. My lack of response antagonised him even more. I knew by his eyes that round two was beginning. The woman's terrified expression begged me not to let her down.

Suddenly he charged and we tangled. He had a frenzied power but his muscles were flabby. I pinioned his arms and forced him against the wall:
"Cool down, take it aisy."
I felt strong and in control. He slackened, and confident that the sap had been squeezed from him, I pushed him near the corner of the hallway. But as I turned to attend to the woman, he launched another attack, clambering on my back, clawing and ripping my shirt. Whirling on the floor together, I heaved and shunted, but he hung on gamely, his body sliding and grabbing. Looking for a hold, he tugged at my baton strap sticking from the top of my pocket. The possibility of disarming me was his undoing. I wrenched him off. Turning I brandished my baton. He was on his feet and swung a punch which I countered with the stick

forcing his fist open. This made him hop, but he came at me again, a low staggery kind of attack which I side-stepped, then connected again with my baton giving him a good few welts across the shoulders which creased him against the wall. He was on the run with no place to hide, and I made my decision;
"You're under arrest."

He came quietly. The neighbours had gathered and cheered as I led him out.

The SS bounced upright when we made our appearance. I gave him an account of the arrest. He was delighted with my evening's work, but instead of inflation, I felt hugely deflated. I had done my duty, but I had used force and would have to vindicate my actions to a judge in an open court. God had a thimble of praise and a bucket of worry:
"You did well. Remember you're duty bound to act in such situations. You'll be goin' to court in the morning. We'll make out a sheet for the prisoner and after charging him, you can take the morning off."

All of a sudden I didn't want the morning off. Mentally I was still in battle - wrestling, fighting, watchful. I tried to concentrate on the present but the memory of the fray kept winding me back. I wasn't helped by the sight of the S S battering the guts out of the typewriter with glee.
"Assault," he recited the charge out of his head as he pounded. "Assault one... Garda... contrary to..."

The Bully shuffled back and forth making out the recognisance.
"What about bail, S S?"
"Custody," snorted the skipper, banging the typewriter with emphasis.

The thought of appearing in court was a new heartburn. I had never given evidence in the charge courts before. Now I had to climb into the witness box, take the oath, sit in the hot seat, give the facts, be subject to cross-examination and prove my case. Would I be able?

And I also realised something else. I had wanted a prisoner so badly, to prove myself to myself, to the S S and my colleagues. Now I had accomplished this, but at what price? I was still considering the new scenario when the SS thrust the charge sheet into my hand with instructions:

161

"Read that over to him, caution him, and we'll see what he says."

My hands trembled as I saw for the first time my name as complainant
on a charge sheet. Underneath was laid out the defendant's name and the
indictment. Settling myself I read the charges, cautioned him and asked
if he had anything to say in reply.
"You're guilty. Aren't you?"
The demand came from the S S glaring over my shoulder at the defendant. The prisoner nodded miserably and the skipper nearly blew my
ear-drum from its socket with his next instructions.
"In answer to the charge he indicated he was guilty. Write that down.
Get him to sign it and you witness it yourself. C'mon now. Hurry now.
Brostaig."

I went to get a file cover, trying to waste as much time as possible, but
he was laying it all out for me on a copy of the charge sheet.
"There's our evidence.... Justice, he was acting the bowsy, beating his
wife. I cautioned him but he wouldn't give over. I restrained him but he
assaulted me so I drew my official baton and subdued him. That's what
you'll say. Remember keep to the facts. Never waste words in the witness box."

Later in the mess hall I tried to eat but couldn't. I was coming to grips
with the present but even more fearful about the immediate future. How
would I manage?

Suddenly I was no longer alone; the mess hall door was crowded with
colleagues:
"Are ye all right? We heard you were called into action. You did your
stuff. Good man. He's a bad yoke. The last time he cut up rough, it took
two to bring him to ground, but we heard you massacred him. Fair play.
You have to stand up to his type."

My trapped thoughts raced, fixing finally on one of Little John's gems
- the family of the police, the camaraderie, the sticking together when
the chips were down, the picking each other up. The code of the job.
Yes! I had experienced this from the S S tonight, now I had got a second helping from the lads. As I trawled back over events from the
moment I wheeled in the prisoner till I was handed a copy of the charge
sheet, I realised both contributions had been huge.

But even with such encouragement, I couldn't sleep that night. My mind was all over the place and my body ached with the many abrasions it had suffered in recent combat. To pass the time I went over and over the night's events, concentrating mainly on the evidence. Finally, I resurrected the S S's dictation and learnt it by heart.

Next morning at the Bridewell lock-up my prisoner was a sorry sight. Together we made the trip along the dungeon-like corridor to the holding pen directly under the court.

There followed the most daunting period - waiting for my case to be called. Custody cases were invariably first on the list which meant I would have full house for my debut. I sat and waited. Ten minutes after the half-past ten start the clerk bustled in and called out: 'All rise'. Everyone stood as the judge entered and took his seat on the bench.

Up to now the court had been fairly full but the judge's appearance was the signal for the place to really bulge. The swinging door continually swung to and fro as people came and went. I hoped I wouldn't be first on the list, and my wish was granted as the first, second, third and fourth cases went ahead.

I learned a lot during that brief respite. First, when a case was called, the garda in charge identified himself by moving from the fringes of the crowd towards the bench. Next he took the few short strides to the top of the stairs to shout out the name of the prisoner thereby signalling his release from the pen. Then, the prosecuting garda climbed into the witness box to await the arrival of the defendant on the dock.

At this point all present held their breath their eyes bunched on the landing waiting for the prisoner. Each new arrival created a palpable swell of emotion from family members, interested parties or supporters in the gallery. But the court grew silent as the garda took the oath and the facts surrounding the arrest, charge, caution and reply were noted. A judicious pause here: time to allow the gallery to assess. As the misdeeds were stated, public attitudes ranged from compassion to horror. The direction taken by the bench varied. Most were remands. The more serious cases including those arrested on warrant were kept in custody, resulting in a tramp back down to the hold. Others were pleas of guilty causing bated breath until the verdict was greeted with an exhalation of relief or disagreement.

The judgement was often followed by a period of uproar, until blasted into stillness by the clerk or the garda in charge who sat at the judge's right hand. 'Order in court'. Or 'next case'.

The pervading atmosphere in court was one of anxiety. I thought it impossible for anyone involved to relax in an assembly so saturated with emotion and potential confrontation. I knew that one word out of place could destroy my credibility or scar forever the reputation of the defendant. I listened to the oath, in particular to the three references to the word truth: the truth, the whole truth and nothing but the truth....

Finally it was my turn, my name ringing out loudly for the first time through the portals of a court of law. I stand, move towards the balcony, and call out the name of my prisoner lurking at the bottom of the stairs. Then I'm on the stand, three short steps. The court room hushes as he appears in the spotlight. Momentarily I feel a tinge of pity for him. But the eyes are back on me. The judge is ready:
"Yes, guard."
The oath. Good audible voice. I rattle it off. Pause. No problems there. The judge nods me to begin my evidence and I launch into an account of arrest, charge, caution and reply. Then the spotlight switches back to the defendant, and his reaction which is one of shameful guilt. Again the judge indicates I should proceed.
"I'm prepared to go ahead, Justice."
"Fire away, guard."

I was off, reciting the S S's dictation. Within seconds it was over. Another anticlimax.

That court appearance caused me to reflect on the whole issue of using force in an arrest. I had beaten up a fellow human being. Sure he deserved it, but that didn't make it any easier. For days and weeks, the memories persisted. I needed time to assimilate and put them in context.

The protection of life, but to what extent? Use such force as is necessary, but remain cool throughout the confrontation. Drawing my baton had been my instinctive reaction to his attempt to disarm me. Did I draw it in anger, or to defend myself. I didn't know. Did it matter?

The passage of time calmed me down to some degree and other insights helped. First there was the recognition of the extraodinary demands of the job, plus the satisfaction that came from feeling righteous. Also I had the acknowledgement from the neighbours, my colleagues and the courts. But deep down I still had to come to terms with the emotional impact of using force.

I had always been able to defend myself. When I was about fifteen, I had worked for a farmer Arthur W. who had looked after me well, with no stinging in the humour department. One day a tinker strolled into the yard looking for a stray pony. He was about seventeen, and much bigger than me. The farmer took him aside and promised there would be a shilling in it for him if he could take me on and better me. Before I realised, my opponent was on top of me fighting with the desperation of one who didn't finger many shillings. He took me by surprise but when I warmed to my task he cooled down pretty fast and he didn't earn his shilling.

But the fight with the violent husband was something else. Never had I witnessed such ferocity. I felt capable of overpowering him with my fists but I was supposed to use my baton if attacked. Of all the weapons I'd handled, this was the most powerful, and would take the most getting used to. From that realisation another crystallised. There would be other occasions when I would have to use my baton meaning there would certainly be further problems to grapple with.....

The night tour slid by into weeks. Since the arrest I had new respect for the S S who occupied a corner table in the mess hall where no one dared intrude. I had also grown in awe of his appetite. Each Monday night before going on duty he arrived with a full pig's head rolled up in a newspaper and clutched under his arm. After parade the largest skillet was rummaged from the cupboard under the sink and filled three quarters full with water. Then the ugly looking carcass was placed inside.

Until midnight it simmered merrily, with the S S paying periodic visits to the furnace to tend the offering and regulate the gas. During each trip he would stir and scoop out some of the gurgling fluid, supping it expansively. After about two hours a huge onion would be added. Later as we gathered to eat, the offensive offering was ceremoniously paraded into the mess hall and placed on God's private altar. Next, he produced a long bread pan, and laying it on the table sliced through its middle end to end. Then he plastered slabs of the frothy bacon on one side before cementing with the other bread half. A pot of tea was supplied, and he would stir the scalding brew with his forefinger.

As feeding began he chewed slowly at first then extending to rapturous grinding. Meal over, he was reluctant to say grace as he prodded the remaining carcass. Now and again almost impulsively he would carve off another morsel and chew it ponderously until at last the remains would be locked away until the following night. The head lasted three nights.

The Black had warned me about its final scraping before consignment to the bin:

"Watch him, there'll be nothing left. He's even prod the nostrils to unearth anything lurking inside."

The relationship between the pig's head and the S S was of long standing. The first time I saw the feasting, The Bluffer had a special story. Apparently some years before the S S had needed a heart operation. The story goes when they patched him up they stitched a piece of pig's bladder to his innards. According to The Bluffer one wag said: 'Pity they didn't sew on the snout as well, it'd be an improvement on his mush'.

The second month of nights was twice as hard as the first. Two decades of normal routine had been overthrown and adjusting to nights remained very difficult.

During the first month I had been on fire, flying over the beat. However, the second time round I began to appreciate the value of a sturdy pair of legs. I discovered that after a few hundred yards of patrolling on the unyielding concrete my feet heated up. Within a mile or two they had swelled, and if I had to stop they became stiff and sore. I dealt with this by balancing alternatively on heels and toes to help circulation.

The meal break was a killer with the feet stiffening up completely until they felt like lumps of concrete. I used to change my socks and shoes for the second half. The Bluffer believed that a soaking in salt and water was a good antidote. 'Feet for the beat. Petrol for the car', was one of The Black's sayings as he sailed by me in the patrol car.

But exercise was positive also, and while the night stayed fine and I had a good wad of leather between my feet and the concrete, I was well able for it. As regards footwear I swore by the all-leather shoe - George Webb, Winstanley or Lee. The Black favoured a boot, and The Bluffer swore allegiance to the Donaghy's vulcanised.

Around this time a new disability came on the market - athlete's foot. It wasn't long before the S S was scribing the ailment in the occurrence book:
"Sick report. Member reports non-effective, suffering from athlete's foot. Haaa... What's that? A new disease, some athlete that Bluffer, a born trapeze artist."

It was true. Nothing fazed The Bluffer. One day we were discussing the amount of sick leave he could wangle, and I began to pry:
"You were sick for two days last week, anything serious?"
"Aw no, I was refused a day's leave, but I wanted the day off badly, so I built myself up, and sure didn't I wake up that morning feeling so poorly, I had to go sick?"
"Built yourself up?" I asked.
"Yes," he replied. "It's amazing. I had to get the day off, so when leave was refused I took it so bad that when I woke up that morning you know what? I was terrible sick. All I can say is if you think really hard and believe you'll be sick, it'll happen. At least it does for me. Ha. Ha."

The whole sick scenario intrigued me. Non-effective was the official title, also referred to as 'throwing a sick, malingering or dossing'. At the time, much of the sickness seemed to last 48 hours to the minute - the maximum non-effective period without going to a doctor. Anxious to get a better insight, I consulted Little John on the subject. As usual his diagnosis was spot on;

"There are delicate members and some are injured on duty, but most of us are fairly hardy or else we wouldn't be in the job in the first place. But a lot of fellas are notorious for neglecting their health. They think they're tough skiving off a few days, for example saying they're sick with the 'flu' but really they could be ignoring something more serious."

A conversation soon after with The Bluffer confirmed this. He struggled in to the mess hall one night from patrol and collapsed on the chair

167

opposite me. Reaching down he peeled up the trouser leg. I saw his ankles had swelled badly and there were knotty, bluish veins further up the leg:

"Why don't you look after them?" I asked. "An elastic stocking, even."
For the first time ever he looked vulnerable, before snorting:
"Would you wear them women's yokes around here? What if the latchicos found out? No. I've managed so far and now that I'm on the back straight they'll carry me the rest of the journey."

At night the city purred with life, but with less people as the night progressed. After midnight it began to scale down to its lowest and at four or five in the morning the clicking heart of the traffic lights was often the only sound. At about five o'clock I had the squawking of seagulls filling the air and the scampering pigeons. At home the pigeons were shy, confining themselves to a gentle cooing from the topmost branches. But here they were on my beat and under my feet.

The early morning racket started with the milkman and newspaper vans, to be followed by squealing buses, car horns and children as traffic built up. I would normally finish duty at 6am, go to bed immediately but needed time for the events of the night to thaw out of my system before I could sleep. What often followed was fitful slumber, littered with numerous noises and disturbances. The station pulsed with life 24 hours, but really hummed from 9am to 5pm.

A night arrest meant getting the morning off, giving time to wash, tog out and parade before the assizes at half ten. But normally I would get up about two o'clock in the afternoon, still feeling like a wet rag.

Usually a cup of tea was all I could manage. The dinner would be stowed away in my locker for later, when I felt like it and sometimes not eaten at all - an unreal half-life half-sleep existence.

Out in the sun meant headache or drowsiness. The only training I could manage was a bit of listless jogging. Indoors was little better, resting on an easy chair meant falling into a fitful stupor. Sand in the eyes. Tiredness. Lethargy. Putting up the feet and closing my eyes for about ten minutes was one of Little John's suggestions. I tried it, and it helped. A good wash or shower before going on duty was also refreshing.

I was finding that while the early, and late on alternative days was bad, the month of nights was a killer. I often wondered why these duties were called 'the regular'. To me they should be known as the irregular. I hoped I would get used to night work as it was an essential part of the job. Nonetheless I was getting accustomed to the S S's roar and used my eyes and ears to gauge the mood of the day.

At parade time he set the tone with one of his many commandments. The first night of the month he preached of commitment to our duties before turning and knuckling the notice board:
"The annual mission is on in Mount Argus. Father Clarence will expect a full turnout and I'm directing you all to parade clean and regular."

The following evening I made my way to Mount Argus and was impressed by the beauty and splendour of the church. The place was packed. I had never seen so many big men under one roof. They stood, sat, knelt and prayed. The preacher Father Clarence was spellbinding; and having heard the charismatic Passionist in action I was convinced that whoever decided that he should bestow us with spiritual guidance must have been divinely inspired.

Meanwhile the month stretched unbearably because I didn't think I would get any of my four nights off. The Bully said the S S was like a bear this weather and it wouldn't be advisable to go within hearing distance of his lair.

In early May I had one day off, none in June, two day's annual leave in July and two monthly days, and the same in August. Now it was September, I was on nights again and things were not looking good. But surprise, surprise, as a reward for producing the prisoner, the S S gave me three nights off over the second half of that month. They were much appreciated. Ten days off out of one hundred and fifty.

In early October I was back on days, and detailed for the station, relieving The Bully. At first I was terrified of the inner sanctum, but I soon settled down. The first morning the phone rang beside the S S who was buried in his occurrence book. Between the third and fourth blast, he rolled his eyes at me and back before speaking to himself:
"I wonder would that be for us?"
I picked up the receiver and got an earful:

"It's that cat again. The tom. Last night he did it again. My begonias ruined. I was talking to Mrs Daly at Mass this morning and she has the same problem. Can ye not control them? Do you not have the humane killer? A nice guard said he'd come down last week, but he never appeared."

Suddenly the S S was beside me, gesturing with his hand as if winding up a gramophone. This was my cue to let her go on which she did for another few minutes before hanging up suddenly.
"What was she on about today?" he asked.
"Cats," I replied.
"Aye, it's Monday. Tomorrow it'll be dogs. Did she mention the weather at all?"
"Yes, she said it was a fine day but a bit dry."
"Ah yes, if it's raining tomorrow, it'll be too wet. She's harmless. We have a few of those craythurs in our patch. All they want is someone to listen to them."

A striking feature of the public office was the open fire. To the lads it was known as the 'hob of hell' as some of the S S's more ferocious broadsides were delivered as he stood in front of it his palms screwing the heat into his ample backside.

The station cleaner replenished and cleaned the fire each morning. One day when I was doing relief jailer she bowled in armed with an ash-shovel, brush and bucket. God was transcribing some letters to the Pharisees or some other needy group, and she bent over the hearth, attacking the ankle deep ashes with gusto.
"Good morning, Josie."
Amazingly it was God who spoke.
Josie was a yellow skinned slip of a woman who looked at death's door. But the S S regarded her benignly:
"Stoke her up there, Josie. There's my girl."
"You're the devil," she retorted, adding to my amazement. Could she talk to God in this way and survive? But he was smiling:
"Yeah, I like my bit of hate... Ha, ha.."

She laughed with him, then hopped back into the fireplace, using her body as a cowl and proceeded to attack the heap of ash. As she *scuabed* and shovelled, God rose, moved to one side and watched admiringly.

After a while she pulled back from her labours allowing a film of ash to cascade out and become sucked upwards towards the sunlight. God spoke again:

"There Josie, check my halo, and see if it's straight."

As the year progressed I became more accepted - though still being the recruit I had to take what was dished out and try to keep smiling. Otherwise you got extra rations of slagging. But if you laughed it off or showed you could take the flak, they usually laid off.

One character had it in for me from day one. He wasn't in our unit, but still went out of his way to humiliate me. Typical was his attack when I got my first prisoner:

"Well now, if it's not the red-arse recruit. I hear you got a prisoner at last. Mickey Mouse assault? Ha. When will you catch a thief, a real prisoner? Waiting for one to give himself up. Ha. Ha.?"

I usually tried to smile my way out of this but it only made him worse and he put the boot in when he got me on my own. Also, when we met in the mess hall he began to really turn on me. This was a worrying development. How to handle him?

One evening in mid-October I was chatting over a cup of tea when he came in behind me.

"Can any of ye understand what that bogman is saying?"

Everyone ignored him, but he wasn't put off as he tapped me on the shoulder and continued his prodding.

"We'll have to apply for an interpreter for you."

Again there was no response.

"Now Pudsy Doyle, let's start again."

I tried to laugh off this attack but I found myself clenching my fists in anger. He had now parked himself across the table from me. Suddenly, something snapped. I jumped up, shifting the table and sending a couple of mugs cascading into his lap. Immediately I was surrounded by the lads:

"Lave it over. Break it up."

Little John propelled me out to the fresh air, then upstairs where he calmed me down with words of common sense. It wouldn't look right for a recruit to be brawling in the mess, he said, and sure nobody took any notice of your man. He went on and on. After he left, I was still upset. What would people think? I had been insulted, ran away and swallowed it. I'd be the talk of the place.

Could I live with that?

I shouldn't have to put up with this carry on. No one should. But what could I do? My eyes fell on the latest letter from home. As usual Moma had the family news. One story starred my father. Apparently he had been collecting sticks in the turf shed, and my baby brother Thomas not realising he was there, had barred the door. According to Moma it was the quietest hour of the week until my father was released.

Suddenly from my library of memories came another of my father and the day he went to war.

It was a humid summer day with the threat of rain and we had a field of hay to be cocked. He had been in town early and came home in an awful state. Heeling out the messages on the table, he ignored us, and stared into the mirror until he put on his very cross face. Then turning, he tore into the bedroom and wrenched out the side bar of the bed with a box wrench. He threw the bar over his shoulder, marched out the front door and over the bohereen with the rest of us in tow.

Our mother was away, otherwise we would not have been treated to such excitement. After a good part of the journey to Puck he came within striking distance of a farmer who had a bit of a loose tongue and greased every bit of local gossip until it became the talk of the parish. As usual the farmer was in the dyke of the road. But when he saw my father's black face, he skedaddled indoors. Luckily for him too as our militia put on a bit of a spurt and arrived with the rasp of the bolts. That seemed to cool things down, and apart from a march past or two my father held his temper and went home to the haymaking.

On our arrival Moma had mellow words for him;
"I see you were on a crusade. Did you put the fear of God in him?"
"No," he replied. "But I put the fear of Tom Dile in him."

Now it was my call to arms.

I charged downstairs. The corridor was tallow coloured beneath the stuttering fluorescent light, but near the door of the public office the glow spilled out resplendently onto the figure of my tormentor. Pretending not to notice him, I turned and walked away to where the light was swallowed up by the basking darkness. I waited. I felt powerful. He came confidently, childishly crooning insults until both my hands collared his throat. His neck was soothing and pliable, like a velvet football, as I wrinkled his taunts into submission. He backed away fearfully as I pushed him into the glare, my face jamming into his. No words were spoken. Disdainfully I released him and he crawled along the wall and away from me.

That was the end of my persecution. From then on he wore a cloak of respect tinged with fear whenever our paths crossed. Within the hour the grapevine was thick with stories of my deed. At first I thought there might be an enquiry but Little John allayed my fears;
"What you did was right. But don't gloat."

From the start a group that interested me greatly were the detectives. They hung out in an enclave down near the back door opposite the cells. Occasionally, I witnessed frenzied activity between the cells and their door. Once, I saw a wild-eyed individual being jockeyed from cell to office accompanied by loud voices.

The plain clothes staff seldom appeared around the public office and their door remained firmly closed. The first time I spoke to one of them was a bitter cold morning in October. At about 8am I snuck in the back door for a heat from the stove. Throwing off my waterproof I came face to face with a young detective who had arrived from another station to work with our plain clothes section. As we talked he began to cook a massive breakfast of rashers, sausages, eggs and toast. He had a wealth of fascinating stories and before I left he thrust a rasher and sausage sandwich into my hand with instructions to get it inside me.

From then on, I often drifted by their office but the door remained firmly closed.

One day I was in the public office when a phone message came for the detective unit. I headed for their door, knocked and waited until a voice told me to come in. Inside a gnarled-looking detective was lying back on his chair, feet thrown on the corner of his desk, phone cradled between shoulder and cheek, and two hands raised as if he was about to conduct a sonata. As I stood, he indicated with an impatient forefinger where to put the note - and stopped talking. Obviously I had disturbed a vital chat under the Official Secrets Act. Then his eyebrows signalled me to leave.

At the door I noticed the map of the District plastered on the wall, its skin punctured with clusters of red and green-headed pins. Later I discovered these referred to crimes committed and detected - though The Bluffer had his own slant:
"Firing darts at a map of the district is the nearest some of them chancers will come to trapping the villains that are successfully plundering our patch."

I considered this a bit harsh. But it gave me an insight into the rather grudging relationship that existed between the uniform and plain clothes staff.

One morning shortly after, our parade briefing was interrupted by the arrival of the detective sergeant. His perennial garb was a lightweight overcoat coloured white under its epaulets with the remainder weathered to a porridge hue. This garment was never buttoned and depended for support on his two arms which squeezed tightly into its side before disappearing into the trouser pockets.

God was absent and the young parade sergeant waited respectfully as the detective came to the tail end of the parade - and to me. Then his eyes flicked back to the sergeant. He had made his selection and my skipper nodded his approval for me to leave the parade. Bursting with curiously, I followed the detective out the back door and into the back seat of a battered car. My captor sat in front. The driver was the detective to whom I had delivered the note. For a while they were silent, then:
"What do you think of your man?"
The driver angled his rear view mirror on me:
"Not bad, a bit green about the gills, but better than nothing."
"Yeah, I see what you mean but he's all we can muster."
Then the D/Sgt turned back to me:
"Are you good with wimmen?"
I was startled but answered immediately:

"Well, a while back I got a statement from a lady about a traffic accident and I had no problems with her."

The two in front laughed.

"Green is no word for the youngsters that depot is turning out. She'll be safe enough with him," said the driver.

I hadn't a clue why I was being kidnapped, but before long we squeezed up a deserted back alley and stopped. My captors got out and beckoned me to follow. Up a creaky stairs, over in a corner almost hidden in a maze of steam, lurked a little gnome of a man squatting over an ironing board.

"Welcome gentlemen, How's business?"

"Fit him out for a monkey suit," the D/Sgt cut across him.

Soon I was being stripped and my body stuffed into a corset tight dress suit.

Next I was programmed.

"You're going to a dress dance tonight. Taking a lovely girl. You should be honoured. Her father is well-in and you could do worse than make an impression."

I had no option but to follow orders and go through with the masquerade.

The dance was a very sumptuous affair. The girl was more interested in her father's alcoholic intake than in me, and well she might. He had been taken captive by the detectives, his sole concession to movement was a sleight of hand to and from his inside pocket. Later when the show was over my assignment was not complete until I had escorted both the by now paralytic father and refined daughter home with strict instructions that both should enter their front door simultaneously.

It was through the detectives that I paid my first visit to Dublin Castle; the history of which I had long been interested in. It was also the headquarters of the plain clothes members, often referred to as the basilica of detectives.

My first visit was memorable, if not informative.

For some time I realised that a particular detective had me under cover. It was December and my month of nights had come around again. One

day in the first week I was lazing around the mess hall with a few hours to kill when he approached me:
"I have job for you."
I jumped at the opportunity. I had discovered that uniformed members were sometimes seconded to the detectives and such conferral was momentous. He drove off towards the city, displaying an interest in me and my background. I gave him the whole spiel, my family and how a long overdue visit was on the cards for Christmas. He seemed to be lapping it up, expressing lashings of condolences on the Spartan existence of my family.

Suddenly he turned to me;
"You'll give me a dig out. Won't you?"
"Sure, of course," I replied, having been caught on the hop. He continued to look at me, forcing me to elaborate:
"I'll do what I can."
"You're in St Raphael's, aren't you, our credit union?"
"Yes, The Staff shoves a pound a week into it. Why so?"
"I need a tenner fast. They're based in the Castle and that's where we're headed. I'm in the red with them but really skint and nowhere else to go. You know how it is. I'd have a better chance of getting a smile from a dead man than a bob from the manager, but with you there's a chance. All you'll say is that it's your first loan application and you need ten pounds desperately to send to your poor mother in Kerry for Christmas. Will you remember that? And for my sake, put on your most innocent face, or he'll run you. Go on, say it a few times till you've got it right."

I felt a right impostor but was stuck, having given my word. Soon, we were barrelling in under the archway to the castle yard. In the hallway the driver gave me more injections:
"Now you know it by heart. Remember you have to be fierce convincing. Your man will smell it a mile off if it's not dead on."

The room was large with rows of benches. I had two full ones to negotiate before reaching the manager at the top. He was a bulky, florid character, with a big, inscrutable wise-looking head, and a pair of thick-rimmed spectacles perched halfway down his heavy nose, threatening to slide off at any moment. Everything about him looked intimidating as he sized up each applicant. Yes, definitely the confessor type - listening, deliberating. He put the heart crossways in me, but I was already com-

already committed to a sin of intent. I had given my word and now had to lay on an Oscar winning performance.

As the numbers moved forward and dwindled, I tried to build myself up for my ordeal. Immediately in front was a character who looked as if he had come not for money but a blood transfusion. He had eyes only for the manager and as he moved closer he sought to hypnotise him with audible mutters:

"Paddy there, one dacent man, would give you the shirt off his back."

He was next to take the hot seat:

"It's only a fiver. You know how it is, Paddy?"

"I do." The banker's eyes bored into the borrower. "What do you want it for?"

"I need it desperately for Christmas."

"I see now, and what are you going to do with it?"

The interrogation was too much as my neighbour exploded into truth:

"To drink it. I need it for snake oil."

"Refused. Next."

He left muttering about the lack of Christmas spirit in some people.

It was my turn. But my tutelage was in smithereens. I blurted out my tale of lies only for Paddy to snorkel me with one eye and allow the other to squint toward my tutor's shadow lurking in the doorway. A dry smile crept on his lips and he spoke a single word of rejection:

"No."

As I rose he leaned towards me and whispered:

"If you're stuck, give me a shout next week. On your own."

I was looking forward to Christmas. Already I had spotted presents for the family and was determined to take the home front by storm. Now it was all down to my annual leave being granted.

Ten days into the month I lashed in my application covering Christmas. A few days later, I got it back. Granted.

I was going home for Christmas.

In the meantime, rumours were flying concerning an outbreak of Foot and Mouth disease in England. It had been on and off in the news for a while until, overnight, someone somewhere stamped their foot or opened their mouth and the disease became our problem.

The day before my leave was due to start, the exigencies of the service reared its unsympathetic head.
The S S made no bones about it.
"You're going to the border tomorrow."

That was it. No explanations, no apologies. The government of the day had heeled the safety of the cattle industry into the lap of the guards. The requisitions were made. The recruit was available and would fit the bill.

Chapter 13 - INTEGRATION

I almost revolted. I had thought my star was rising, but now it was light years further out in space. Six months on the job, approaching my first anniversary of joining up, what did I get as a present? A transfer against my will. Send the recruit. Another stick.

I had arrangements to change, but I did nothing, just sat and sulked, full of dejection and a fierce antagonism towards the S S. However, before I overflowed, The Staff found me. We sat in my room and he talked:
"It's tough. You're thick about being sent. Try and control it. You have to go through with it. You'll need to arrive at the border in a half-normal frame of mind or you could wind up on the rocks. You'll want your head well strapped on up there. The temptations will be enormous. You could easily go off the rails and come back a different man.

"Now listen carefully. The S S is impressed by the way you're shaping up, but if you cut up rough or throw the head, no better man to put the boot in. You're still only a recruit and expected to do as you're told. But buck up, I'll have a chat with your border sergeant, he's a personal friend and a sound man, he'll keep an eye out for you. Now, c'mon with me."

I trailed after him to his office:
"Now let's see, wellingtons, pull ups, extra raincoat, gloves, torch. Take them. Money now. How are you fixed?"
He had his wallet out urging me to take a few notes but I had enough, and anyway he would be forwarding my pay. This good-natured human being started my engine again, and even though I was only in first gear, his advice helped to keep me going.

Next day, others weighed in with more counsel. As usual The Black coaxed a smile:
"Bring plenty of shampoo. It could turn out to be a hair-raising experi-

179

ence."

Later the S S appeared to see me off. I said nothing, letting him know I was still fed up. As usual his words carried a hint of a threat but he ended with the merest twist of commiseration:

"This is a good station, one of the most respected in the country. Its reputation is travelling with you. Come back in one piece."

There was no handshake, just a not-unfriendly slap with the knuckles of his fist on my elbow. That was it.

So one afternoon in mid-December I stepped on board a bus bound for the border. Already aboard were twelve apostles, assigned from other Dublin stations, all looking equally abandoned. Hours later we reached the village of Muff, Co. Donegal, where we shuffled into a tiny station and gave our identities. Accommodation was up for grabs. I opted for a hotel in Moville because I liked the sound of the place, and had a vague memory of an old time saint once living there.

Next we were informed there would be four weekly tours of duty each consisting of six hours and as there would be no relief, we would have to bring our food with us. Feeling like a martyr I opted for the worst tour for the opening week - midnight to 6 am. After that the bus took me off up the Inishowen peninsula to the quaint little town of Moville.

As I booked into the hotel I noticed a map on the wall in the foyer. I realised I was almost as far away from home as I could be while remaining within the shores of my native country.

The following morning I discovered two other members Noel and J.J. had arrived during the night and were on the same tour of duty as myself.

The first night on duty on the border is an unforgettable experience. Alone under the dark canopy of the sky in an alien environment is very unsettling. Such displacement needs time for adjustment. Darkness alters the physical aspect of any scene. Already during my city tours, I had learned to sharpen my senses and reactions. Now I was on full alert.

Also, while I had become used to standing still for short periods, the prospect of having to remain almost motionless for six hours caused foreboding. Of course, I could walk the length of my beat, a dirt track, limiting my movement to two strides either way and one for the about turn. Underneath the tiny bridge a trickle of water was my only company. This stream marked the frontier.

As if to share my mood the skies opened in a bizarre welcome. Another baptism. The cold scuttery rain drove me under the bridge arch for shelter. Standing in the inch of water, I was grateful for The Staff's wellingtons as I stamped my feet and blew the icy cobwebs from my lips, all the while feeling sorry for myself and blaming the SS and the Foot and Mouth epidemic for my predicament.

When the shower cleared, the night settled into an overcast, eerie stillness, gradually enveloping me in a heavy shroud of depression. I dredged for some semblance of comfort and remembered again The Staff's words: 'It's rough but anyone who tells you otherwise is not in touch with reality'.

It certainly was rough - and very real. Since I joined the force my capacity to absorb punishment had increased. Now, here I was experiencing the ultimate Christmas bonus. Instead of going home I was dumped at midnight in the back of beyond with nothing but the memory of a brief briefing to sustain me.
'You're all going out to different points, one man per location. Transport will drop you off and collect you afterwards. All you have to do is stand there and keep and eye on things'.

I had heard it all before, different words, same meaning. But as most of my experiences to date were unique, I was continually struggling to understand them. And this latest escapade had introduced an additional and potentially fatal ingredient - idleness.

During training and since, I had been changing from a man of action to one of reaction. But now I was being reprogrammed for inactivity.
With movement gone, other senses become more potent. First my eyes picked out the nearby landscape of hillocky boggy fields. Second my hearing, after the commotion of the city, had to become re-attuned to the stillness of the country at night time.

As if to consolidate this reawakening, a three piece orchestra came to perform a gig in a nearby hedgerow - a deep bass frog croaked to the tuneless cricket, while overhead the dithering snipe soared in celebration that at least one patron had turned up for the performance. Quietly I drew my coat around me and stood on the grass margin until another shower of rain drowned out the sound of the ensemble. It was intermission time as I clambered back under the arch. From far away I heard the lonely yelp of a collie dog seeking company like myself.

The shower turned into a persistent pelter and drove me further into my dome where I stood hunched. My previous melancholy evaporated and was replaced by other thoughts. I was making new discoveries. If my mind was constantly active and concentrated, I could maintain a consistent level of interest. So my thoughts could become invaluable allies.

To help pass the time several now took flight to home and back, taking in all the stops along the way - Templemore, Dublin and Muff. I concentrated on the happiest period of my life - the quiet secure confines of home. Again I saw Moma reading from one of her many books. This was the story of the saint of Moville, and now in this place I recalled it. St Finnian, the Abbot of Moville had set out to convert the local chieftain, Tuan who was feasting and merrymaking. When he got the message that he was due for conversion Tuan slammed the door in Finnian's face. However, Finnian said he would picket the castle until Tuan made himself amenable to salvation. This impasse continued throughout the night until Tuan and all his household were converted.

And so my solitude lent itself to endless memories of my youth and developing years. As a child, I loved to be out at night with the moon for company. Now that heavenly body burst from over the hill and shafted its beam brilliantly on my lonely vigil. I remembered what my father had said: 'There's a man in the moon boy'. I smiled at the thought. I was warmed by the fact that the selfsame moon was also shining down on my home at the far end of the country. Man, if you're up there, tell them all I was asking for them.

I had an unexpected response. A cow conferred a mournful bellow over the fence. I thought she had come to give herself up. Desperate for any company, I addressed my visitor, urging her to pass the word to her pals that Number Forty had arrived to protect them. By way of acknowledgement she flung her head and trailed off into the night. Obviously the rest of the herd felt secure as during the first week of duty she was my only caller, apart from my relief, pick up and drop off, I met no one.

Back in the hotel Noel and J. J. told of similar adjustment to their first night on duty.

The second night I was a bit more settled. For the want of something better to do, I tried to remember the lectures on the Foot and Mouth. It was contained in a lecture entitled The Diseases of Animals Act, newly minted legislation, and the hand-out had floated on to my desk near the end of training. Initially, the instructor made a bit of a skit out of it, quoting obscure diseases such as epizootic lymphangitis, parasitic mange and foot and mouth disease.

I remembered it was the last class before lunch. I detected endless possibilities in this far-fetched piece of legislation so had raised my paw and enquired about the causes of Foot and Mouth disease. I got my answer:
'Do you still ate your toe nails, laddie?'

As usual the joke was on me.

However, my question had tickled the humour department and others chimed in so much that the instructor started on page one: 'Effects of the Foot and Mouth Disease'. As he forged ahead, I tried to keep the devilment going:
"This foot and mouth now. If I saw it coming down the road, what would I do? My power, like?"
This had him flicking pages until he read:
"Report it to the Department of Agriculture. You may stop any person committing an offence under the Act, and if his name and address are unknown to you or if he fails to give them or gives one that is false or misleading you can arrest him. Also you can stop and detain such animal". "How would I do that? If it was a bull that came at me?"

The query was ignored so I tried again:
"How would I know it?"
"Ye'll know it when you see it."
The classic answer.

We went to lunch and forgot about Foot and Mouth.

But I had tempted fate and now it was pay up time.

The symptoms of the disease were mouth tenderness and inflammations on the hooves. Now my imagination was flowering with visions of wild, mad, roaring herds of steers gathering just over the hill ready for an invasion. Any minute now they would come tearing at me, mouths slavering on painful stumbling hooves hell bent on spreading their dreadful disease all over the republic. I was Cuchulainn defending the Brown Bulls and Heifers of Ulster against a marauder far more deadly than Queen Maeve of Connaught. Cocking my ears I listened. Not a sound. Sure every self-respecting animal was tucked up in bed not wandering the countryside. They were in, housed and fed and I was the one out in the cold protecting them.

Some duty.

But if our duty was cold and barren, our accommodation was warm and caring. I had become friendly with the son of the family who ran the hotel and after the first day he had a routine mapped out. Good film in town. Walk to Greencastle. The Inishowen. Malin.

One night I was all togged out ready for duty when he appeared and took my photograph. When the film was developed I dispatched one home to my parents.

Throughout the week of nights, the cold remained intense and the greatcoat was less than adequate. I wondered did any of the powers-that-be ever bother to test the garment in such harsh conditions before making it standard issue for the force. Four nights into the week I woke with a rasp in my throat and felt I was coming down with flu. I had considered my health as indestructible and had been drenched on duty many times. But now I was exposed to fog and dampness as well as cold, for a lengthy period and had succumbed. I was determined not to report sick and fought the bug with reckless obstinacy. I didn't want to be the first human casualty of Foot and Mouth disease.

Magically a cure appeared beside my bed. Bottled, illicitly distilled. I didn't mind, took it as a night-cap and sweated out the fever in my sleep. Did such imbibing break my abstention pledge? I decided not, as it was for medicinal purposes only. Also, I realised the need to retain heat during my lonely vigil and remembered the tip of an old watchman I used to meet on night tours in Dublin. 'A sheet of brown paper creased across the chest was as good as an extra skin', he said, and guaranteed to keep out the cold.

Next day I got two sheets of strong paper, cellotaped them together, cut out a hole for my head and made a long bib back and front. This, along with fifty press-ups every half hour did the trick. Though I wondered if I were rendered unconscious by the galloping herd of my fantasy, and whipped into hospital, what the staff would make of their brown paper mummy.

About half way through the week I decided I would go insane if I didn't hear the sound of another human voice during the long hours of darkness. Next day I borrowed a transistor and for the rest of the tour I had Cliff and Elvis and Radio Luxembourg, the station of the stars, pretty appropriate as I listened to it under the night sky.

Three days later I got an urgent letter from my mother conveying a message from my father. He was glad I was minding the border and should forget about coming home this Christmas. Instead I was to ensure that the disease was not allowed in as he had a few great yearlings and if anything happened he would have to sell out.

Christmas came, memorable for Donegal hospitality. The hotel owners went out of their way to ensure that we felt like part of the family. After the new year, I rotated my tours to different unapproved roads. They were all the same, quiet and dusty.

As the New Year passed and the days lengthened and I got used to the job, more forgotten memories of the border came to me and helped pass the time. These originated in my early youth from stories my parents told me. Once, when I was about eight, we heard on the news that a young Limerick man had been killed on the border. A few weeks later my father came home from town with the words of a song in honour of the slain man. I was ordered to learn it off and had to sing it whenever requested. I recall the time my American relations visited, and I was commanded to sing. I agreed on condition I could serenade them from my bedroom with the door closed.

I remembered the huge plastic map of Ireland beside the blackboard in primary school. Often my day dreams trekked off along the ominous black line stretching from the top of Louth up over Monaghan, skirting the southern side of both Lough Erne's almost to Bundoran on the Atlantic and straggled north to Lough Foyle. I imagined the border as a visible division where differences would be obvious. Now I was amazed at the similarity on either side. The suggestion that the Six Counties was inhabited mainly by Protestants who were totally different from us was proving to be inaccurate. Each Saturday I visited Derry, meeting police and people and found we were much like each other, except for accents and uniforms.

My sergeant had also been transferred from Dublin. He had a pair of smiling blue eyes, and a kind word whenever he dropped and collected me.
"It's an experience. You'll be the better man for it. Cheer up Forty, remember when you're that age, I'll be nearly retiring. Here, check out my speedometer. We don't want to be breaking the speed limit on these busy roads."
"Go on, I'd say, the needle hasn't moved yet. Get me home to bed."

After the first week, the next three flew. And suddenly I was going back to Dublin.

This caused a new set of reflections. First, my duties had been easy. The sole requirement was to be present and correct in the blue. However, to remain still and silent for long hours was very difficult and I had learnt a new and valuable attribute: patience. Also I had developed the knack of occupying my mind with provocative, humorous and imaginative thoughts. In fact I had learned to dream awake, and in the process had become more self-knowing and self-aware than ever before.

Back in Dublin, there were two surprises. The Squirrel was gone, jacked up, stuck in the half sheet, and was now inside the wall of a seminary. I was glad for him.

The other surprise was a delight. On my first day back I was having a cup of tea in the mess hall when the S S darkened the doorway and crooked a finger at me:
"Where's your D 9?"

I resurrected the leave form noting again the cancellation scrawl and gave it to him.

"You need a break. Go on away home to your family for yourself. Come back to me in a week."

Already he was folding the form and placing it carefully in his tunic pocket.

"I'll look after this. It'll be between us."

I was thrilled. A week off buckshee. Before night fell I was in Kerry.

At the cross-roads I stopped. Having looked forward to this moment so many times I wanted to soak in the atmosphere. But things had changed. First, it was unusually deserted, there was no on around, something I had never envisaged. Second, a crop of brawny rushes had claimed squatters rights to the alder tree that had shaded and sheltered me many times.

But the scene and its memories still intoxicated. Just to stand there and look away across the bog which seemed almost to submerge out house. Up to Nauntinane. Down the slope to where the languid Laune nourished the fertile plain and away up the incline to the Maclicuddys looking splendid after a snowfall.

As I looked I heard a step behind me. A friend brought me up to date with news:

"The lads have scattered. Paddy's Day gone out, three or four headed for England and a few more have gone working on the beet. Things have gone dead around here."

As we talked I remembered Big Andy's prophecy:

'Apart from your family, there's nothing here for you. The days of the labouring man are numbered'.

Nearer home I met the ex-member prowling between the gaps. In his mind I knew he still patrolled the streets of Dublin. While I had often avoided him in the past, now I felt privileged to spend a few minutes with him on my way home:

"Who's your skipper?"

As I began to tell him, he interrupted and was off in his own inimitable way.

"Ah now, you may say. That man is a legend. He's forgotten more about the job than any training centre. You're fortunate to be under his umbrella. Hard to get to know, but if he's on your side you're away on a hack. I served with him once. Listen to what he says, remember every word, as in a few years his equals will be history...... Let me tell you, in the world of the guards, the D.M.A. is the only place for a young lad like you to become a man. Now, I take it once you've seen the folks, you'll not be wasting your time down here."

Before I could reply, he was off again:
"Do you have a mind for the drink?"
I told him of the abortive initiations of The Black in that regard. He stamped his feet and burrowed his eyes into mine:
"Stay off the beer. The greatest curse in the job. How's the legs?"
"Grand," I answered, but he wanted proof and I had to pull up my trousers:
"Turn around. Aha, no discoloured veins. They'll do the thirty all right."

Home at last to my parents, but here too things were different. In fact, there was the biggest change of all.

Before leaving home I had depended on them for everything. This meant that the disciplines of having to fend for myself had made training very difficult. Also, the decision-making associated with my on-the-job training had influenced me further until I had become a totally different person. But now I had come back to the beginning, seeking consolation and renewal but discovering neither. When away I had visualised my early life as an escape route from present problems. Now I was back and faced reality. Time had moved on. My friends had emigrated. The cross-roads were only a memory that would never be the same. These external changes nudged me closer than ever to my parents.

That first night Moma and I sat and talked into the early hours:
"We had Mary for Christmas but missed Danny and yourself. Wasn't it great he made such a recovery? And your photograph was a great Christmas box. It's in my bag. It reminded me of one day in the valley when you were in short pants. A travelling woman came calling and before she left she had a good look at you and said. You'll be proud of that child. He'll wear a uniform."

Armed with my training precepts and experiences I traded my recent life against hers. She had an ocean of words, reminiscences, and nothing could diminish her pride that her prayers were answered, I had persevered and she had a son in the guards. For me it seemed as if I was looking at her for the first time. She was always thin but now she looked positively skeletal. When asked she admitted to still cycling the road dragging bags of messages, sewing patches on trousers and mending socks with the light of a candle. At least she now wore glasses and was hopeful we would soon have electricity.

As usual my father had a few small jobs lined up. The drain had scrawed up again and needed to be dug out. The first day we attacked the job with shovels and hayknives. At first it felt good to have an implement in my hands, but after a few twists of the handle I discovered the skin of my palm was burnt to a scorch. My father had no such problem. He took off his coat, bent over and kept at it. But I noticed that his shoulders had shrunk a bit and his movements had changed. The always purposeful gait had become a bit staggery and fretful. But his trademark, the horse shoe nails hitching the gallowses to his trousers were still intact.

The next morning my body ached from the unaccustomed stiffness associated with manual labour. I lay on, savouring the old familiar sounds - the geese patrolling the ash heap, Gyp's sharp growl from the hedge heralding a passer-by on the main road, and more immediately the raucous crows whom I had often catapulted from the roof but who had obviously built a chimney nest during my absence. As usual there wasn't enough time for lying in. I heard my father's determined tramp on the kitchen floor:
"Is he getting up at all today?"
Moma's quiet answer was in my favour but he would have none of it.
"Tis no day to be wasted in the bed."
He banged a door or two until I abandoned my rest.

Later I found him knee deep and barefoot in the swampiest part of the bog swinging the scythe with the ice clinging to each newly shorn sward. I stood for a while, watching the bend of my father's back and the powerful swivel of his upper body. Now almost 70, in his early days he had moved mountains. More recently he was reclaiming a twelve and a half acre spread too damp even for the snipe.

As I looked, he stopped to sharpen his weapon. He was sweating in the cold, panting as he scraped the whetstone on the steel blade. Next month when the days lengthened he planned to redrain the sweatiest portion of the bog. I recalled Moma's parting words as I left the house that morning:

"That bleddy bog. It'll be the death of him."

The trip home opened my eyes, mind and heart. I went back over the events since my arrival - my meeting at the cross-roads, my chats with the ex-sergeant and my mother, my father's addiction to slavery. He hardly talked to me unless we were harnessed together to some job. The images came fast and furious. My life had been grafted from this place. I had brought it with me, yet left it behind. The last year apart, physical hard labour had been ingrained into me. I did it without thinking, my mind uninvolved except to get the job done as quickly and efficiently as possible. Now, standing on home soil and looking back over the year, I became aware of a different tilt in the fulcrum of my life, another perspective. I had been given a choice, something my father never had. The mountains, the bog and the economic conditions had charted his course through life.

During my training and early on-the-job period I had been like the many sprats I hooked in the Laune on balmy evenings. No use to anyone, fit only to be thrown back. Some day they would be worth catching. In a way I had been spawning for the past year as well, and while I hadn't yet reached my prime, the transformation was becoming more apparent. Friends and neighbours commented on my transformation. It was the way I walked and looked at them.

In a way I felt like a celebrity. My neighbours endowed our capital city with undeserved distinction, and some of the reflected glory fell on me: 'It's a tough place up there, I hear fierce things on the wireless, how do you stick it?'

Some people at home credited me with special powers. One was Seanin whose jewel in life was his son and heir. Seanin had great plans for this offspring, chiefly that he would marry well and present him with a litter of strong sons to cultivate the farm. The father had canvassed the local parishes but nothing suitable was on offer.

Then at the Killarney races the son had made his mark. Armed with copious pints he corralled a comely maiden and finally wound his way homewards full of glee - and good news. He had found a wife. Unfortunately, the next day all he could remember was that her Christian name was Susan and she was from Dublin.

"Never mind," Seanin proclaimed. "Young Dile is up there. He'll find her."

I began to see a similarity between my father's line of work and my own. I began to appreciate that in my work I too would be irrigating, cultivating and reaping but for higher and more permanent stakes. The towering mountains and the sweaty bog had been replaced by high rise flats and concrete pavements. The rural peace had been overtaken by a bustling metropolis that never slept. The capital city, with its smell, noise and people who slagged me because of my accent and background yet challenged me to look them in the eye and protect them as well. My home which had called me back couldn't hold me. Now I was rushing away. In the city sprawl I had discovered peaks and valleys more appealing than any in my own county.

I saw other people in a new light too. Now, at last, I could identify with the ex-member, his tales of the guards, his reminiscences on my S S, his pride in the job and the affirmation he offered: 'you'll not be wasting your time down here'.

This was the life my mother had planned for me. She had been the instigator in chief, plotting my course like a master mariner. There would be no more arse and knees out of the pants for her second son. I would wear clean shoes, get a week's wage without haggling, have the chance to make something of myself and a pension at the end of my days. Going home offered a new perspective. The last year had been difficult, but I had survived and this was a powerful incentive to persevere. There was the realisation that I had changed, become more of a thinking rather than a doing person. Also, I had begun to appreciate a new life-style. Living with electricity and running water along with a gradual build up of confidence. Finally, I was convinced that before me lay boundless possibilities for excitement, experiences and adventure.

Coming home had put things in context and another encounter before I returned to Dublin underlined the change. I was driving to Killarney with my father and as we rounded the bend at the Laune Bridge we came upon a fight - two car loads of a wedding party, decked in dress suits, flaking hell out of each other. A year ago I would have stood back and enjoyed it or joined in. Now I automatically went between them and ended it.

My father and I drove off again:

"The law of the jungle," I said to him, quoting the S S.

"Ah no, boy", my father had an answer. "They're great friends usually, but now and again the sap rises in them. They knew who you were though."

Here it was again, an acknowledgement of who I was, what I had become, and what I could do.

Till then I had figured you needed the uniform to act. Now I knew different. In or out of the blue, once a policeman, always a policeman.

The last day of my holiday I cleaned out the cow house with my thoughts as potent as the sweltering manure. I realised they were straying progressively back to Dublin, flying away from my old home to my new home, to my station in the city.

What was happening up there? Who was the S S cracking the whip at? Any excitement? Hate to miss anything.

That was it. I stuck the pike in the heap of dung. New prongs had been added to my life - the Dublin Metropolitan - the tuning fork of the Garda Siochana.

My farewell to my parents was loving but not sad. Nobody ever willed a train to break the speed limit as we crossed the Irish plain and I drew nearer to Dublin. Roll on steel wheels, get me back to my constellation of characters. I missed you.

Action stations. Here I come.

Chapter 14 - ALTERCATION

Back in Dublin all I wanted was to be out all the time. Beat duty was a constant learning experience and there was the overpowering expectation of walking into something big. At parade time when the S S allocated beats, I was already ahead, charting my course. Usually I concentrated on the busiest locations, heading there immediately before running my eye over the rest.

The tensions of the job were ever-present. Every car horn or summons for assistance stirred the pulse. Dozens of people interrupted my patrol looking for directions. Then there were confrontations - reports of crime, traffic accidents or emergencies any of which could - as Little John said - lead either to a slap in the mouth - or a cup of tea.

Throughout that first summer and early autumn, the wave of lost souls looking for my guidance had served me a daily dollop of embarrassment - eventually compelling me to seek advice from The Bluffer:
"Ho, ho tourists. They're a summer pest."
"No," I cut in, "what I need is a..."
"Bluff," he finished my sentence before taking off:
"If you've no idea of directions, it's vital you don't let on. Remember, you're expected to know all things past, present and to come. Pretend to know, that's the secret. At the beginning, be supremely confident. Next, use confusion and distraction by getting them to look away - pointing as if their destination is just down the road is a good bluff. Then give them a spiel of right and left turns with a bevy of traffic lights thrown in. By the time you're finished, they'll be up the creek again, but too embarrassed to ask for a repeat.

"Another tip, if after all this they're still confused, tell them where they're aiming for is fierce awkward to get to, and they'll probably get lost again, so their best bet is to make further enquiries down the road a bit. Of course, if you're in a hurry or having a bad day, just tell them straight on, and then get lost yourself."

Typically this advice had me floundering as well, and I sought the council of Little John:
"Get a street directory. No messin.' If you don't know, tell them you've just arrived on transfer," he said.

The next day armed with his advice I went to the local bookshop and picked up a directory. It was slim and fitted into my back pocket but had almost a hundred pages of street names laid out in alphabetical order - with even three Killarney's - Street, Avenue and Parade to make me feel at home.

Directly opposite each address was a grid reference which corresponded to a designated section of a foldup map. Unfortunately when opened, the map sprang loose and stair-cased to the ground. This was too much and I made no purchase - as the prospect of rummaging through pages as the tourists waited did not appeal.

In the meantime I was getting to know the main tourist attractions in the city and already could put some visitors on the right track. The foreigners were difficult. They shovelled maps out of car windows into my face. But I had the biro to prod them on as I traced over the main routes.

The Irish rural native wasn't put off so easily. They wanted an itemised account of every gateway, tree and telephone pole en route. For them, all I could do was come clean... 'well, actually, I just arrived up yesterday myself'...

Some of the country people were from my own part of the world and occasionally if they spotted me, they jammed on the brakes in the middle of the road or pulled into the kerb without indicating, wound down the window and saluted me. I recall one such incident when a driver hailed me;
"Sergeant Jim O'Sullivan comes from north Kerry. A broader man than you entirely. I know he's stationed somewhere around the city. I told him I'd give him a shout when I was in the big smoke. I wonder would he be on duty around around here by any chance?"

One day I was caught out badly when a car sailed by me then spluttered to a halt and hooted me to its side. I noted the Kerry registration and realised the car belonged to a neighbour:

"Where's Croke Park?"

Here was a nettle burn, I wished the ground would swallow me up, as I hadn't a clue. Imagine a Kerryman living for three quarters of a year in Dublin and not having visited our city shrine! Wait until the news reached home.

But when I related this story against myself The Bluffer had a better one. A few years earlier his county had made it to Croker. Their opponents were first-timers and most pundits reckoned they would need more experience before they made the breakthrough. In the run up, The Bluffer had a field day goading the underdogs. On the day of the match, an opposition supporter stopped him for directions:

"How do I get to Croke Park?"

"Practice," was the crushing reply.

Since that afternoon in the cinema with The Bluffer, I had contempt for lie-ups. However, as time passed I discovered that they were as much part of pounding the beat as oxygen and movement. I remembered that day at home when the big policeman called. At the time it seemed as if he was only drinking tea and gossiping, but he was doing far more.

As The Bluffer often said: 'there's dossing and there's dossing'.

The S S kept in touch his own way. There was the example of his pub-raiding foray. The Bully had his own assessment of this:

"The S S.... Now, he gets dry once in a while and breaks out, it's also a reminder that he's master of all he surveys."

And indeed the S S was an expert at developing and updating his local knowledge. This was confirmed for me a few nights after the pub raid when the S S was called to the phone at the tail end of parade. The Bully filled me in:

"It's the publican from there a few nights ago, the S S has the hammer-lock on him." Within the public office the S S boomed out:

"Aye, you'd be wanting to get back to me on those few things, it'll be in your own interest, in the meantime mums the word."

Since my second month of duty the S S had begun to fire a daily ration of messages, cautions and files at me. These could refer to a simple enquiry or passing on an important message. It could be cautioning someone about an adjourned court case or to renew a licence. My favourites were files which could be anything from a lengthy interview to taking statements. They all gave me an excuse to knock on doors and speak to those concerned.

While this type of monitoring radiated from and was ajudicated on by the S S I felt every other member was watching me as well. In fact I had no sooner arrived at the station than the process of dissemination had begun. Beginning with my appearance, accent, habits and progressing to my attitude to authority, discipline and my duties - from day one every move I made was scrutinised. I knew that just like wearing the uniform, this universal scrutiny was another cultural initiation I had to accept. I also knew that from these judgements would come either distinction or disapproval.

From day one I had been intrigued by the peculiar use of the descriptive adjective which classified members into various categories within the job. The most prestigious accolade of all - above and beyond all rank - was to be called the sound or solid man. To gain this one had to be as steady as a rock under a landslide. Fearless in a row. Able to take the flak in court, or from a supervisor. Possess a sense of humour and be capable of giving and taking a slagging. One had to be competent on paper and have a good measure of common sense. Finally, one had to make spot-on decisions and think on their feet.

Such a sound man was perfection and by general consensus revered. From that point the classification percolated downward in order of demerit to encapsulate thick, round, windy, pernicity, gildy, bluffer, cribber, dosser and waster.

At this stage I could see myself falling into several of the foregoing categories from time to time. Sometimes I felt I was a cross between a bloodhound and a puppy, a lion and a lamb. Yes! even a bit mulish at times but mostly a willing workhorse.

Calling to people's houses was an education. They were often anxious when they saw a uniform at the door, until I explained who I was and the matter in hand, My role model again was the calm reassurance displayed by the big garda who came to our house to enquire about my bicycle.

"Good afternoon ma'am. Not a bad day. Can I talk to you? May I come in, please?"

This was my standard approach on the doorstep. I took it easy, recalling that my mother's initial response to the policeman was to leap to the defence of her home.

I remembered the way he behaved. First, the respect shown to my mother, the way he gave us time to settle in his presence, his relaxed manner, his gentle voice and economy with words. I remembered the sequence of chat, first the state of the country, the weather, only then came my interrogation with occasional concise questions. I remembered the non-appearance of the notebook to commit anything to paper until near the close of proceedings. The relaxation over tea, with the parish for dessert.

Once my business was out of the way the conversation usually drifted to the family I was visiting. Sometimes there was some query or problem and I was the right man in the right place. Normally this led to a cup of tea, a symbol of acceptance. Later, I felt the verdict would be: 'He wasn't too bad, only doing his job'.

Back in the station I continued to settle down. There was a distance between the married members who lived out and the live-in cuckoos of which I was the nestling. Numerically, the former were a lot stronger, a conscientious bunch whom I felt carried the bulk of the workload. We rubbed shoulders when our units crossed and usually there would be some carry over from the previous tour to ignite the parade room. Invariably this consisted of a bit of slagging or craic. Often I was the butt of this argy-bargy but I had to take it as I was still the recruit, parading at the end of the table, last to be told off and fair game for the stick of the day.

I was beginning to get to know some of the staff of the other units who worked opposite to me, starting or finishing as the case may be. When taking up duty it was noticeable how the finishing crew rushed to cast off the suit of armour, in contrast to the slow ponderous warm-up before we took up the slack. Most would have a few words, but this was more courtesy than interest. My pedigree remained unproved and I would win acceptability through progress.

While each unit was separate, independent, circuiting the clock, and each maintained their own was the premier unit, each had a grudging respect for the other. This was most evident when handing over the reins at the end of the tour. This was usually done proudly with the assurance that each had kept things ticking over:
"Anything big?"
"Ah no, a few prisoners, all charged and bailed. One lodger bunking down in trap two, drunk, not a bad sort, slip him when he sobers up and show him the short cut home. That chap annoying you in the near pen is a bad yoke. We lifted him from the nest an hour ago. There's a sheaf of bench warrants on the information clip for him. Pat Joe McCarthy will be in at ten bells to take him to the assizes."

This was typical repartee at the early morning turnover, perhaps followed by the S S's growl on discovering a member had gone sick resulting in rejigging the duties.

My live-in comrades held the most fascination and considered themselves superior in every way to their counterparts who lived out. The mess hall was the stamping ground where they pontificated on the events of the day, zealously guarding their preserve as if they were a protected species.

I realised that the mess hall was the cradle of comradeship where members were bonded together. Most especially after some exacting duty, they appeared there to draw breath, wash their hands, have a drink of water, play back the incident or just let off steam. This release was an almost daily occcurrence and a valuable insight into the wear and tear on members. Typically Little John described this function:
"Members returning from the field need to draw breath and slake the thirst of battle before returning to the fray."

Even though I wasn't competent enough yet to make a contribution, through listening I got valuable insights into the culture of the job and the people doing it. I was also struck by the atmosphere in the mess hall when a serious incident occurred. Virtually every member would light up with a suggestion, a motive, a culprit or a remedy - and many of the conclusions were spot on:

"The word on the street."
"A sham I was talking to."

Great stuff, but for me an impediment as I had zilch to contribute.

I'd hardly seen The Black since my return from leave, but within hours I had been updated on events. Indeed it was the talk of the station - a row in camp is always news. When one of the protagonists was The Black it meant a battle, but when the other was the SS, it was more like World War 111.

I had observed that the relationship between gardai and sergeants was at best lukewarm. In the case of The Black - the SS had his knife into him from the word go. They were like two grizzly bears stalking each other, and while the SS had bigger paws, The Black resorted to sniping guerrilla tactics:
"Oul' JCB hands. Dirty paws. Did you see the cut o' him?"
This referred to the the SS's hobby. He had acquired a small plot of land in which he cultivated vegetables. The Black latched on to this:
"With his maulers, he doesn't need any spade."

But the SS was the supreme dictator whom most members never dreamt of taking on. I had already received sound advice from The Owl:
"If the SS gives out medicine, swallow it down, close your mouth and walk away. No answering back or questioning his authority. He'll always have the last word."

Behind his back, of course, the SS was filleted daily. Niggles and undercurrents of unrest thrived in most stations. Within units they usually fizzled out, as members realised that if they didn't pull together the spin-off could be disastrous. But if the conflict crossed units, things usually got worse before they improved. Another crucial element was the personalities of those involved. Usually the more hard-nosed could hold out indefinitely until the sap was squeezed from their milder opponents.

Occasionally a wound developed, festered and grew septic. This was the core of the confrontation between the S S's regimental discipline versus The Black's disregard for even the slightest decorum. Two thick men at each other's throats.

"Thick men, also known as round men. They just keep rolling along grinding down the opposition," said The Owl.

Hostilities between the S S and The Black had broken out when I was on the border. The opening salvo had been fired by the S S a few days before Christmas when he had giving The Black a bit of a chawing over philandering drink - otherwise known as hawking.

Hawking was another heirloom impregnated into the culture of the job. It owed its origin to the early days of the force when times were bad and presents of food and drink were left in by the public. Christmas was open season when the hawks filled the sky more than at any other time of year. Exiled to the border I had missed the crack. Apparently the week before Christmas, the smell of strong drink filled the air and many local business people surrendered themselves to our station laden with barrels, bottles and cakes. The delivery of these consignments was fraught by casualties, as inevitably the ring of steel disintegrated and goodly portions of the precious cargo was skived away by individual members for their private consumption.

In the case of one disappearing shipment, the S S had picked up the scent and fixed responsibility on The Black. Never a man to stand back, the skipper met the Black on the corridor and went straight for the jugular. For once The Black sang dumb, disclosing only name rank and number. This intransigence infuriated the S S stoking him into a ferocious broadside which ruffled The Black but didn't rout him.

However, that night the S S waylaid his suspect in the back yard shifting his loot. This took The Black off his guard and startled him so much that he spewed out a rope of porter, spattering the wall beside his superior. The subsequent row would have ended in blows if the patrol car had not sped into the yard. This sent The Black skulking off, and left the S S in a quandary. If he did things by the book and put it on paper, the Christmas spirit would be non-existent. If he didn't act, he would lose face. And so it was on the following day an envelope was waiting for The Black. And it wasn't a Christmas card. More like a farewell card. The S S had shifted him to another unit.

Since my return I had observed The Black only at a distance. Apparently he had taken to the bottle like a Cow and Gate baby. I had long realised that drink played a significant role in the lives of many members, with only The Squirrel and myself on the abstention list.

One evening during my second month of nights doing car relief, I had a first hand example of The Black's thirst.

"Did you hear that?" He stuck the car to the street outside a substantial pub.

"No," I said.

"S..Sh.. There it is again. You ears aren't trained yet. There's a noise coming from the back of the pub there. You'd better check."

I jumped out and tore round the back clambering over empty barrels and scattering a flurry of wailing cats. But there was nothing to find so I made my way back to discover my partner loitering at the front door of the premises.

"Gimme your baton." He flung it at the alarm box causing it to blare out.

"Just to be on the safe side, that's the best way to get in the key holder."

Soon a bleary-eyed owner put in an appearance. Before he could open his mouth The Black laid a spiel on him:

"Just patrolling by there a while ago, the young lad here, just outta training, fitted out with fierce keen ear-flaps, swears he heard something round the back. I think it's all right but to satisfy him, you'd better open up."

Before I knew it, we were inside with The Black on the nearest high stool breasting the bar counter and ladling out instructions at me:

"You check the place out, upstairs first. Hurry up, this man has a bed to go back to."

Then to the keyholder;

"Fierce busy night, Fumes and dust rising to bate the band, Me throat is parched."

On my return The Black was still hanging me out to dry.

"There he is now. The hard. Insisted that there was something up, even though I told him your place was the most secure around. But he wouldn't listen. I don't know what the force is coming to. Men, how are you, boys more likely. Doesn't even take a drink. Aaahh, listen, I'm sorry for dragging you from your bed."

"You'll have one, lads."

The keyholder was resigned to the fact that he wouldn't get rid of the Black without setting them up. This he did, The Black lowering a few jorums in rapid order.

Sadly The Black and the drink were inseparable and as time went by I witnessed his dependance on the gargle. As a rule he bowled in at all hours well oiled up and took over the show in the mess hall.

"The Road Traffic Act. That's all the go now. Stop a vehicle. Run your eye over it. The driver squirming in the cockpit. A captive audience, you might say. No fun any more. Now I recall the three card trick, thimble-riggery, trick o' the loop. Ever hear of them country?"

I had to confess I hadn't, but he was off again:

"Kite flying, cock fighting, bear baiting, shaking and beating rugs, slides on ice or snow, ringing doorbells, piercing casks?"

I still shook my head but he was on another slant:

"Talk about cask piercing. Years ago I was stationed close to a brewery. There was a heatwave that summer, the sweat was running off me so my first mission was to make myself known to the staff of that establishment. Before long I had the low-down on the running of the place and naturally the brewers had to cough up for my extra attentiveness. At the start it was a few pints here and there, but a month of nights nearly withered me till I discovered after painstaking detective work that one of the grills was insecure. This was my passport to a daily session. After the break each morning I would stretch my legs to that particular grating on the path outside the brewery. My contact would unlock the grill and pass up a bucket of top class brew fresh from the malt. I would drink it down in one go the nectar cascading like Niagara... ah.. when I think of it.. those were the days."

During those drinking stories I felt out of place, unable to make a contribution. I felt it was unglamorous to be a teetotaller and there was an obligation to break out. However, a streak of obstinacy coupled with the promise made to the ex-member back home prevented me.

Around midday one day during the third quarter of January the S S collared me.

"I want The Black, he's on nights, he's up in the scratcher so dig him out. It's urgent."

This decree gave me my first peep into The Black's billet. If proof was needed of the desirability to remain on the dry, that visit did it. Inside was as dark as a confessional and I groped for the light switch. Immediately there was an eruption from a bed at the far corner of the room:

"Put off that friggin' light."

It was The Black roaring and wrestling with the bed clothes. I grinned as I made my approach, flinching as a boot flew past me smashing to smithereens the light bulb near his bed. His section was now bathed in the dull glow of the single bulb beside the door.

As I approached he remained immobile, gave a few groans then a long moan like a death rattle tremoured his body. Next, he ran his outstretched fingers across his face as if trying to prise off the top of his head. Yes, definitely in the horrors. Finally, he rolled sideways out of bed on to his knees. At first I thought he had the Morning Offering in mind, but one hand trailed under the bed to reappear clutching a bottle of Lucozade. With one swig he downed the contents:

"Am I supposed to be on duty?"

"No," I replied. "Your on nights."

"Thank Jaysus. What am I doing up, so?"

"The S S wants you downstairs."

At the mention of the skipper he turned away.

"Me head. Where's the cold tap?"

I stood back as he took off in a wobbly trot, his body crouched and palms outstretched as if at any second he would horizontal himself into a few press-ups. He filled the sink and buried his head in it before turning and shaking it like a water hen. It was the first time I'd seen him in the flesh and was amazed at the prime condition of his tawny body in contrast to his ravaged face.

Whirling away he grabbed a towel, threw it over his head like a prize fighter, climbed on to the balls of his feet, and began to prance, dance and sing.

Suddenly he turned to me:

"C'mon put up your dukes... The Brown Bomber versus the Crown Prince, Madison Square Gardens, December. 1935."

He was off shadow-boxing his reflection in the mirror before turning again and shaping up to me. My instincts had me raise my arms in defence. Immediately he adopted a prizefighting stance and stalked me with deadly intent. I aped his moves, my mind reeling back to training and all I had learned about fisticuffs. I kept my eyes on his as he swung at me with abandon. I realised he was deadly serious and all I could do was back away and turn him.

Suddenly a step on the corridor signalled the end of round one. The Black peeled away and stumbled back to the sink where he shovelled another basin of water over his steaming upper body. The Bully stood at the door, patting his watch, indicating that my sparring partner was needed downstairs. The Black turned to me:
"The S S - What's his beef now?"
"I don't know, but he wants you."
"How's his form?"
"He said t'was urgent."
"I'd better face him. Did you see ere a pair of socks walking round?"

Woollen twins, definitely deserving the long service medal for devotion to his crubes lay plastered on the radiator.
"Aw, not them. The window sill and the other radiator should have an underpants lying at half mast. That new fangled Burco is a great yoke. I did my laundry in it last night."

In fact his illicit use of the Burco boiler was round two in the prize fight of the new year. This time there was no sparring. The S S hit him with a barrage so vicious that the paint nearly peeled off the walls. The S S was livid. Earlier when he had turned the spout in the new boiler to scald his grain of tea, he had noticed the discoloration and immediately smelt a rat in more ways than one.

Well, he drank no tea but had The Black for lunch instead.

The ensuing brawl lasted well over the regulation three minutes. It spiced up the on-going saga between the two and while round two went to the S S he was placed in an unenviable position in the overall bout. He had already forced The Black to cross units, now he would have to take further action. But he was a wily operator so he played down the issue, merely administered a public bawling out and humiliated his sub-

ordinate into cleaning and replenishing the Burco. It was no knockout, and The Black, revitalised by the sympathy vote reserved for the down-trodden, was still well ahead on points:
"The Black has done it again. Did you hear the latest. Ha. Ha."

These incidents broke the monotony. We waited for round three until the Black administered a seemingly permanent knockout blow.

Shortly after Christmas, a duck had arrived for the S S compliments of the new yard man. They had discovered a mutual interest - poultry - Rhode Island reds and pullets. The yard man also favoured duck who he claimed laid the most famous blue eggs in the city. It wasn't long before the S S was breakfasting each morning on a fresh duck egg.

Early in the new year S S duck took up residence in the station. This was contrary to regulations but nobody dared question the S S's authority. His latest relation was confined to a tea chest covered with lettuce wire and billeted in a backyard shed.

This time from drink, socks and underwear, The Black progressed to more devious skul-duck-ery. One morning when the S S came on duty he found lying in state on the kitchen table the remains of the station duck with a note picked to its backside which read: 'S S. Duck. RIP'.

On this occasion there were no messengers needed as the S S took The Black's door off the hinges and slewed him almost out of existence.

After the duck's demise a pall of disquiet hung like incense over the station. The S S took long walks to the scene of outrage in the back yard. He had lapsed into a cold, calculating silence, his face heavy and brood-ing, more potent than any fury. The Bully's bulletins were brief reports of dark, muttering tantrums and fuming monosyllables, while rumours abounded of heads rolling and sworn enquiries. Those who knew the score said that one way or another The Black's carcase would be cooked.

Although The Black appeared unshaken by his death sentence, he began to favour the gargle even more. While on duty he kept up a brusque, hard-man stance. Off duty he was in rag order, a daily heavy drinker until around midnight he would barge into the messhall turning the place into a frenzy with wild tales of law and disorder.

One day at the brow of the stairs I saw The Black with an arm lock on Files accusing him of carrying stories to the S S. As a rule nobody minded this summary dealing with Files who had a long record of violating breaches of The Offences Against The Police Act. While it was acceptable to slag and talk about each other, even crossing units, running with scandal to a supervisor or officer was beyond the pale. That day The Black was like a bull with nostrils flaring, mouth dripping hatred.
"You're nothing only a natterjack toad. The leaving's of cuckoo's spit, I'll rip the gonads outta you."

I went between them and Files slid along the wall to safety.

About this time another individual who crossed units when The Black was shafted came to my attention. He had been a quiet, unobtrusive type who barely acknowledged my presence. But when I returned from the border I noticed the transformation. He had either grown a few inches or straightened himself up. He had cleaned up his act with a weekly haircut and spent his time fawning over the S S. Little John gave me the low-down:
"That's The Spoofer. His most fatal flaw is that he talks faster than he thinks. In other words, he's a mouth. To add to his misfortune he hasn't much between the ears.

"You see, it so happens that the interviews for the skippers are coming up later on, and the Spoofer is making a burst. Promotionitis. That's his problem. It's the same every time interviews are in the air. He suffers from delusions far above his station. He'll be at it now for all he's worth, throwing shapes at the S S and the top brass and trying to stroke the next rank.
"You watch him crucifying the public and spoofing to all and sundry about his great return of work. Another thing, he'll be missing first Fridays from now on, doing nine of them up in the church. He'll try anything. Sure he was at the same crack during the last run up for all the good it done him. Afterwards he was like a sick cat whinging, blaming the system, the board and everyone but himself.

"Unfortunately no matter how many arses he licks, he hasn't a snowball's chance in hell of making the list. There's one or two in the clique around here being groomed for promotion and the rest of the field just won't be there at the finish."

Spoofers, grievances, stroking, cribbing, cliques. Before training I had no inkling of these words but they were to develop into some of the most emotive expressions in my vocabulary. What struck me forcibly was how the word promotion affected even the most placid individual and guaranteed an opinion from everyone in the mess hall.

A few days later at a checkpoint I had personal experience of The Spoofer's transformation. Half-apologetically he slithered up the driver's side of the flagged down vehicle:
"Good morning sir, fine day... sorry for the inconvenience."
He leaned forward placatingly, placing two palms on top of the open window as he continued:
"Who would you be now? I think I know the face."

Identity supplied, the chat would become even cosier, with The Spoofer calling the driver by first name, and giving only the merest glance at the car:
"I'm sure you've noticed John, that ould tyre there needs a bit of a remould, great invention that, and you might throw in your driving licence and certificate of insurance or exemption to some station. You're own station. Would that suit? Yes? Good. That would be? Yes... I know it well. Do that so, good man. No hurry with the documents, you've ten days whenever you're passing. I'll let you go now. The day is brightening a bit, thank God."

Not a notebook in sight as The Spoofer wished the driver God Bless and safe home.

However, the exhaust fumes had no sooner singed his trouser legs when he was all action. Out flashed the notebook and be began to recite aloud:
"The chancer. Name and address, number of car. Yes. I have those. Offence? Rear tyre excessively worn. Aye, after the rub up he got, no way will be bother producing. Ah ha, there's one sham who'll be definitely hearing from me."

In spite of all these goings on the passage of time decreed I was making progress. There was nothing definite but I felt a smidgen of acceptance since the wife-beating arrest. Meanwhile the station waited for the S S to get dug out of The Black. The Owl as usual had a wise word on the pair of them:

"We're our own worst enemies, supposed to be protecting the public but we can't even look after ourselves."

Around that time an incident showed the S S at his most potent. It concerned a baker who had come under the spell of the District Detective Unit. The lure of crime detection had taken over this character, body and soul. This affected his profession to such a degree that his employer was sick and tired of reminding him that he was paid to leave his fingerprints on the dough and not burn all the evidence in the oven. But he was wasting his breath as the baker spent his day craning out the window looking for potential thieves in the nearby carpark.

At the slightest suspicion he would abandon his bread and sally forth to seek out villains. The word was he had a path worn to the detectives' door with whispered information on would-be criminals.

In the end he got carried away and arrived to the S S with a cringing prisoner in tow:

"I arrested him for the detectives." He informed the S S.

"What did you do wrong son?" the latter enquired.

"I got caught." was the snappy reply.

"Simple larceny, Section 2." The baker piped up, "lock him up and let him stew. He's done a stack."

Well, if he had he escaped on that occasion as the S S cut up rough giving him and the pseudo-detective their marching orders out of the station and later slating the plain clothes members for giving the job a bad name.

As the new year gathered momentum, I began to notice a difference in the S S's attitude towards me. I realised he was giving me a chance to prove myself. I felt my pedigree was being monitored as he sought to inculcate me into the fold. I also realised that from these judgements either a distinction or repudiation would eventually be conferred.

But I was still adrift in a turbulent sea of influences and desperately seeking my own safe passage. In this respect I decided to proceed with care, keep my mouth shut, options open, talk to my three wise men, (The Staff, The Owl and Little John) and watch the S S like a hawk.

Chapter 15 - INSTRUCTION

The conflict between the S S and The Black remained number one on all popularity charts. Daily the rumour machine spewed out reams of gossip. The Black was thinking of lashing in a transfer, but the prime boys kept talking him out of it. They were the cute ones working on a hidden agenda, as while he held the spotlight, they could get away with murder. The S S remained his usual imperturbable self, though it was noticeable he had taken to leaving his office, patrolling the corridors and carrying out spot checks in the messhall. Word was he was bent on flushing out The Black. But he was keeping tabs on me as well.

Prior to my stint on the border I had entered a few summonses under the Road Traffic Act which were due for hearing the first week in January. On the day of my transfer I had one leg on the bus when the S S hauled me off:
"You have a number of summary prosecutions pending. I'll arrange for adjournments so you needn't attend court."

He met me on my return from leave:
"You're back. Them summonses are up shortly. Check your pigeon hole for the new date. Caution those involved, and don't let it slip your mind."

I did as bid only to discover the court was on the next day. Grabbing the phone, I rang the station covering the defendant's address and requested that he be cautioned for court.

The next day I attended the assizes but the defendant did not appear. I gave my evidence, secured a conviction and he was fined a few quid. I thought no more about the incident until a few weeks later when The S S hauled me in:
"Them summonses you had pending. You never cautioned the defendant to be in court. He was on to the boss this morning with a major whinge

209

and there's a stinker of a file on the way. Why didn't you caution him?"
"I did," I said. "I arranged to have it done."
"How did you do that?"
"I left word with someone in his local station to do the needful."
"There's no such person as someone in this job. His identity, name or number? Let's have it."
I had neither and he laid into me.
"That please explain has horns on it. You'll be blocked at the very least and lucky to get away with just that..."
"What can I do?" I said, and my chagrin must have showed, as his growl changed to a kinder tone:
"You've a long time to go in the job and there's a valuable lesson to be learned in all this. At least you're a man, not afraid to own up to a mistake. Some of the hardchaws round here would do well to follow suit. Now, here's a bit of advice. Remember, no matter how bad things seem, there's nearly always a way out. In this case, here's what you'll do. Pay the fine yourself. It'll be a lesson for you. I'll look after the paperwork. It'll be between us. All right..."

I agreed immediately, thankful to get a pardon and particularly for the opportunity to preserve my dignity in the messhall. I could imagine the repartee from some, if word seeped out:
'Did you hear the one about the recruit? Bringing people to court and paying their fine himself'.
Fair play to him he was as good as his word and not a whisper was ever mentioned about my mistake.

More important, though, was the part played by the S S. It seemed I had stumbled on a way of getting through to him. My involuntary cry for help had drawn a response. He had saved me a certain blocking.

My beat was still there to be prowled and I was getting to know a few locals. Since my fretful first days, I had worked hard and had become adept at focusing on people. The majority reciprocated. Older people nearly always had time for a few pleasant words. The middle-aged were more preoccupied. Teenagers and the younger fry gave a mixed response to my uniform, from admiration, to blatant disregard to showing off.

At this stage maintaining maximum visibility, stopping cars and covering the trouble spots was becoming child's play. With each passing day I was becoming more aware. However, I craved excitement and believed that out there some notable event existed with my name plastered on it.

My sometime companion was The Bluffer. Once I saw him at a distance standing in the shady side of the path and headed in his direction. On arrival he had evaporated into thin air. It was only after a minute inspection of the ivy-clad wall, I discovered a small section had crumbled and facilitated his escape. He was impossible to find if he didn't want discovery, covering his tracks so effectively that snaring him was out of the question.

"I didn't see you on your beat at 4pm. Where were you then?" The young sergeant enquired one day.

"Aw, but I saw you Sarge. You were outside the supermarket at the time. It didn't seem like you were looking for me."

He knew every inch of his patch and was a real will-o-the-wisp, leading the section sergeants a merry dance as they sought to locate and mark him down on their beat cards.

Indoors he licked up unashamedly to the S S. Indeed, after a tiff between them it was an education to monitor his attempts to get back on the right hand of God. His favourite ploy was to choose a situation where the S S had issued some controversial edict. Later within earshot of his superior, The Bluffer would launch into an eulogy of praise of his superior, ending:

"It amazes me how one head can carry all that man knows."

Since my first arrest The Bluffer seemed to have abandoned any ideas of initiating me into his regime, but still displayed great pleasure in reminding me of his multiplicity of lie-ups and underlining my lack of progress in that field. In a strange way, I was growing fond of him, but had my mind made up. For me dossing was tedious. I was anxious and fidgety to be out and about.

One afternoon early in the New Year the old lady in the tiny corner shop which was on my beat crooked her finger at me.

"Do us all a favour around here, son. There's a gang carrying on at night across the road. They're not even locals so you might put the run on them."

I had noticed a group acting the maggot once or twice and had asked The Bluffer about them:
"Ah, they're gurriers, young gougers, they're harmless."

The shopkeeper's complaint came to a head a few nights later when I passed by and gave them the eye. In return they avoided my gaze and quietened down. Continuing I rounded the corner and slid in under an awning tightening up against the door. Almost immediately, the raucous pell-mell came after me. I retraced my steps towards them. Two ran, but the biggest and boldest stood his ground.
"Go home.. Now," I ordered. He gathered himself up as if to go, took a half step, and stopped.
"Why should I? It's a free country."
"You're acting the blackguard, committing a breach of the peace, and I'm telling you to go."

This moved him on a few more steps, but he was still full of insolence, so I gave him another nudge:
"Your name, address and date of birth?"
Grudgingly he muttered the particulars.
"Father's name?"
That stung and he dropped his lower lip. At least there was some bit of discipline at home. That decided me:
"Now, I'm cautioning you about your behaviour. There's to be no more hanging around here. If you persist, I'll have to take action. Do you understand?"
He didn't like being told what to do, but I kept hustling him.
"For the last time, I'm telling you. Go home."
He walked a few paces but turned on me again:
"You're making a show of me, I'm doing nothing."

I had my cape in my hand. I swung it in his direction causing him to turn away and bend forward. His backside was too inviting and I connected with it with my boot. That put the run on him. Over in the shop a few people stood admiringly:
"Good on you guard. That'll put manners on him."

That night the teenagers father called to the station enquiring for me and picketed outside until I arrived. I expected confrontation but told him what happened. He accepted my explanation without question:

"I'm, a widower and out all day working. He's a bit wild, so I appreci-ate your interest. Anytime you see him hanging around, put the run on him," he said.

The lady shopkeeper and myself became great friends and through her I soon knew everyone in the immediate vicinity. She reckoned I was a bit on the thin side and needed fattening up, and so she tempted me with bars of chocolate, which I politely declined. Afterwards, anytime I stuck my head in, she pulled out a large bar of Cadbury's Dairy Milk, splin-tered it with her bony hands and scattered the squares in front of me: "There now, I can't sell it, so you'll have to take it."
I tried to return the compliment by buying a few messages.

By this time I had got to know others who worked the beat. These included the milkman, postman, night watchman and rat catcher. There were others introduced by colleagues, but it became obvious I would have to develop my own contacts.

There was one regular I made no progress with. An old man, he never looked at me, only gathered speed and glided away from me when we met on my patrol. Whenever I looked expectantly at him, he ignored me, keeping his head down as if he had lost his last shilling. There and then I determined to salute him the next time we met. A few days later as he approached, I had my speech prepared.
"Good morning, not a bad day, thank God."
But at the critical moment, I froze. Struck dumb by his lack of recogni-tion, my intentions paralysed by his inflexible reaction to my presence. It was an unusual sensation, as if my uniform prohibited me from mak-ing free with an unwilling respondent.

I regretted the missed opportunity a few weeks later when I was back on night duty. Around midnight I was summoned to a traffic accident. On arrival, I knew it was serious. The stricken car driver languished across the bonnet of his car. The pedestrian scrunched up on the roadway like a baby in the womb. It was my silent friend and I knew instantly he would never avoid my eye or anyone else's again. Loosening his shirt collar, I felt blood seep from the corner of his lips through my fingers. Groping gingerly I tried to parcel him up in the worn raincoat which he had filled adequately, but now seemed massively oversized. Suddenly I sensed the touch of his hand. It was cold and tremulous but instantly

213

recognised my presence. I breathed the Act of Contrition.

"O my God, I am heartily sorry...."

Soon there was the hustle and bustle as the ambulance came and went.

Afterwards I felt very alone. The sightseers were three-deep but as had been the case in the past I felt very isolated. As if by divine intervention, assistance came from an unlikely source. The S S materialised out of the gloom.

"I thought you might need a hand. How're you getting on?"

I showed him the progress in my notebook under the street light.

He grunted acknowledgement, then said in more reverential tones:

"The hospital was on. He's passed away. You've a fataler."

That put a clog in my mouth and caused me to drop my head. He revved me up with his familiar trademark, a rap with the back of his hand on my side arm:

"C'mon. Let's have a look."

As he prowled round the scene, he kept me talking:

"What's the first thing you did?"

"The Act of Contrition."

"Good. We could all do with a prayer or two at the end."

"Witnesses?"

He threw that at me over his shoulder as he moved round the scene taking all in.

"Three," I replied. "I have the particulars. They are.."

"Point of impact?" he cut across me.

I had that as well, and pointed to the load of muck and glass before ushering him on to where the body had lain, and a dark smear staining the road.

"Where's the driver?"

"He went home. But I have his particulars. He's producing his documents at our station."

"Hmm, imagine how he'll sleep tonight. You held the car?"

"Yes, we pushed it up in the grass margin over there. It'll have to be examined, won't it?"

"Of course, let's have a look."

I watched as he scrutinised the vehicle. It was as if he were trying to locate the exact portion of the car that had come in contact with the

deceased. Then he had a go at the tyres. Afterwards he strode off flashing his torch along the route taken by the vehicle before the accident.
"Skid marks?" I prodded. "They're not back there, they measure approximately thirty feet up ahead."
By way of reply he scraped the sole of his shoe along the road:
"Slippery. Road surface damp. Was there a mist at the time?"
"Yes."
"Did you make a note of that?"

He had read my mind. I had forgotten that detail and now wrote it down.
"Measurements?" He whipped out the round measuring tape gave me the ring and my head to the edge of the roadway. He called out the distance which I copied. "There now, behind your shoulder, the telegraph pole is a permanent landmark. Measure from the point of impact. You'll need a good rough sketch of the scene."
Then he called out the measurements of the skid marks and the distance between them and the position of the body and the point of impact. Finally there was the width of the roadway. I used two pages of my notebook to draw the sketch and note the measurements.

Next he summoned me to him.
"This is serious stuff, a tragic accident involving loss of life. Two different families are going to be very upset tonight and for a long time to come. You're involved as well in a way. You'll be fortunate if both parties don't end up tugging outta you, looking for answers. Do all the simple things right. Get it all down in your notebook and you won't go far wrong. Tomorrow you'll have to go to the mortuary with a member of the deceased's family and get them to identify the remains. Then you'll have to attend the post mortem and do likewise for the pathologist. Let me warn you, autopsies aren't for the faint-hearted. But I think you'll be up to it. All right?"
He looked hard at me, and even in my brittle state I was conscious of the enormous effort he was making on my behalf. At that instant I would have agreed to almost any suggestion he made.

As we walked back to the station he repeated his earlier advice calmly, again explaining the significance of the occurrence, the loss of life, the effect of those involved, matters of conscience and guilt. Finally he talked of the effects on myself. I would experience sadness, upset and shock:

"This may be a criminal matter, if not a civil one. Some day you could be summoned to the green-domed courthouse and asked to explain all." Here he halted, turned and faced me:

"As a matter of fact, here's a headline for you. In any serious case, think of them courts, particularly the higher up ones, and work backwards. If you do, you won't make many mistakes.

"Now getting back to this fatality, the parties involved will probably be looking for you over the next few days so it'd be better to work days for a while."

"What can I say to them?"

"Very little, except offer your sympathy and keep them abreast of the ongoing investigation. If you have a problem, give me a shout. The car driver now?" He stood again: "Did you give him the oral warning?"

"No." I said. "He was decimated so I got him a lift home and told him drop into me tomorrow night at ten bells. I can do the needful then."

"Good lad."

He was leading me through each step of a very serious investigation. This was real training. The master tutor at work, allowing space between each comment or question to make sure it sank in. No rush. Take it easy. The way I had expected things to be. It was a priceless lesson and I concentrated on every word.

We walked in silence for a while, my thoughts racing over the events of the past hour. As if reading my mind he doled out enough time to reflect before speaking again:

"The witnesses now... they're important. It might be worthwhile to bring them back to the scene before they make their statements. Anyway, I'll give you a hand with them. Now, first we'll have to make out a preliminary report for the Super."

On arrival at the station he reverted to his imperious self. First he read the messages The Bully had stacked carefully on the cover of the occurrence book. All the time he beckoned me to remain in his shadow. Finally he loaded up the typewriter and without halting he banged out the heading on the paper:

"An Garda Siochana. Dublin Metropolitan Area."

Next it was our division, district, station, and date all on the right hand side. Then he placed his outstretched hands over the keyboard and laid this gem on me.

"Now we'll type little and say a lot. Never forget when you go to press there'll be others reading your report with fresh minds. Some of them won't be interested in what you did, but what you did wrong."

Then he put his head down and rattled the machine into action. He addressed the report to himself, flicked the lever on to the heading: 'Fatal traffic accident at...'

Then he was off banging away calling out here and there for details from my notebook. Near the bottom of the page he read it aloud and it was perfection. Factual yet concise. Then he administered the final accolade, typed my name rank and long number at the conclusion.

He was the first member to adorn a document with my full rank. Next he addressed the report to the Superintendent. Finally he turned it out of the machine, segregated the pages before laying them carefully on the table.

"Now sign that, and keep a copy."

Later when I went to bed I thought again of the life of the man who has died. What were his last thoughts? Why did he appear so aloof? What was bothering him? Sleep eluded me and my mind took off on a constant trawl over each individual second of the incident culminating in inconclusive question and answer time. Eventually I entered a kind of dream world from which suddenly I would bolt upright, grab my notebook and feverishly check some point only to discover it was covered.

Next day I had a visit from the old man's daughter. He had been living with her and she had her hands full taking care of him. He was very independent, slipping away at every opportunity and inclined to wander. The fact that he was almost totally blind had been a real worry; it was good to able to tell her that I had met her father on my travels. She had a good cry, and by the time we went to the hospital mortuary she had left a lot of grief behind. I brought her home and she showed me her father's room. Through this incident I experienced at first hand the uniqueness of an occupation that allowed me a peek behind the curtains of a home where tragedy had visited and view the impact on the family.

Later that evening the morgue attendant welcomed me to his domain. "Your first wan," he indicated towards the old man laid out on the slab. I could only nod in agreement as I stood reverently in the presence of death.

"You'll get used to it after a while."

But I found the whole scenario rather offensive. The pristine hygiene, the unnatural function about to be performed, above all, the cool detachment on the attendant's face. Having been at a few wakes at home I expected some display of reverence but there was not a single holy picture or crucifix in sight.

The pathologist bustled in, asked me a few questions about the accident before moving on to identification. I was free to go.

Back on the street the sight of live people going about their business was revitalising.

This then was my first official date with death. Admittedly I had been in its presence many times. Whenever anyone died at home my mother was sent for to lay them out. From my mid-teens I went with her, my job being to lift and turn the corpse to enable it to be washed and dressed.

But this was totally different. This was duty. The protection of life and the investigation or explanation of death. Where did my responsibilities begin and end? How could I deal personally with the effects of this shocking experience? Was I supposed to be coated in an impervious shellac that rendered me immune to such incidents, and, in my case, had they forgotten that final varnish?

Another thought that confused me was the attitude of the public to a fatal accident. Maybe it was shyness, but how could they stand there and not offer any help? Death, violence, suffering, it was all dumped in our lap. They caused it, we cleaned it up. Who did we go to when we were in difficulty? Or were we meant to suffer in silence? I had no answer.

However, I was thankful for two pillars of support, first the S S whose bulky presence sheltered me, and who had been transformed from an cantankerous old codger into an understanding human being. Secondly, The Staff who sought me out that evening:

"You've had a fataler. Don't bottle it up. Get it out of your system. It's never easy dealing with loss of life; they say if you get used to it, you cease to be a human being. Keep the head up and work away."

Later that evening when I visited the scene, I discovered nature had its own way of tidying up. The sudden squall earlier had washed the dark red stains from the road. All that remained now were the tiny crystals of glass sparking dramatically against the ebony tar.

As the days passed I noticed the S S was keeping a special eye on me. A few days later when I was alone in the mess hall, he took me for a walk in the yard where he had more wise words for me:
"You're suffering a bit. There's nothing printed in any book about the job that'll explain how you feel. All you can do is rely on the support of people. Just as the driver of the car and the old man's family are in bits, so are you. Talk it out and get it off your chest. Then try and settle it in your mind and stop picking at it. You'll get used to living with it after a while. It was the same for all of us the first few times. In this job there's no facility to condition against such happenings and no time to dwell on things. You must carry on till your next experience which again could come when you least expect it. Some say we become immune to such happenings. I suppose we do in a way. I often think it's a pity that happens."

I found the on-going investigation was good therapy. A chance to express the memory of the accident out of my system. Taking statements from witnesses was another learning experience. the S S went through them painstakingly, then sent me back to their doors with almost a dozen queries of ambiguity to clear up.

In accordance with his edicts I liaised with the families involved and felt the absence of any blame on either side most commendable. I had anticipated feelings of antipathy from the family of the deceased but they exhibited a serene resignation which made my enquiries somewhat easier.

About a fortnight later I realised that the car driver was still deeply upset. That spurred me to considering a reconciliation between himself and the family of the dead man. I floated the idea by, The S S and he gave it his blessing, provided both parties were in agreement. The initiative worked well and I felt particularly good about it.

After that a sense of peace descended on the station. 'Calm before the storm', said Little John, when I asked if hostilities had ceased between the S S and The Black.

But before the month of nights was up The Black hit the headlines again. It had been on the cards for a spell. Already the S S had handed him the half sheet for a few indiscretions and word was he was to be shafted to the back of beyond.

Anyway, he went from bad to worse until finally he caved in. It was his atrocious driving that did for him. One evening while on a driving patrol as he rounded a corner he met a sturdy concrete wall. Immediately on impact he turned to the member with him:
"How're you?"
"All right," the other replied.
"Well then," continued The Black, "any second now I'm going unconscious. When I do ring for an ambulance and if anyone asks you what happened, tell them you were writing in the car log book and didn't see a thing."

The Black was duly carted off to hospital and the crumbled remains of the patrol car towed back to the station. Within a few hours a full investigation began and a retinue arrived at his bedside.
"What happened?" The six million dollar question. The Black turned his head gingerly and stared wanly at the speaker.
"Ooohh, me back, me head.. ooh no, me memory. I'm awful sorry but I just can't remember a thing."

And so he lay in state with his injuries and his recollections proving mighty slow healers.

While The Black was hospitalised, The Bluffer plied us with a litany of his motoring convictions. Years ago The Black wrapped the patrol car around a telegraph pole on a straight stretch of road with no other vehicle involved. Everyone waited for his explanation but he remained tight-lipped until directed to put pen to paper, he reported as follows:
"I was proceeding on my patrol at a reasonable rate of speed when suddenly a cat ran onto my path pursued by a dog. Naturally I took corrective measures to avoid a collision which would certainly have ended in loss of life. Unfortunately, I crashed in the process."

The Super' wrote back. A snorter.

"I'm not happy with the explanation as to the cause of this accident, and particularly with the follow-up enquiries. I now direct the following:

"An immediate and exhaustive search of the area should be carried out with a view to locating the uncontrolled dog. In this regard I direct your attention to the register of householders which should be part of your station records. Also, as you are no doubt aware the Finance Act 1925 requires that a licence must be taken out annually for each canine over one month of age. Now if this legislation is being enforced a cursory check with the Revenue Commissioners coupled with a few enquiries at the scene should lead to the identification of the dog. Report developments forthwith."

This was buckshot, shrapnel liable to blunderbuss the peace and tranquillity of the station. Undoubtedly it would leave supervisors and gardai at each other's throats if a plausible explanation was not available. It could lead to a visit from the officer and more than the dogs in the street would be howling. As so often in the past, The Black came up with the goods:

"Unfortunately I can't describe the dog. I just glimpsed him out of the corner of my eye. Anyway, it was the cat I was trying to avoid."

On another occasion he came a cropper when serving in a country station. This time his excuse was that while driving down a country lane a sheep jumped over a small wall on to the bonnet of the car damaging it badly. His Super' wrote back:

"Given the amount of damage caused to the official vehicle I am inclined to think the sheep was a horse and it jumped over a six foot wall."

For my part I was bewildered at the ongoing enmity between the SS and The Black. One day the opportunity arose and I asked the The Owl, why couldn't they sort out their difficulties man to man?

I got my answer:

"First," he said, "there's rank involved. Then there's reputation. But most of all, it's the different breeding. The Black is a gallery man, good for the crack and possessing a certain native cunning but not over-endowed with grey matter. He's sailed close to the wind throughout his service.

221

"The S S is different. He is no fool. He is a deeply proud man who will steer a straight course all the while aware that The Black and his influences would destroy and plunder his charts given half a chance. That's why he's on his neck and will eventually keelhaul or shipwreck him."

I decided that given my recent experiences if there was a ballot between The Black and the S S for flavour of the month my vote would go to the latter.

Chapter 16 - DISCRETION

Spring was giving way to early summer but the longer days did nothing to urge The Black to leave his hospital bed and rejoin the fold. But as someone said who'd be in a hurry back to the wooden spoon? There was no spring in the S S's step either. He sat back like a big tom-cat and waited.

The image of the fatal accident still haunted and exploded into life at waking time each morning. By this time I had prepared a file on the case for the state solicitor.

I still had my beat and lots of advice to chew on. I was amazed how statements which I considered as woolly at first hearing now gave me food for thought. 'One day you'll walk around a corner straight into a big case. It'll be the making or breaking of you'.

I couldn't wait.

One day my attention was drawn to a fracas outside a new supermarket.
"I've been robbed," the irate shopkeeper blazed at me, "there she is gettin' on the bus. Quick, nab her."
I was off like a greyhound, missing the bus but not the car behind it. Janey! This was great, directing the driver in and out of the traffic, holding my hand on his horn. Ahead the bus trundled along, with the conductor and passengers staring back at our keystone cop chase. Eventually the bus stopped. Without even thanking my jarvey, I jumped aboard and grabbed the prisoner. She was only a slip of a woman, and her wan, pale face was full of shame:
"I'm sorry," she kept whimpering at me under her breath.

I grabbed her bag, the evidence, containing a pound of sausages, a loaf of bread and a half pound of butter. It didn't matter. She was a thief and my excitement was underlined by the butter melting into my sweaty palm.

She came quietly and soon we were in the station.

As usual the S S celebrated the arrival of a prisoner by rising to his massive height. But on this occasion there was no rejoicing. To my surprise he showed scant regard for what I thought was a fairly good piece of police work. Somewhat taken aback, I laid the facts before him - with trimmings:

"She stole items of food from the supermarket and tried to get away on a bus. I had to commandeer a passing car to chase her for nearly a quarter of a mile until I made the capture."

He considered the prisoner, then gave me a look of intense irritation as if I had lagged his mother. Suddenly he addressed the woman:

"C'mon in here, me oul' segocia."

Almost as an afterthought, he threw over his shoulder at me:

"Make a sup of tay."

He brought her into the parade room and sat her down. I expected the grilling to start immediately - how many times had she stole, and so on. But there was no inquisition.

I went to make the tea.

Later I found him back at his desk roaring down the telephone:

"You should be ashamed of yourself. You and your likes sprouting up outta nowhere squeezing the life out of the little corner shops that fed you. Screwing every deuce out of unfortunate wimmin with young families. Building up profits without a thought for the poor. Now, I'm warning you, don't get me going or I'll be down to wrap that hank of sausages round your miserable neck."

I stopped outside the door? What was happening? Here was the opposite to all I had learned. Sure the women had mouths to feed, but she had been caught stealing, and even though it wasn't much, it was still a crime.

I went in with the tea:

"Where's the biscuits?"

Janey! I thought. I'd never seen biscuits in the station. But the local shop had them and soon I was back with a packet.

They were not for the S S

"Come here, me oul' craythur. You're famished."

He opened the packet and offered tea and biscuits to the prisoner. I was ignored and watched amazed. A prisoner being hand-fed by the S S. I couldn't understand it.

Suddenly he turned, snagged my upper arm and hauled me along the corridor and into the back yard.

"The common touch. Ever hear of it?"

I hated such riddles and just stared at him.

"We must never lose the common or human touch," he continued. "What it boils down to is this - we are human beings empowered to deal with fellow mortals who have sinned against society. Can you relate to that?"

He looked hard at me.

"You're not getting my drift? Right, we'll start again. By and large, we enforce the law and line up those responsible for punishment. Do you understand that?"

"Of course," I replied. "That's what I learned in training."

"Ah yes, training," he cut across me. "But this is the real world, and a most imperfect one at that. We mustn't forget that many underprivileged people have particular difficulties. This is understandable when you consider problems such as unemployment, poor living conditions, lack of education, pressure to survive. Our patch is full of such unfortunates. I know that poor woman in there and all belonging to her for years. She comes from poor but honest stock and there is no way she would take a penny's worth without paying for it unless she was desperate. Also this was her first time, and everyone deserves a chance. What I'm talking about is discretion. Do you understand?"

I understood. I was being introduced to another dimension... the grey area. People committed crime and I was expected to act. But there was more, another layer was being superimposed on the training lectures. I now must examine all circumstances and judge each case on its merits. I should be just but fair. Everyone deserved a chance.

Along with this lesson, I learned another. It was necessary to take it easy on my patrol, to slow down, and where possible give more thought to

225

my actions. There was more to the job than capturing prisoners. I could advise, admonish, caution - all discretionary powers dependant on circumstances. The stringent powers drummed into me in training were now being balanced out by first hand practical experience. All of a sudden I remembered the chance I'd been given half-a-dozen years before by the big policeman sitting in our kitchen and the words of Little John fell into place. 'Learn by experience. Learn by mistakes'. Yes, and yes again.

Discretion - the half way house between arrest and summons marked my first shop-lifting case indelibly on my mind and revealed the humanity of the S S. He was a man like my father who would take an iron bar to an neighbour one day but would help pull his animal from a bog hole the next. The S S too would be hard on the villian, but showed an abundance of goodwill for genuine people in distress:

"If you see someone out late at night and think they're up to something, bring them in and we'll find something for them."

Never happy with that statement by the S S, I had run it by Little John: "Ah yes, I've heard that being trotted out by the S S when he's a bit off colour. He claims that while people are out and about at night, there's liable to be trouble. Get them in off the streets safely, then we can relax. That's one of his commandments. The Dublin Police Act. He swears by it."

Now the S S's approach to the shop-lifter opened a new window on the statement. I began to realise that 'bringing them in', didn't necessarily mean that charges would follow. Discretion.

At a deeper level my social conscience was changing. I had brought to the city the impression that all poor people were gougers. The S S's handling of the poor woman had changed all that. Have no preconceived ideas. Another piece of the jigsaw was fitting into place.

Indeed when I looked back over my past ten months in the station, it appeared that the S S was moulding me, bringing me along slowly by a planned design. I also felt that he had kept his eye on me in case I became too comfortable under the shadow of The Bluffer or The Black.

In spite of all the S S remained a stickler for time, duties and productivity. If I sneaked in even a few seconds early from patrol he would lacerate me and roar me back to my beat. Not being clean or tidy or a bit slow on parade resulted in another telling off. Usually though my work rate was last on his list, he knew I was a trier and that was proving to be my continual salvation.

This was another awakening for me, a lesson in judging people. Before the border I had been afraid of this man, unable to look him in the face. Now respect and gratitude were replacing fear. Little John had said it would take two years to get a handle on the job. I was now almost a year out of training and I had made an important breakthrough. I felt I was on the right track. I was beginning to fit in and that was a mighty good feeling. I began to reconsider my attitude to live-in colleagues. I knew I had to maintain harmonious relations with them if I wanted to remain within the circle.

The Bluffer was still on my unit. When the S S was about, he was like a mouse. Outside, he did his own thing. More than anything he missed his old sparring partner, The Black. They ignited each other. They were both close to retirement. Once I heard The Bluffer confiding in The Owl:
"I've only fifty pay packets left, If thou'l Black goes, I'll be on the high road as well."
But for now he remained on beat duties. For him this was a drudge, thirty years of penance and suffering.

I didn't mind the beat at all. For me walking was never hard work and I was always on the look-out for action and excitement.

One day at parade the S S read the riot act:
"Bicycle thieves. They're cleanin' out our patch. What are ye doing about it?"
I copied The Bluffer and looked away as if in deep thought. But later I got the lowdown from The Bully. Apparently a local school was being hit hard. The Bully produced a sheaf of stolen bicycle forms. I made up my mind to try to advance the case. That day I poured on my beat with deadly intent. As usual two words went with me - prevention and detection. I decided the sight of my uniform had prevented enough, today I was going to try my hand at detecting.

227

The school was tucked in off a side street with the bicycle shed- accessible to the public - at the rear. Most conveniently the shop of my friend the old lady overlooked the shed and soon I was upstairs armed with a pair of her binoculars. However, it wasn't long before I discovered that surveying inanimate objects was extremely boring. My eyes kept straying to the street where there was people and traffic. During my first period of surveillance the most frequent sighting was the patrol car cruising up and down with monotonous regularity. Of course, God's spiel had impelled them to action as well, but I prayed they would get a call to the far side of the district.

As the school bell sounded I had nothing to show for the day. The old lady however was a unexpected source of intelligence:
"I've been talking to a few people and they say a stranger has been seen around off and on during the past few weeks. He's a chubby chap going light on top."

The next day after my break I headed for the school like a bloodhound. I skirted the perimeter from the far side. Rounding the corner I walked straight into him. A small fat bald man. He looked at me and the eyes nearly fell from his head with guilt. He was mine. Clasped in his pudgy arms was a child's bicycle. Oh joy! He had no answers as I rattled out the questions: make of bicycle and saddle, size of wheel, location of number. I arrested him on the spot. He was a sniveller and when I got him to the station the S S knocked a few more pounds off his carcass with roars and bangs on the counter:
"Stayling from young ladeens. You're some boyo. It's not cycling from now on you'll be but walking a tight rope. You're for the high jump. C'mon. Own up. How many more have you whipped?"

The tongue lashing smote the prisoner to silence. He spluttered as the S S crumpled his shoulder like a napkin and propelled him towards the cells.
Then he turned to me:
"Good work. Now you have to build up you're case. Go down to the school and root around, hopefully it's stolen from there."

I did as bid but an owner was not forthcoming.

The discovery shook me but the S S had no doubts.

"He's guilty. Look at the state of him. Leave him in the cell to sweat a bit. Let's have a look at the bike."
Grabbing the cycle, he twirled it upside down, peered under the saddle and central axle:
"Aha, I knew he was a wrong one. He was at the number, it's filed. Quick, get the car, you're for Ballistics."

For all I knew I could be headed for Cape Canaveral or was due to be fired into outer space. But no, I was on the way with the suspect bike to an address in John's Road.

My destination was a run down compound surrounded by a high fence with a few rows of poorly strung thorny wire on top. But I got a warm welcome from the man in charge who reminded me of the biggest cattle dealer who made an annual pilgrimage to Puck. I was in desperate need of vindication that my bone shaker was stolen. As he listened he broke into a huge grin as if I had recovered the crown jewels. Then he started on the bike.

First he whipped it on to its saddle and bars, produced his pen knife and scraped and scratched around the number Then he applied a solution and eventually resurrected a letter and a few digits. He explained where the bike had been altered and repainted in certain areas, adding that it definitely appeared to be a wrong one. Following this he made a phone call to Kevin Street garda station and we waited. Then great news. Kevin Street cycle staff confirmed the bike had been stolen a week earlier from another school on our patch. Immediately we rang the S S.

However on my return to the station the climate had changed for the worse. I was met by the D/Sgt:
"We've had tabs on that sham for a while but you snapped him."
This delivered, he loitered watching me dragging the bike from the boot of the car. I felt annoyed. So I had spoiled the crime of the century? But I said nothing and after a few further growls the D/S perked up.
"Put on your civvy coat and come on. Let me do the talking."

He took off for the cell, twirled the flap on the peep-hole and rammed back the massive bolt at the same time. Within, my prisoner lay cross-legged on the bunk but jumped up at our appearance, staggering against the wall. Immediately the D/S tore into him.

"Stand up. Look at me. What are you hiding over there for? Show a bit of respect. We know all about you. Haven't we been watching you for a while. The game is up now though. Caught by the short and curlies. Disgraced you are and all belonging to you. Name and address in the paper. Middle-aged man jailed for stealing child's bicycle. Ha. We'll put the brakes on you, me boyo. Come on, give us a few lines of a statement. Speak up. C'mon now. What have you to say?"

Before the prisoner could cough up a syllable, the D/S reached in his pocket and produced a folded document, waving it menacingly:
"All right. You've had your chance. This is a warrant to search you're gaff. I'm off now to round up a posse and we'll tear your place apart."

Then with a nod he beckoned me outside the door:
"That bit of bird seed might make him sing. Be nice to him for a while."

Back in the cell the prisoner cringed near the far wall, his eyes fixed on the entrance as if expecting a firing squad.
I stood in front of him and smiled.
"Are you all right? Can I get you anything?"
This had an effect as immediately he was on his feet pacing back and forth:
"Is he gone? I'm an effin' eejit but he's a madman. Can I talk to you?"
I nodded but he was off:
"Well, there's no point in denying I have a few more bikes stashed, but not at my gaff, mind you. I'll go with you if you promise to keep that other header away from me. If he gets to my gaff, I'm ruined."

I was thrilled. My first confession. I realised that the D/S had done the donkey work, but I'd finished it off. I couldn't contain myself and had to share the good news. Out in the corridor I was delighted to see the gaggle near the public office. It was the S S and the D/S for once in deep conclave. Halfway to them, I was already blurting out:
"He's admitted and he wants to go with us and show where the rest of the property is stashed."

Without acknowledgement the detective rushed back to the cell door. I made to follow, but the S S had words of calm for me.
"Hold on now. Take a breather. Let them put the finishing touches to the case. I'll see you get due credit."

Later that evening I got another drive in the detective unit's car. This time the sweating prisoner was squelched between myself and the D/S. Again the detective kept up a barrage of talk, but now the pressure was gentler:

"You'll be all right. You're not the worst. Anyone that admits his guilt is game ball by us. We'll look after you. Put a word in the right ear. We've checked you out and you've no previous. Take a bow to the charges and the Probation Act is yours."

Later the detective had a few rare words for me:

"That's it now, not a bad little case. We'll take it from here. There's a bit of tidying up to be done, and you mightn't be able to handle it yet. But it'll be a mark for you."

Indeed it was. I got the acknowledgement of the messhall and, more significantly, I noticed the S S's eyes lingering a little longer in my direction than at any time since I'd first walked into his station.

Chapter 17 - EXHALTATION

We were into early summer. Since The Black's banishment, Joe was the car driver on my unit. He was slight, but had an elegance of character less apparent in more pugnacious colleagues. In this too, I was changing. I used to feel one had to be big, strong and tough to survive in the world of the gardai. But I began to realise that a balance was necessary - between brain and brawn, sensitivity and strength.

Joe was a pleasant, conscientious garda. One early summer's day we set out on the 2pm-10pm patrol. He cruised the limits of the area systematically as we talked about our mutual interest - sport. I had become enchanted by a new game on the television called tennis. My initial interest was awakened when the commentator talked about seeds and sets. It put me in mind of home and the sorting of potatoes and onions in preperation for sowing. But these tennis players were no farmers as they flitted across the screen swiping at a fluffy alley ball. I soon saw that tennis was an intricate game of skill.

I had little experience of television until I arrived in Dublin. Back home there was only one 'box' in our locality. That was owned by the Corcoran family who lived about a half mile away. It was a special treat each Thursday evening to go there and watch a series called 'The Fugitive'. I'll never forget the introduction; 'A Q.M. Production, starring David Jannsen as Richard Kimble, an innocent victim of blind justice'.
We loved that programme. After it, we looked at 'Get Smart' with its anti-hero Maxwell Smart- known locally as the poor eejit with the sore nose from getting it caught in the same door each week.

I dragged my thoughts back to our patrol. It was very quiet and as usual I wanted adventure:
"I wish something would happen."
"Look out when it's too quiet," replied Joe.

But perhaps my wish was to be granted because the Control room gave us our first call of the tour:

"Call to 27 Coolroe Street. Report of a missing person."

"Only a missing person," I grumbled, "what about a bit of excitement?"

"Not to worry," Joe countered. "Expect the unexpected, and remember the eleventh commandment - keep an open mind."

Soon I was in a spotless living room and being confronted by the woman of the house, who managed to combine coldness and fussiness. This was lace curtain poverty. The windows and doors were done up to the nines but the further in I went, the more the need for the decorator's hand. She brought me to the kitchen. I gave her the opportunity to let off steam until she became more relaxed. This was usually successful in settling things down, allowing the person to unwrap their particular dilemma.

She went through the routine, walking the floor, pulling the curtains, and peering out the window:

"Why did you park so close? What'll the neighbours think?"

There was annoyance and bitterness in her tired eyes.

Suddenly she sat down opposite me and lapsed into silence. I spoke:

"You called for us Ma'am. Can I be of assistance?"

This was the key. Immediately her strident voice quavered.

"I don't know what to do. I'm very worried about my only daughter. She's married a few years but lately herself and her husband are not getting on..."

"Where is she now?" I prompted.

"She was here this morning, looking terrible, we ended up having a row and she ran out the door. I'm afraid something is going to happen. I just have a feeling. I don't know what to do."

"If you give me her address, we'll go up and check it out," I said.

"God! would you ever? I'm totally distracted. Can't think straight. She's up in the top one of them new skyscrapers. I'd be terrified to go up there myself."

Something about the incident concerned me and as I climbed into my seat I was already giving Joe the lowdown. He too felt the sense of urgency. Within minutes we were there. I jumped out of the car, into an

234

elevator, hit the top button, and rode up to the address.

Immediately I began thumping on the door which was saturated in puce coloured paint. There was no response except a hollow eerie echo that ricoched along the balcony. I planted my ear close to the door but heard nothing. Next I peered through the letterbox and viewed a nondescript hallway, but then got the characteristic whiff. My God! It was gas.

Joe had followed me. We broke the door down. We ran in. The gusts billowed out and fought to engulf us. It was an inferno without flames, attempting to throttle us to a standstill. But we didn't stop and willed ourselves into the cauldron.

She was all ready for the coffin, her body carefully laid out on the floor, hands joined reverently. The sight almost took my breath away again, but I swathed my nose and gritted my teeth sufficiently to repel the poisonous gas. Over in the corner the cooker doled out its invisible hiss of death.

At first I thought the note tightly clasped in her hand was a prayer. Anyway, we didn't stop to read it but dragged her out to the balcony. Her body reeked with the smell of gas, but there had to be life. There must be. The alternative was unthinkable.

My first aid drill came into my mind bang on cue. Eliminate the source. Remove the victim from the affected area. Lay them in the rescue position. Loosen upper clothing. Clear all obstructions, Open air vents...

Then it was straight into artificial respiration. Head tilted back, pinch nostrils, open mouth and seal lips over mouth. Blow into lungs until the chest rises. Urgently, Joe and I took turns applying mouth to mouth. It wasn't easy, particularly as I got the impression that she was trying very hard to die. So it was an awesome feeling to see life returning.

We called an ambulance and its wailing siren added further eeriness to our operation. A local doctor arrived and the medical people did their stuff and soon the groggy but recovering casualty was stretchered away.

Later when I unfolded the note I read of despair. The staccato sentences were frightening in their economy. She said a lot in few words. Apparently herself and her husband had not been getting on and that morning he demanded his freedom and walked out. That was the end. She had written of the rows and the threats.

"You said if I killed myself to leave a note, so here it is."

She continued with expressions of love for her husband.

" Till death do us part."

He had gone, now she felt suicide was the only answer.

In the immediate aftermath, the drama took some time to sink in. I got into the car and prepared to log the result of the call:

"Call to.. re missing person."

I noted the earlier entry. I realised it would take several pages in my notebook to do justice to what had happened, but all I committed to immediate posterity was a fistful of words as we resumed our patrol:

"One female casualty to hospital,... suffering from gas inhalation. Not serious."

Later the doctor confirmed that we had saved her life. There was more excitement when the evening papers hit the stands. They gave us the front page: 'Kiss of life in nick of time'.

This was a sublime moment. Cloud ten. One for every floor I had ascended to. Fame surrounded me, but I felt no hero. Later there was talk of a citation but it came to nothing. Not that I minded. I realised that no commendation would compete with the cherished feeling of saving a life.

It was indescribable.

Now I really felt entitled to look the world in the eye.

But more than anything the incident set me up in the station. It had a multitude of side effects. One of the most pleasurable was the inner glow I felt every time I was in Joe's company. Words were unnecessary. The drama had stitched us together forever. Along with that I learned a valuable lesson which copperfastened his earlier advice:

'The eleventh commandment. An open mind. Every summons for assistance should be taken seriously'.

The incident also made me realise the anguish, depression and despair that can drive someone to attempt to take their own life.

Over the next few days I relived the incident again and again. The moment when we burst in the door and danger stared us in the face. Our reactions and our actions. I realised I had no thought, no fear, just an overwhelming desire to act. What was behind it? Maybe it was the tendency to have a go, a fierce desire to succeed. I recalled days when I leapt high on the football field more in hope than in expectation only to make a marvellous fetch. It was instinct.

I learned more about myself. I discovered I had a sixth sense to adorn the other five. Up to then, I had been most proud of my sight and felt that a garda without a good pair of eyes was not fit for the street. But now I began to appreciate an awareness of gut feeling. This had shown itself in the unease I had experienced when talking to the young woman's mother. I was also gratified that I could recall crucial elements of training when needed - such as first-aid drill. Perhaps other realisations would assert themselves from now on. I hoped so. I recognised the need to balance the physical and mental approach and so act instinctively, rather than impulsively.

I was now nearing the end of my first year of on-the-job training. It was still very much a learning process. One answer for which I knew I would get full marks was that excitement and adventure introduced its own dilemmas.

Another was the need for a clear head when recording and reporting incidents. Since my first arrest, and particularly since the fatal traffic accident, I had become adept at isolating details in chronological order. In this the notebook was of crucial importance. I had logged the salient features of the fatal accident methodically in order to have the facts at my fingertips and to avoid the possibility of a cock-up resulting in being served with a please explain.

Recording the chronology of the lifesaving incident was more difficult. I felt it would be impossible to coherently explain my actions on paper. I took advice from Little John:
"It's very difficult to record the exact thoughts that whirl through your mind when you sweep into action," he said. "You will remember the actions before and after but in the heat of battle you're working on basic instinct."

The S S's response to the drama was to collar me in the corridor and give me his verdict - with a sting in the tail:

"You accomplished the primary duty of a policeman. Well done. Don't let it go to your head. By the way, you're going back on part two training in a fortnight's time."

That put the shroud on my spotlight. I was going back to Templemore. I loathed the thought. Within days of my arrival at the station, I had compressed many memories of that institution into an impregnable bunker in my mind, locked the door and thrown away the key. But now in my moment of glory, these memories began to escape, to gloat and overpower me with almost frightening intensity.

As the fateful day approached I felt the tug of the place ever tightening. Strangulation. The only glimmer of hope was the realisation that this was the final hurdle to clear before I was free of the stigma of being the recruit. Also, I knew that I had worked hard, I was proud of my record and felt I was good enough.

The morning when I got off the train at Templemore, the Devil's Bit wore a sombre bonnet in keeping with my state of mind. It began to rain. This forced my head down all the way past Lacey Avenue until the corner when I turned left and faced the entrance. As if in recognition of my diffidence, the elements flew into a frenzy and blew me through the gate.

Inside much was changed. The Gander had taken flight, but it was good to see my drill, physical education and police duty instructor still doing their stuff.

That evening I visited my old quarters and stared away across the plain to the now bareheaded Devil's Bit.

There was an exam the next day. The questions were fairly basic, concerned with powers of arrest and the more important legislation. After that I settled down for a month. I soon realised we were being treated totally differently from our previous sojourn. Apart from the morning parade and paying respects to the Guardroom, we were left to our own devices. It seemed as if they had brought us back only to have a look at us and make sure we were still alive.

I soon realised that the D.M.A. numbers on my shoulders were a passport to every gathering.

"What's it like on the outside?"

"I'm hoping to get the country. It's easier there."

"They say the D.M.A. is tough."

"As who says?" I asked, mimicking the S S before adding, "let no one tell you otherwise, it's tough."

What's it like on the outside? This query was a perennial chart toppper, but one I had never asked in training, being so busy holding myself together. Instantly I was imbued with a mission to give the recruits the benefit of my experience. Mentally I planned this initiative. I had a lot to tell them, how could I put it all in perspective? Where would I start? I began to break down all I had learned. In reality, I was still up in the air myself, propelled by many and varied nuggets of advice which floated like comets across my mind. As I settled down, various snippets of comment came to me:

'They only want bogmen in the guards, uneducated men who don't ask questions and do as they're told'.

Who said that? Never mind, I discarded it, unwilling to burden impressionable trainees with such negative inaccuracies.

Where to start? There was so much. I had to get it right.

I transported myself in spirit back to their world. My incarceration. One memory came to the fore - the weeks I imprisoned myself in the distant toilet to transcribe legions of definitions on paper.

That evening I made a decision. Armed with my daily diary and official notebook, I began to prepare. First, I punched a dozen or more half sheets of paper together. Next, I sat, thought, and wrote. My exercise went late into that night, the next and the one after. I began with leaving home. Then came the recollections of my training. I was amazed how the suffering of that sixteen months made those memories so acute. Raw edges still remained, but writing them down and reading them over offered a new depth and meaning. Best of all, I discovered many conclusions dripping from my pen.

The distillation exorcised many ghosts, and I discovered I was in a position to give the recruits an honest appraisal of my experiences of the job to date.

I watched their expressions of interest and intent as they fired questions at me. I recognised myself in their faces and my own unrequited thirst for enlightenment at their stage of training. What could they expect? What will it be like? Does training become easier?

"It depends on your life before training."
I explained that in my opinion those who leave home and work in civvy street for a while are the more rounded individuals when they come into the gardai as they're already equipped with a bit of worldliness.

"So why are you joining up? What did you know about the force before? Did you know anything about training disciplines? You see, when you come in here, all you bring is your background and your life experiences. But you'll need more. You need to have an open mind and a streak of physical and mental toughness. That's my recipe for where you are now. It's tough, but you must be tough as well to survive."

More questions. It was my signal to share my philosophy on the difference between training and the real job. I started out from the moment they would arrive in their stations. The first impressions, meeting their skippers and colleagues, living in or settling into digs. I introduced them to the characters that populated the job. Then there was the crack, the slagging, the ever-changing environment of working in a unit.

Then I moved on to their duties, concentrating on what I knew best, the three relief or regular. Their first parade. Being shown around the beat. Facing the public in uniform for the first time. The lie ups.
This drew a protest:
"You're having us on."

We talked back and forth. I told them about walking the beat. I gave them everything from people looking for directions to the occasions when things go wrong. I underlined the significance of time. Time to fall in step with the pace of their new station. Strict timekeeping for parading for all duties. Also time for rest, relaxation and reflection. The importance of physical exercise to remain fit. I talked about the special relationship that could be forged between the recruit and his sergeant. Sergeants had a lot on their mind. They were often preoccupied with several problems and may seem uninterested in the dilemmas of a new recruit. I underlined the importance of choosing the right moment, and how to approach the superior officer. Take a step at a time. Early feelers were crucial in any search for advice or guidance.

Then I began hammering home core points with emphasis. Each recruit was an individual. But he was also becoming part of a disciplined organisation and would have to mesh into the existing structure. They could find themselves serving in any of the 700 odd stations round the country depending on, yes, I was actually quoting it 'the exigencies of the service'. They would be armed with many laws which they might have to apply on the spur of the moment. They would have fretful times but there would be advice and help often from unexpected quarters.

"No-one knows what street, road or bohereen they will end up. Every confrontation has the potential for injury. You'll need your wits about you as you're fair game for any criminal or anyone else who fancies his chances. The only protection you have is your fitness, strength and the official truncheon. This is a powerful weapon, and if you can get by without using it, you're better off."

As the days passed I realised I was really getting through. I laid on a continuous steam of the gospel according to Little John, The Staff and The Owl with a few epistles of my own.

"You'll meet tragedy and suffering and become wound up in the consequences. It will be difficult coming to grips with those situations but the only way through is to get advice and learn from men of experience who have suffered themselves. Try to get them to spend time with you and learn from them. Remember.. good judgement can come from bad experiences...

"There's another cardinal rule - the need for loyalty. This has kept the force together over hard times. Some people call it the ring of steel, others the thin blue line, but it's more. When the chips are down and some of us are quaking in our boots, others will stand up and be counted. Sometimes a benefactor can come from an unexpected quarter. There is so much to the job- the one to one word of advice, sticking together and supporting each other, burying our dead and not crying in public. We are at the butt end of many jokes but we always hold our heads high. A

241

guard may go down, but there's anther to pick up the baton. And generally we have the public on our side, and they're the real judges in society."

At the end of one chat, a recruit came up and thanked me:

"You should be up there in the classroom telling us all this," he said.

I gave him some one-to-one advice - an extra transfusion of my experiences in the city and on the border.

Each evening I met and talked with the group. Again some of the comments gave me food for thought:

"You're lucky. Exciting things always happen to you."

I began to identify with my own development during the past eighteen months. From being uncomplicated and ordinary, I had become extraordinary. The wealth of experiences gained during training and on the streets of Dublin, the people I'd met - all had had a profound effect. As a child my father had shown me the physical way. When I left home I had been a physical heavyweight but mentally I was only in the flyweight class.

During training my self-respect and enthusiasm had been temporarily extinguished. I'd found it difficult to form relationships arising from a lack of understanding and trust. The training had been bruising, no doubt about it, and it had left its mark. Now on my return I realised that while the slate hadn't been wiped entirely clean, my daily diary was proving therapeutic. Along with that came the realisation that it was time to bury the ghosts that had haunted my training and move on. The job was too serious to harbour grudges..

I was becoming a fully fledged garda.

A month later I was back in the station. I had a great welcome. Each and every colleague had something to say to me. Even The Black had left strict instructions that I was to visit him in his 'sick' bed. What a difference twelve months in the job had made. Even in the month I was away in training, I had missed so much.

Little John brought me up to date on station events. Privately the S S was talking of creasing the half sheet and retiring. The Bully was saying that if God went, he would go too. But the forecast was that the S S wouldn't budge until himself and The Black had a rematch. The latter still reclined in hospital crowing that a trapdoor hadn't yet been invented that could swallow him.

The Bluffer was getting away with even more. The Spoofer's reign of terror on hapless motorists continued. But those in the know said this would fizzle out when the promotion list came out at the end of the month. Files alias the mess man had considered introducing a green ration for some of the heavyweights until The Owl threatened to move house. The Staff just smiled and smiled.

And what of myself? I felt I still hadn't found the real Doyle. In six months I would be 21, a man. A few months after that I'd have my first two years under my belt. Hopefully, then my expectations of being a real guard would be fulfilled.

I couldn't wait.

The first day back on duty the S S told me to hang on after parade. When the coast was clear he ushered me along the corridor to the back yard. "Read that," he commanded, thrusting into my hand a sheet of paper with an official looking stamp on the top right hand corner. It was from the training centre and contained my assessment and conclusions from the training officers. Towards the end I read:
"A sound type with plenty of intelligence. He has a good knowledge and is very good at the practical aspects. Suitable for retention in the force."

As I read it I nearly burst into tears. 'Sound man... very good at practical aspect'.

Fair play to them. I couldn't have written a better epitaph for myself. I stood there, holding the precious testament in my hands. How I had suffered for it! I could have stood there forever, savouring the moment.

Suddenly the S S snapped the correspondence back:
"You've served your time and you've got your papers. We'll file them away in the archives. A sound man. You've got top marks. Good. Now, we'll have to work hard to make sure you live up to it."